Passing Off

The Law and Practice Relating to the Imitation of
Goods, Businesses and Professions

Third Edition

David Young, QC

LONGMAN

© Longman Group Ltd 1994

ISBN 0 75200 0330

Published by
Longman Law, Tax and Finance
Longman Group Ltd
21–27 Lamb's Conduit Street
London WC1N 3NJ

First edition 1985
Second edition 1989
Third edition 1994

Associated offices
Australia, Hong Kong, Malaysia, Singapore and USA

A CIP catalogue record for this book is available from the British Library.

Printed in Great Britain by
Mackays of Chatham PLC, Chatham, Kent

Contents

Preface

This book deals with a branch of law which prevents one trader from taking unfair advantage of the reputation which some other trader has built up for himself. However the law of passing off does not confine its protection to traders. It extends to authors, artists and others whose reputation is a valuable asset to them and who may suffer from unfair competition.

The first edition was derived from the book *Passing Off* by E Holroyd Pearce (now Lord Pearce) published in 1928 by Solicitors' Law Stationery Society. Whilst essentially a rewrite, it retains most of the cases and extracts of cases referred to in Lord Pearce's earlier book. As well as dealing with the principles of the law of passing off, it collates decided cases topic by topic and deals with procedural matters such as the evidence required in support (trap orders and survey evidence) and the relief that can be obtained (interlocutory and final). To adopt Lord Pearce's words in the preface to his earlier book, in all branches of the law which depend largely on fact it is difficult to know how far to include cases determined solely on the facts of the particular case. In this book an attempt has been made to include any cases, that although decided on fact, indicate the angle from which the court views such cases, and the legal principles which guide it. Certainty is not possible: but a close study of the decided cases may lead to an accurate forecast.

The third edition is an update of the first and second editions, taking account of the impact of the Trade Marks Act 1994, which comes into force on 31 October of this year. There is a fuller treatment of most of the topics, in particular, unfair competition, injurious falsehood, the impact of EEC law, and Chapter 10, Practice. With the practitioner in mind a checklist has been provided, which sets out the necessary requirements before launching proceedings. Also, an Appendix has been added, which includes pleadings precedents compiled with the assistance of Colin Birss (much appreciated).

It is hoped that this book may be of practical use to members of the profession, and that it may convey an intelligible account of the law of passing off to the traders and others whom it protects.

In assisting in the preparation of this Edition I am very grateful for the assistance of Justin Turner.

David Young
6 Pump Court
Temple EC4
September 1994

Table of Cases

Table of Statutes

Table of Statutory Instruments

Chapter 1

The Principle of the Law

The law of passing off has been formed chiefly for the protection of traders and for the prevention of commercial dishonesty. It was stated by Lord Morris in *Parker-Knoll Ltd* v *Knoll International Ltd* [1962] RPC 265 at 278 (HL) that 'trading must not only be honest but must not even unintentionally be unfair'. In the Advocaat case (*Erven Warnink BV* v *J Townend & Sons (Hull) Ltd* [1980] RPC 31 at 91 (HL), Lord Diplock stated: 'Unfair trading as a wrong actionable at the suit of other traders who thereby suffer loss of business or goodwill may take a variety of forms, to some of which separate labels have become attached in English law. Conspiracy to injure a person in his trade or business is one, slander of goods another, but most protean is that which is generally and nowadays, perhaps misleadingly, described as "passing off".'

1 Passing off—its origins[1]

Like the torts of slander of title, slander of goods and injurious falsehood, the tort of passing off originated from the cause of action for deceit. At common law before the passing of the Trade Marks Act 1875 there were two species of improper use of trade marks; first, as a species of property rights, there was the wrongful taking of another trader's trade mark affixed to or used in physical relationship with that person's goods. Such a trade mark was wrongfully appropriated by a rival whether the same was taken innocently or deliberately (see *Millington* v *Fox* (1838) 3 My & Cr 338) and whether the whole of the mark was taken or essentially the whole mark. This is the forerunner of the registered trade mark, first registrable under the 1875 Act.

---

[1] For a history of the cause of action, see *Singer Manufacturing Co* v *Wilson* (1876) 2 Ch 434 at 453 (Mellish L J) and *G E Trade Mark* [1973] RPC 297 at 325–327 (Lord Diplock).

The second species of wrongful use was originally a case of fraud where the rival made a false representation as to the nature of his goods or business.[2] It differed from an ordinary action for deceit in that the plaintiff, instead of having to prove that the defendant's false representations had deceived him, had to establish that members of the public or trade were or were likely to be deceived by such false representations. At common law, at least, where special damage could not be established proof of fraudulent design was originally a necessary ingredient[3] even though the Courts of Equity would grant injunctive relief if a likelihood of deception could be established irrespective of any fraudulent design.[4] This second species is the forerunner of the common law action of passing off, the subject of the following chapters.

2 Passing off—its ingredients

The action for passing off is brought by one trader against another and not by the persons (ie members of the public) upon whom the deception is practised.[5]

Representations which give rise to the deception may take many forms—the defendant may expressly intimate to members of the public or trade that his goods or business are the goods or business of the plaintiff; or, as more frequently happens, the defendant may indirectly and by implication lead members of the public or trade to suppose that his goods or business are or are connected or associated with the goods or business of the plaintiff by trading under a similar name, or marking his goods with a similar name, or getting or dressing them up in such a way that an unwary purchaser will be deceived into thinking that they are the goods of the plaintiff.

As was stated by Lord Parker in *A G Spalding & Bros* v *A W Gamage Ltd*

---

2 *Blanchard* v *Hill* (1742) 2 Atk 484 (Hardwicke L C).
3 See, eg *John Rodgers* v *Neville and William Rodgers* 5 CB 109.
4 See *Reddaway and Co* v *Bentham Hemp Spinning Coy* (1892) 9 RPC 503 at 507 (CA); *Cellular Clothing Coy* v *Maxton and Murray* (1899) 16 RPC 397 at 404 (Lord Halsbury).
5 Cf the Merchandise Marks Acts 1887 to 1953 and now the Trade Descriptions Act 1968 for the protection of the public from deception—such Acts do not give rise to any civil action for breach of statutory duty on the part of the competing trader, even though he may sustain actual damage as a result of the deception—see *J Bollinger* v *The Costa Brava Wine Co Ltd* [1960] RPC 16 (Danckwerts J); *H P Bulmer Ltd* v *J Bollinger SA* [1978] RPC 79 at 109, 110, 137 (CA) *Erven Warnink BV* v *J Townend & Sons (Hull) Ltd* [1980] RPC 31 at 94 (HL).

(1915) 32 RPC 273 at 284 (HL) 'the basis of a passing off action being a false representation by the defendant, it must be proved in each case as a fact that the false representation was made. It may, of course, have been made in express words, but cases of express misrepresentation of this sort are rare. The more common case is, where the representation is implied in the use or imitation of a mark, trade name, or get-up with which the goods of another are associated in the minds of the public, or of a particular class of the public. In such cases the point to be decided is whether, having regard to all the circumstances of the case, the use by the defendant in connection with the goods of the mark, name, or get-up in question impliedly represents such goods to be the goods of the plaintiff, or the goods of the plaintiff of a particular class or quality, or, as it is sometimes put, whether the defendant's use of such mark, name, or get-up is calculated to deceive. It would, however, be impossible to enumerate or classify all the possible ways in which a man may make the false representation relied on.'

In *Cadbury-Schweppes Pty Ltd* v *The Pub Squash Co Ltd* [1981] RPC 429 at 490 (PC) Lord Scarman stated, 'The tort is no longer anchored, as in its nineteenth century formulation, to the name or trade mark of a product or business. It is wide enough to encompass other descriptive material, such as slogans or visual images, which radio, television or newspaper advertising campaigns can lead the market to associate with a plaintiff's product, provided always that such descriptive material has become part of the goodwill of the product. And the test is whether the product has derived from the advertising a distinctive character which the market recognises.'

The basic principle of the law of passing off cannot be better expressed than in the words of Lord Halsbury in *Reddaway* v *Banham* (1896) 13 RPC 218 at 224 (HL):

> For myself, I believe the principle of law may be very plainly stated, and that is that nobody has any right to represent his goods as the goods of somebody else. How far the use of particular words, signs, or pictures does or does not come up to the proposition which I have enunciated in each particular case, must always be a question of evidence, and the more simple the phraseology, the more like it is to a mere description of the article sold, the greater becomes the difficulty of proof, but if the proof establishes the fact the legal consequence appears to follow.

Reddaway v *Banham*, known as the 'Camel Hair Belting' case, has been described as a landmark case in that it concerned the use by a trader of a term which accurately described the composition of his own goods which nevertheless amounted to the tort of passing off because such term was understood in the market in which the goods were sold to denote the plaintiff's goods. However, it was concerned with the classic form of passing off of one trader's goods by a rival's with the consequential diversion of potential or actual customers and the rival was accordingly restrained from using the words 'Camel hair' in such a manner as to deceive purchasers into the belief that they were purchasing belting of the plaintiff's manufacture. It is to be noted that there was no absolute bar on the defendant's use of the words 'Camel hair', only a restraint on further misrepresenting his belting as or for the plaintiff's belting.

Lord Halsbury's statement of the law was considered by Lord Parker of Waddington in *A G Spalding & Bros* v *A W Gamage Ltd* (1915) 32 RPC 273 at 283, 284 who added the following gloss: 'the proposition that no one has a right to represent his goods as the goods of somebody else must, I think, as has been assumed in this case, involve as a corollary the further proposition, that no one, who has in his hands the goods of another of a particular class or quality, has a right to represent these goods to be the goods of that other of a different quality or belonging to a different class.' In an earlier passage Lord Parker stated: 'Nor need the representation be fraudulently made. It is enough that it has in fact been made, whether fraudulently or otherwise, and that damages may probably ensue, though the complete innocence of the party making it may be a reason for limiting the account of profits to the period subsequent to the date at which he becomes aware of the true facts. The representation is in fact treated as the invasion of a right giving rise at any rate to nominal damages, the inquiry being granted at the plaintiff's risk if he might probably have suffered more than nominal damages.' The invasion of the right to which Lord Parker was referring was (he said) the invasion of the right in 'the property in the business or goodwill likely to be injured by the misrepresentation'.

Spalding v *Gamage* was a case where the defendant had issued an advertisement announcing a sale of the plaintiff's footballs at very low prices. In fact the footballs to be sold by the defendant were an inferior class of the plaintiff's footballs to those advertised and the plaintiff claimed to have suffered damage because the defendant's advertisements had interfered with the sales of the plaintiff's footballs. It was argued for the defendant by Sir Duncan Kerly that since no footballs had been sold before the issue of the writ, no action lay for damages because damage to reputation could only be recovered where the damage was caused by a purchaser's unfavourable reaction to the goods purchased. This argument was not accepted by the House of Lords, Lord Parker at 283 defining the tort in terms of the making of a false representation rather than any act of passing off, Lord Parmoor, at 289–290, stating that offering to sell constituted an actionable wrong and that there was no artificial limitation on the damages that could be recovered for that wrong. On the inquiry as to damages the Court of Appeal held that the House of Lords had decided that the tort of passing off was complete with the advertisement and the defendant was liable for all the resulting damage therefrom.[6]

The above principle of law as stated by Lord Halsbury and Lord Parker is not confined to passing off of one person's goods for those of another, but extends to passing off of one person's business as or for another's or for a business connected or associated with that other. See for example, *Office Cleaning Services Ltd* v *Westminster Windows and General Cleaners Ltd* (1946) 63 RPC 39 at 42 (HL).

3 Passing off—the protection of goodwill

The basis of all passing off actions is the protection of goodwill. Goodwill was defined by Lord MacNaghten in *CIR* v *Muller* [1901] AC 217 at 223 as 'the benefit and advantage of the good name, reputation, and connection of a business. It is the attractive force which brings in custom.' In *Star Industrial Coy Ltd* v *Yap Kwee Kor* [1976] FSR 256 (PC) Lord Diplock stated 'goodwill, as the subject of proprietary rights, is incapable of subsisting by itself. It has no independent existence apart from the business to which it is attached. It is local in character and divisible; if the business is carried on in several countries a separate goodwill attaches to it in each. So when the business is abandoned in one country in which it has acquired a goodwill, the goodwill in that country perishes with it although the business may continue to be carried on in other countries.'

In the 'Budweiser' beer case (*Anheuser-Busch Inc* v *Budejovicky Budvar NP* [1984] FSR 413) Oliver LJ held that a plaintiff must establish a business or trading presence in this country in order to establish the necessary goodwill and that a 'spill-over' reputation from abroad was not sufficient.[7]

4 Passing off (classical type)

In an action for passing off of the classical type where B's goods or business are represented as B's goods or business (or a particular type or quality of B's goods) or as goods or a business connected or associated with B with

---

6   (1918) 35 RPC 101; cf Lord Diplock's formulation in the Advocaat case (p 7 below).
7   See Chapter 2, below.

the consequential diversion of custom from B to A it is necessary for B to establish the following:

(i) the necessary goodwill in the particular name, badge or livery (ie get-up) which denotes either B's goods (or a type, characteristic or quality of his goods) or his business either exclusively or his and some limited number of other persons[8] *and*

(ii) that the manner in which B is marketing his goods (or B's goods of a particular type or quality) or carrying on his business is likely to deceive or confuse a substantial number of persons in this country (being either members of the trade or public) into believing that such goods or business are B's goods or business or are connected or associated with B or are B's goods of a different type or quality.

5 Passing off (false trade description)

The action for passing off is not, however, confined to the classical type of case. Thus in *Samuelson* v *Producers Distributing Co Ltd* (1931) 48 RPC 580 (CA) it was held to be passing off to represent falsely that the defendant's film 'His First Car' was based on a music hall sketch called 'The New Car', of which the plaintiff owned the copyright. It was stated by Romer LJ at 593 that 'the cases in which the Court has restrained passing off in the popular and usual sense, are merely instances of the application by the Court of a much wider principle, the principle being that the Court will always interfere by injunction to restrain irreparable injury being done to the Plaintiff's property.'

The right being invaded would seem to be a right of property, the property being in the business or goodwill likely to be injured by the false representation.[9]

In *J Bollinger* v *The Costa Brava Wine Co Ltd* [1960] RPC 16 it was

---

8   See *Dent* v *Turpin* (1861) 2 John & H 139 (Wood V-C) and *Southorn* v *Reynolds* (1865) 12 LT (NS) 75 (Wood V-C) in which one of two traders was held entitled to obtain an injunction without joining the other. See also the Champagne case which came before Danckwerts J in two stages, the first stage (reported at [1960] RPC 16) on a preliminary point of law, namely does an action for passing off lie at the suit of a class of persons alleging that the defendant is causing them injury by the use of the name of a locality which name forms part of the goodwill of the plaintiff even though such persons do not have an exclusive right to such name; the second stage (reported at [1961] RPC 116) on the trial of the action; approved of in the Advocaat case [1980] RPC 31 at 93, 95 (HL).

9   See *A G Spalding & Bros* v *A W Gamage Ltd* (1915) 32 RPC 273 at 284 (HL); *H P Bulmer* v *J Bollinger* [1978] RPC 79 at 94, 95 (CA); and *Erven Warnink BV* v *J Townend & Sons (Hull) Ltd* [1980] RPC at 92 (HL).

admitted that the action was not a 'passing off action' in the classical sense that there was any allegation that the defendant's product (Spanish champagne) was passed off as wine produced by any of the plaintiffs individually; nevertheless it was held by Danckwerts J that the plaintiffs (12 producers of champagne from the Champagne district of France) were entitled to prevent the defendants from selling sparkling wine in this country as Spanish champagne on the grounds that such wine may be considered to be genuine champagne. The ratio decidendi of this case was followed by Cross J in the Sherry case (*Vine Products Ltd* v *Mackenzie & Co Ltd* [1969] RPC 1) and by Foster J in the Scotch Whisky case (*John Walker & Sons Ltd* v *Henry Ost & Co Ltd* [1970] RPC 489). It has been suggested that the Sherry case altered the law of passing off to make the requirement of the likelihood of confusion or deception unnecessary. This would not appear to be correct. Cross J in considering the Champagne case concluded at [1969] RPC 23, 29 that the deception arising from the label 'Spanish champagne' was not that the public thought that they were buying a wine from France but rather that the public might think that they were buying the genuine article. In other words, that the defendant, in so labelling his goods was selling them under a false trade description likely to injure the plaintiff.

The ratio decidendi of the Champagne case has recently been considered by the House of Lords in *Erven Warnink BV* v *J Townend & Sons (Hull) Ltd* [1980] RPC 31. The plaintiff was a producer in Holland of an egg and spirit drink known both in Holland and England as 'advocaat', having some 75 per cent of the share of the market in England in such a drink. The defendant produced an alcoholic egg drink from a mixture of dried eggs and Cyprus sherry which the defendant marketed as 'Keeling's Old English Advocaat'. As Lord Diplock stated, the plaintiff had no cause of action for passing off in its classic form, not being able to establish that any purchaser of the defendant's product supposed or would be likely to suppose it to be goods supplied by the plaintiff or to be Dutch advocaat of any make. The findings of the trial judge which were accepted by the Court of Appeal and not challenged in the House of Lords, were inter alia that: (1) the defendant's (Keeling's) product had no natural association with the word 'advocaat', being an 'egg flip'; (2) that members of the public believed that in buying 'Keeling's Old English Advocaat' they were in fact buying advocaat; and (3) that the defendant's deception of the public had caused damage to the plaintiff. The House of Lords, in reversing the Court of Appeal and restoring the injunction granted by Goulding J held that the plaintiff had established that there was a valid cause of action for passing off in that the defendant's product was being deliberately and falsely misrepresented as the genuine article, namely advocaat.

The facts of this case differ from the Champagne, Sherry and Scotch

Whisky cases in that the name of the product for which protection was sought was not a distinctive product coming from a particular geographical locality bearing the name of such locality. Indeed the Court of Appeal felt able to distinguish the Advocaat case from the earlier 'drink' cases on the facts. In differing from the Court of Appeal, Lord Diplock said (at 96) 'if a product of a particular character or composition has been marketed under a descriptive name and under that name has gained a public reputation which distinguishes it from competing products of different composition, I can see no reason in principle or logic why the goodwill in the name of those entitled to make use of it should be protected by the law against deceptive use of the name by competitors, if it denotes a product of which the ingredients come from a particular locality but should lose that protection if the ingredients of the product, however narrowly identified, are not restricted as to their geographical provenance.' However, it is to be noted that Lord Diplock qualified this general proposition by adding (at 98) 'of course it is necessary to be able to identify with reasonable precision the members of the class of traders of whose products a particular word or name has become so distinctive as to make their right to use it truthfully as descriptive of their product a valuable part of the goodwill of each of them . . . So if one can define with reasonable precision the type of product that has acquired the reputation, one can identify the members of the class entitled to share in the goodwill as being all those traders who have supplied and still supply to the English market a product which possesses those recognisable and distinctive qualities.' The reasoning being that unless the members of the class are identifiable (unlike, say, producers of butter or margarine) it would not be possible to establish that any particular plaintiff's business will suffer more than minimal damage to its goodwill by the defendant's misrepresenting its product as being of that type.

6 Passing off (general formulation)

In *Erven Warnink BV* v *J Townend & Sons (Hull) Ltd* [1980] RPC 31 at 93 (HL), Lord Diplock (with whom the majority of their Lordships agreed) formulated the action of passing off by reference to five essential characteristics which he stated must be present to create a valid cause of action, namely:

(i) misrepresentation
(ii) made by a trader in the course of trade
(iii) to prospective customers of his or ultimate consumers of goods or services supplied by him

(iv) which is calculated to injure the business or goodwill of another trader[10] (in the sense that this is a reasonably foreseeable consequence) and

(v) which causes actual damage to a business or goodwill of the trader by whom the action is brought or (in a quia timet action) will probably do so.

Lord Diplock was careful to add that because these five characteristics were present it does not follow that a valid cause of action will exist, and cites by way of example the case of the trader who in an advertisement makes exaggerated claims about the quality of his wares compared with his rivals—in law such a claim has been permitted as venial 'puffing' even though a rival's business may have suffered damage.[11]

Lord Fraser, in concurring that the Champagne case was rightly decided, formulated (at 105–106) a different set of five essential characteristics which it is necessary to establish to create the cause of action of passing off. The apparent difference between Lord Diplock's formulation and Lord Fraser's formulation is that Lord Fraser's is directed to the particular facts of the Advocaat case and he expressly states that there must be a reputation in a particular trade name distinguishing the class of goods from similar goods to which a goodwill is attached. Such requirement is implicit in Lord Diplock's formulation because unless there is such a reputation there will not generally be any misrepresentation nor will there be any injury or damage to the business or goodwill of the plaintiff.[12]

In *Reckitt & Coleman Products Ltd* v *Barden Inc* [1990] RPC 341,[13] a get-up case involving plastic yellow lemons (the 'Jif Lemon' case), Lord Oliver (at 406) expressed the elements of passing off (of the classical type) as three in number, as follows:

> First, he must establish a goodwill or reputation attached to the goods or services which he supplies in the mind of the purchasing

---

[10] This, it is submitted, is too narrow. The goodwill which the courts have protected is wider than that of a trader—eg non-trading organisations (see *British Medical Association* v *Marsh* (1931) 48 RPC 565 (Maugham J); *British Legion* v *British Legion Club (Street) Ltd* (1931) 48 RPC 555: Farwell J).

[11] See, eg, *De Beers Abrasive Products Ltd* v *International General Electric Co of NY Ltd* [1975] FSR 323 (Walton J) where the cases on each side of the line are reviewed.

[12] Cf *Anheuser-Busch Inc* v *Budejovicky Budvar NP* [1984] FSR 413 (CA) where it was observed that the criteria listed by Lord Diplock and Lord Fraser are cumulative.

[13] Followed in *Consorzio del Prossiutto di Parma* v *Marks & Spencer plc* (1991) RPC 351 (CA) where Nourse LJ welcomed the return to the classical approach.

public by association with the identifying 'get-up' (whether it consists simply as a brand name or a trade description, or the individual features of labelling or packaging) under which his particular goods or services are offered to the public, such that the get-up is recognised by the public as distinctive specifically of the plaintiff's goods or services. Secondly, he must demonstrate a misrepresentation by the defendant to the public (whether or not intentional) leading or likely to lead the public to believe that goods or services offered by him are the goods or services of the plaintiff. Whether the public is aware of the plaintiff's identity as manufacturer or supplier of the goods or services is immaterial, as long as they are identified with a particular source which is in fact the plaintiff. . . . Thirdly, he must demonstrate that he suffers, or in a quia timet action, that he is likely to suffer damage by reason of the erroneous belief engendered by the defendant's misrepresentation that the source of the defendant's goods or services is the same as the source of those offered by the plaintiff.

Lord Jauncey (at 417) similarly expressed himself as follows:

It is a prerequisite of any successful passing off action that the plaintiff's goods have acquired a reputation in the market and are known by some distinguishing feature. It is also a prerequisite that the misrepresentation has deceived or is likely to deceive and that the plaintiff is likely to suffer damage by such deception. Mere confusion which does not lead to a sale is not sufficient.

Lord Jauncey continues:

However it is not essential to the success of a passing off action that the defendant should misrepresent his goods as those of the plaintiff. It is sufficient that he misrepresents his goods in such a way that it is a reasonable foreseeable consequence of the misrepresentation that the plaintiff's business or goodwill will be damaged. . . . In a case such as the present where what is in issue is whether the goods of A are likely to be passed off as those of B, a plaintiff to succeed, must establish (1) that his goods have acquired a particular reputation among the public; (2) that persons wishing to buy his goods are likely to be misled into buying the goods of the defendant; and (3) that he is likely to suffer damage thereby.

Thus, to summarise, the plaintiff has to prove three matters:

(i) that it has a sufficient reputation or goodwill in the mark, trade mark, get-up, or other indicia in question in this country,

(ii) that the defendant has or it is likely the defendant will practise or enable a third party to practise some form of deception, either on members of the public or trade by means of some misrepresentation,

(iii) that by reason of such misrepresentation it has suffered or is likely to suffer damage or injury to its business or goodwill.

These matters will be considered in detail in Chapters 2 to 4.

7 The tort of unfair competition/reverse passing off

Where the defendant misrepresents goods of the plaintiff as his own, as opposed to his own goods as those of the plaintiff, this is sometimes referred to as 'reverse passing off'. The broad underlying principle to such a doctrine is one of misappropriation. Passing off can be viewed as one form of misappropriation of a party's goodwill or business, namely by misrepresentation. In *Cadbury-Schweppes Pty Ltd* v *The Pub Squash Co Ltd* [1981] RPC 429 at 461–464 Powell J (New South Wales) reviewed a number of the cases on unfair competition; however, the Privy Council declined to consider the case as one other than a case of passing off although had such a tort existed (in Australia) it was a case that, on the facts, could have given rise to such a tort; the defendants having adopted the plaintiff's advertising theme and general get-up for the same type of lemon drink, but not sufficiently similar to cause deception amongst the public. Lord Scarman (at 491) referred to well known case of the US Supreme Court, *International News Service* v *Associated Press* (1918) 248 US 215 at 241–242 in which Pitney J, delivering the majority opinion said 'defendant's conduct differs from the ordinary case of unfair competition in trade principally in this, that, instead of selling its own goods as those of complainant, it substitutes misappropriation in the place of misrepresentation and sells complainant's goods as its own'. Lord Scarman goes on to point out that the development of such a tort has not escaped judicial criticism in the USA itself (eg Learned Hand J in *Cheney Bros* v *Doris Silk Corpn* (1929) 35 F 2d 279). It has also been criticised in Australia: see *Victoria Park Racing and Recreation Grounds Co Ltd* v *Taylor* (1938) 58 CLR 479.

However, in *Bristol Conservatories Custom Built Ltd* [1989] RPC 455 the Court of Appeal refused to strike out a Statement of Claim as disclosing no reasonable cause of action where the defendants falsely claimed that photographs of the plaintiff's conservatories were the defendant's conservatories, thereby seeking to induce customers to purchase conservatories from them as a proven and existing supplier. Had the deceit being practised succeeded, the customer would have been supplied not with a conservatory as illustrated in the photographs, but one from the defendants.

The Court of Appeal were unable to accept that Lord Diplock in the *Advocaat* case was laying down a universal test for the tort of passing off. Ralph Gibson LJ, following *Planter Fuel Economiser Co Ltd* v *National School of Salesmanship Ltd*,[14] accepted that it was immaterial in the minds of the public that the plaintiff was not linked with the illustrated conservatory. As Lord Greene MR stated in the *Phoenix* case 'it is quite sufficient ... to constitute passing off in fact, if a person being minded to obtain goods which are identified in his mind with a definite commercial source is led by false statements to accept goods coming from a different commercial source.' Statements as broad as the foregoing have to be viewed in their context and are not of universal application. Thus, false advertising claims made by one business competitor against those of another, whilst they may be the subject of a claim for injurious falsehood are not actionable in passing off.[15]

8 Enabling others to pass off defendant's goods

8.1 In this country

It is no answer for the defendant manufacturer to say that the retailer or wholesaler is not deceived if he is supplying his goods to such persons in a manner which is likely to deceive the public when offered for sale to them. Indeed it is often the case that members of the trade such as retailers and wholesalers are better versed in the goods they buy and sell than those members of the public who buy such goods so that there is no passing off as far as members of the trade are concerned. In such a case the manufacturer may be restrained from putting into the hands of the retailer goods which are likely to deceive the public. In *Sykes* v *Sykes*[16] Abbott CJ, said 'it was established most clearly that the defendants marked the goods

---

14 [1943] 60 RPC 209.
15 See Chapter 1, para 10, below.
16 (1824) 3 B & C 541, adopted in *Singer Manufacturing Co* v *Loog* (1882) 8 App Cas 15 at 30 (HL). See also *Lever* v *Goodwin* (1887) 4 RPC 492 (CA, get-up case, defendant's sales of soap to wholesale merchants); *Barlow & Jones* v *Johnson & Co* (1890) 7 RPC 395 (CA, trade mark case: Bowen LJ at 419 'if the probable and natural result... is that the immediate vendee, though not deceived himself, will use the name so as to deceive others—his ulterior vendees—it is an injury to take the name and use it in that way, and it is a fraud in equity if it is known by the person who takes it....'; *Reddaway* v *Banham* (1896) 13 RPC 218 at 231–232 (HL); *Upmann* v *Elton* (1871) LR 7 Ch App 130; *Joseph Rodgers & Sons Ltd* v *F M Hearnshaw* (1906) 23 RPC 349 (Buckley J); *Draper* v *Trist and Tristbestos Brake Linings Ltd* (1939) 56 RPC 429 at 435, 439 (CA); *Argyllshire Weavers Ltd* v *Macauley Tweeds Ltd* [1964] RPC 477 at 509, 542 (Court of Session); *Lee Kar Choo* v *Lee Lian Choon* [1967] 1 AC 602 (PC, defendant held to have used marks in such a way as to enable retailers to practise a deceit on the public—injunction granted).

manufactured by them with the word "Sykes Patent" in order to denote that they were of the genuine manufacture of the plaintiff; and although they did not themselves sell them as goods of the plaintiff's manufacture, yet they sold them to retail dealers for the express purpose of their being resold as goods of the plaintiff's manufacture. I think that is substantially the same thing.'

In *Cadbury Ltd* v *Ulmer Gmbh* [1988] FSR 385 the defendants were suppliers to ice cream vendors of bars of flaked chocolate which were inserted by the ice cream vendor into ice cream cornets, thereby passing off such chocolate bars as the plaintiff's 'Flake' bars. Falconer J, in striking out the Statement of Claim as disclosing no reasonable cause of action, held that where a plaintiff's case was that the ultimate purchaser would be deceived by an intervening middleman who was not deceived himself, a 'badge of fraud' held to be supplied by the defendant manufacturer, either borne on the goods supplied to the middleman or separately, such as by the supply of offending labels used by the middleman to effect the acts of passing off on the consumer. In the case before Falconer J the chocolate bars bore no markings and mere similarity with the plaintiff's chocolate bars was held not sufficient to amount to fraud on the part of the manufacturer.

8.2 Overseas

In *John Walker & Sons Ltd* v *Henry Ost & Co Ltd* [1970] RPC 489[17] the defendant supplied to purchasers in Ecuador malt whisky which the defendant knew was to be blended with local cane spirit, and subsequently bottled and labelled. The defendant also supplied the purchasers with empty bottles and certain labels and authorised the purchasers to use other labels bearing the address of the defendant which falsely indicated that the contents of the bottles were genuine blended Scotch Whisky. The defendant was restrained from supplying Scotch Whisky, bottles or labels in a manner calculated to enable other spirits to be passed off as and for Scotch Whisky. It was held that there were two quite separate torts committed by the defendants. First, that of supplying instruments of fraud to persons abroad with the intention and knowledge of their improper use there.

As regards this first tort, Foster J stated 'I would be slow to decide that if a trader in England sells goods and labels which are true and

---

[17] See also *John Walker & Sons Ltd* v *Douglas McGibbon & Co Ltd* [1975] RPC 506 (Court of Session—OH); *J Burrough Distillers* v *Speymalt Whisky Distributors Ltd* (1989) SLT 561; *Johnston* v *Orr Ewing* (1882) 7 App Cas 219 (HL); *Price's Patent Candle Co Ltd* v *Ogston & Tennant Ltd* (1909) 26 RPC 797 at 813 (Court of Session—OH)—'London Candles' in Morocco. Cf. *Def Lepp Music* v *Stuart-Brown* [1986] RPC 273, a copyright case which would apply to infringement of registered trade mark under Trade Marks Act.

has no knowledge of any improper use of those goods in a foreign country, such trader has committed a tort in England. But when I have already held as a fact that Mr Ost, the proprietor of the first defendant, not only knew that the second defendant was going to add cane spirit and sell it as Scotch Whisky but intended that the whisky which was supplied should be admixed, bottled and have the labels put on the bottle describing it as Scotch Whisky, then in my judgment the first defendant's acts in selling those instruments amount to tortious acts done in England.'

In the subsequent case of *White Horse Distillers Ltd* v *Gregson Associates Ltd* [1984] RPC 61 an English exporter of whisky was held liable for exporting whisky for admixture and sale in Uruguay in a deceptive manner, even though he was not directly responsible for the labelling and marketing. Nourse J stated (at 75) 'I do not think that an English trader who exports goods to a foreign country, whether either they or some other goods, in whose manufacture they are used are passed off as the goods of another trader, necessarily commits a tort in England if he does not take reasonable steps to prevent the passing off; even if it is common knowledge that without proper supervision that is the likely result ... In my judgment it is an essential requirement of the tort that the English trader should participate in the passing off. If he not only supplies the goods but also plays a part in their deceptive marketing he commits a tort in England.' In that case the defendants consented to the use of certain brand names and labelling.

The second tort committed by the defendants in the *Ost* case was marketing or enabling the marketing of goods which is both actionable in the country in question and a tort in England. Foster J (at 509) referred to *Dicey and Morris ' Conflict of Laws*, Rule 158 (now Rule 172 (10th ed)) which states that an act done in a foreign country is a tort and actionable as such in England, only if it is both:

(i) actionable as a tort, according to English law or in other words is an act which if done in England would be a tort, and

(ii) actionable according to the law of the foreign country where it was done.

It was held that the defendant's actions were both actionable as a tort in England and actionable in Ecuador and thus also liable under this head.

However, a defendant will not be liable where the deception on the public is perpetrated by the fraud[18] or carelessness[19] of a retailer or

---

[18] *Payton & Co Ltd* v *Snelling, Lampard & Co Ltd* (1900) 17 RPC 628 at 635 (HL); *Schweppes Ltd* v *Gibbens* (1905) 22 RPC 601 at 606–607 (HL). See also *Paterson* v *Kitt Coffee Co* (1910) 27 RPC 594 (Court of Session—OH).

[19] *Hennessy & Co* v *Keating* (1908) 25 RPC 361 (HL).

other third party and the defendant's name or get-up when fairly used is not likely to deceive.

9 Right to bring action not affected by Trade Marks Acts

In order to make it easier for a trader to protect his trade mark, the Trade Marks Registration Act 1875 established a register of trade marks by which a trader could register his mark (if distinctive) in respect of goods on which he proposed to apply it. The Trade Marks Act 1938 (and Trade Marks (Amendment) Act 1984) which have now been replaced by the Trade Marks Act 1994 provide the machinery whereby a trader may register his mark, the object being that when it is registered he may restrain a rival from infringing his mark without having to prove that it may come to denote his goods in the eyes of the public. Whilst the Trade Marks Act 1938 only applied to trade marks in respect of goods, the Trade Marks (Amendment) Act 1984 which came into force on 1 October 1987 applied mutatis mutandis to services. Section 2 of the 1938 Act as amended expressly preserved the right to bring a passing off action (whether or not the plaintiff was the proprietor of a registered trade mark[20]) by providing that 'nothing in this Act shall be deemed to affect rights of action against any person for passing off or remedies in respect thereof'.

Section 2 of the Trade Marks Act 1994 similarly provides that nothing in the Act affects the law relating to passing off. However, under the new Act (s 2) 'trade mark' has been broadened to include any sign capable of being represented graphically which is capable of distinguishing goods or services of one undertaking from those of other undertakings. Such a trade mark may consist of words (including personal names), designs, letters, numerals or the shape of goods or their packaging. However, certain shapes are excluded (viz the shape resulting from the nature of the goods, the shape necessary to obtain a technical result and the shape which gives substantial value to the goods). Furthermore, under the new Act (s 10) the protection afforded to a registered trade mark has been extended notably to include the case where due to the similarity of the sign complained of to the trade mark and the similarity of the goods

---

[20] *Henry Faulder & Co Ltd* v *Rushton Ltd* (1903) 20 RPC 477 (CA), where it was argued unsuccessfully that a trade mark which might have been registered under the Trade Marks Act, but had not been, could not be protected in an action for passing off—this was before the passing of s 45 of the Trade Marks Act 1905 which is the forerunner of s 2; *Great Tower St Tea Co* v *Langford* (1887) 5 RPC 66 (Stirling J).

or services in respect or which the trade mark is registered, there exists a likelihood of confusion on the part of public (which includes the likelihood of association with the trade mark). It also extends to the case where due to the reputation in the trade mark in the UK the use of the sign complained of takes unfair advantage of or is detrimental to the distinctive character or the repute of the trade mark even if the sign complained of is used in relation to goods or services now similar to those for which the trade mark is registered.

As a consequence of this broadening of protection afforded to a registered trade mark it may seem that the common law rights of passing off will be less likely to be involved where there is a subsisting registered trade mark. However, the fact that a registered trade mark may be invalidated or found not to infringe because of defences peculiar to the Trade Marks Act will mean that passing off rights will remain not only as an important adjunct to an infringement action but also as the only cause of action where a trade mark has not been registered or is only in the course of being registered. An illustration of where trade mark protection is narrower than the proprietor's rights at common law is in the case of parallel imports. Section 12 of the 1994 Act extends to goods put on the market by the proprietor or with his consent in the European Economic Area whilst the common law position only applies to Member States within the EC.

10 Passing off action distinguished from trade libel

In an action for slander of title or slander of goods (malicious or injurious falsehood) it is essential to prove that the defendant falsely and maliciously made some representation about the plaintiff's business or goods and that the plaintiff has thereby suffered damage.[21] In *Kaye* v *Robertson* [1991] FSR 62 at 67 Glidewell LJ stated that the essentials of the tort of injurious falsehood are 'that the defendant has published about the plaintiff words which are false, that they were published maliciously and that special damage has followed as the direct and natural result of their publication. As to special damage the effect of s 3(1) of the Defamation Act 1952 is that it is sufficient if the words published are calculated to cause pecuniary damage to the plaintiff. Malice will be inferred if it be proved that the words were calculated to produce damage and that the defendant knew when he published the words that they

---

[21] See *Ratcliffe* v *Evans* [1892] 2 QB 524 (CA) and *Royal Baking Powder Co* v *Wright Crossley & Co* (1900) 18 RPC 95 (HL).

were false or was reckless as to whether they were false or not.' Whilst Glidewell LJ was concerned with a falsehood about the professional reputation of a person they are equally apt where the falsehood concerns a business or goods. It differs from the tort of passing off in that whereas in a passing off action the false representation relates to the defendant's own goods or business, in a trade libel action the false representation relates to the plaintiff's goods or business—whether or not the plaintiff has an established reputation or goodwill.

In *Copydex Ltd* v *Noso Products Ltd* [1952] 69 RPC 38 the defendant falsely promoted his goods as being 'as shown on television' whereas the goods that were shown on BBC were in fact the plaintiff's goods although the product was not mentioned by name. Vaisey J in granting an interlocutory injunction stated 'whether this is strictly passing off, whether it is strictly slander of title, or whether it is malicious falsehood I am not quite certain ... the people who saw (the defendant's) stuff being sold, and who had previously seen the demonstration on television would have said at once, "That is what we saw on the television screen. We will have some."' In contrast in *Serville* v *Constance* [1954] 71 RPC 146 the plaintiff who was the champion boxer of Trinidad and a newcomer to the UK, failed to prevent the defendant falsely describing himself as the champion of Trinidad—the action was one of passing off and Harman J said 'there is no confusion here between Hector Constance and Hugh Serville ... this is the opposite, so to speak of a passing off case—it is the unknown seeking remedies against the known'—query whether an action for injurious falsehood would have succeeded.

This case was referred to in *Bristol Conservatories Ltd* v *Conservatories Custom Built Ltd* (1989) RPC 445 at 464, where the defendants falsely claimed that photographs of the palintiff's conservatories were theirs in order to induce customers to buy one of the defendant's. The Court of Appeal, in holding that there was a reasonable cause of action in passing off, preferred to follow its earlier decision in *Planier Fuel Economiser Co Ltd* v *National School of Salesmanship Ltd* [1943] 60 RPC 209 where the defendants falsely relied on certain tests carried out on the plaintiff's economiser as having been carried out on the defendants, and a list of customers to whom the plaintiff's economiser had been fitted. Lord Greene held that the defendant's conduct constituted passing off albeit the public may not have known of the plaintiff, the misrepresentation being that they were expecting to get the same economiser as those of other satisfied customers (viz one of the plaintiff's).

As stated above it is an essential requirement of an action for trade libel that the false representation is made with malice. Malice in this sense means proving some dishonest or improper motive of the defendant in making the false representation. 'A bona fide assertion of title however mistaken, if made for the protection of one's own interest or for some other proper purpose, is not malicious.'[22] In *Wilts United Dairy Ltd v Robinson Sons & Co Ltd* [1957] RPC 220,[23] where it was found that old stocks of the plaintiff's condensed milk purchased by the defendant and sold as current stock constituted both passing off and an injurious falsehood, Stable J held that a false statement published to injure another person even if thought to be true at the time will constitute malice as will a statement known to be false even if not published to injure.

Thus an action for slander of goods will lie where a person falsely and maliciously makes statements that the plaintiff is not entitled to use a particular name or that he (the defendant) is entitled to a name or other matter[24] or where he misstates the effect of a judgment or threatens proceedings against customers of the plaintiff's goods. However, to establish malice in such cases the plaintiff must show that the defendant knows that his claim is groundless.[25]

Disparagement of goods by one trader of another's may give rise to a valid cause of action if a reasonable man would take the false claim seriously and malice is established. Statements 'puffing' one's own goods at the expense of a rival's are not actionable and the courts have been very reluctant to act as the arbitrator of the comparative qualities of rival products and will only intervene where the statement of fact (as opposed to opinion) is demonstrably false.[26]

In *Ciba-Geigy Plc* v *Parke Davis & Co Ltd* [1994] FSR 8 at 21 Aldous J

---

[22] *Balden* v *Shorter* [1933] 1 Ch 427 at 430 (Maugham J); *Joyce* v *Motor Surveys Ltd* [1948] Ch 252 at 255 (Roxburgh J); *R J Reuter Co Ltd* v *Mulhens* (1953) 70 RPC 102 (Danckwerts J); 235 (CA, affirming Danckwerts J).

[23] Applied in *Redwood Music Ltd* v *Francis, Day & Hunter Ltd* [1978] RPC 429 at 467 (Robert Goff J).

[24] *Thorley's Cattle Food Co* v *Massam* (1880) 14 Ch D 763 (CA, false claim to be solely entitled to secret recipe for cattle food); *Ratcliffe* v *Evans* [1892] 2 QB 524 (CA, false statement in a newspaper that the plaintiff had ceased business). See also *Plant Location International ASBL* v *Yaseen* [1964] RPC 345 (Buckley J).

[25] *Mentmore Manufacturing Co Ltd* v *Fomento (Sterling Area) Ltd* (1955) 72 RPC 157 (CA); cf Patents Act 1977, s 70 and Registered Designs Act 1949, s 26 in relation to statutory threats, actions for patents and registered designs.

[26] See *Hubbuck & Sons Ltd* v *Wilkinson, Heywood & Clark Ltd* (1899) 1 QB 86 at 91, 93 (CA); *De Beers Abrasive Products Ltd* v *International General Electric Company of New York* [1975] FSR 323 (CA), a case reviewing many of the earlier cases on disparagement of goods; cf s 4(1) of the Trade Marks Act 1938 (as amended by the Trade Marks (Amendment) Act 1984) which provides protection for a trade mark registered in Part A of the register—see *Bismag* v *Amblins* (1940) 57 RPC 209 (CA, a case of comparative advertising without disparagement). By reason of s 10(6) of the Trade Marks Act comparative advertising without disparagement will be permissible.

stated 'I have no doubt that statements such as "A's flour is as good as B's" or "A's flour can be substituted in all recipes for B's flour" are puffs and not actionable. However, that does not mean that a similar statement would be a puff and not actionable, if made in relation to a pharmaceutical product. Parliament has thought it necessary to regulate the sale of pharmaceutical products in ways which have not been applied to flour and therefore the common law could apply different standards to statements about pharmaceuticals to those made about flour.'

By s 3(1) of the Defamation Act 1952, special damage need not be proved if the statement in question: (1) was calculated to cause pecuniary damage to the plaintiff and was published in writing or other permanent form; or (2) was calculated to cause pecuniary damage to the plaintiff in respect of any office, profession, calling, trade or business held or carried on by him at the time of publication.

An important consideration where injurious falsehood is alleged, particularly where the grant of intelocutory relief is involved, is to safeguard the defendant's freedom of speech.[27]

---

[27] See *Crest Homes Ltd* v *Ascott* [1980] FSR 396 (CA); *Compaq Computer* v *Dell Computer* [1992] FSR 93 and *Ciba-Geigy Plc* v *Parke Davis & Co Ltd* [1994] FSR 8 at 21–22 (Aldous J); see also Chapter 9, p 142.

Chapter 2

Reputation

The plaintiff must be able to show that the mark, name or get-up or other indicia in question has become known in this country to a substantial portion of the relevant public or trade so that the use of the mark, name or get-up in relation to any goods or services of the kind dealt with by the plaintiff will be understood by the public or trade as meaning those goods or services.[1] It matters not that purchasers or customers do not know the identity of the manufacturer of the goods or the proprietor of the business. See p 43, below.

Lord Hershell stated in *Leahy, Kelly & Leahy* v *Glover* (1893) 10 RPC 141 at 155 (HL) that the party alleging a trade name 'should prove in the first instance that any name which he claims as his trade name has been so extensively used in connection with his manufacture, or with the goods which he sells, that his goods have come to be known in the market by that name; that any one using that name would intend to refer to his goods; and that any one to whom the name was used would understand that his goods were referred to.' In this case the plaintiff failed to establish any exclusive right to the name 'Two D' in respect of cigars.

In *T Oertli A G* v *F J Bowman (London) Ltd*[1] Jenkins LJ said 'it is of course essential to the success of any claim in respect of passing off based on the use of a given mark or get-up that the plaintiff should be able to show that the disputed mark or get-up has become by user in this country distinctive of the plaintiff's goods so that the use in relation to any goods of the kind dealt in by the plaintiff of that mark or get-up will be understood by the trade and public in this country as meaning those goods are the plaintiff's goods.'

It has been held that a reputation not acquired by actual trading or carrying on some business in this country is not sufficient to establish a

---

[1] *Imperial Tobacco Co of India Ltd* v *Bonnan* (1924) 41 RPC 441 (PC); *Dental Manufacturing Co Ltd* v *C de Trey & Co* (1912) 29 RPC 617 (CA); *T Oertli A G* v *E J Bowman (London) Ltd* [1957] RPC 388 at 397 (CA); affirmed [1959] RPC 1 (HL); *Loew's Inc* v *Littler* (1955) 72 RPC 166 (Upjohn J).

passing off action.[2] The basis for this is that without some business or trading activity in this country there will be no goodwill to protect and therefore no damage or injury to the goodwill will be suffered.[2] In *S Chivers & Sons* v *S Chivers & Co Ltd* (1900) 17 RPC 420 at 431 it was observed that 'Advertisement, distinguished from trade, is nothing. No doubt if you have the trade the advertisement assists the trade but to say that a man can by advertising alone make his name known in connection with particular goods so as to assist him in obtaining a monopoly of the goods seems to be untenable as a proposition.'

The mark or name in question may be an invented (fancy) or descriptive word or a personal or proper name (actual or real).[3]

As to the proof required to establish such goodwill or reputation, this will vary with the inherent distinctiveness or otherwise of the name, mark or get-up in question. The relevant date for determining whether a plaintiff has established the necessary goodwill or reputation is the date when the defendant commences the conduct complained of.[4]

1 Plaintiff need not have place of business in the UK

In the Budweiser case[2] the crucial question was what amount of trading activity is sufficient to establish a goodwill in this country which the court will protect. By the relevant date the plaintiffs had a substantial reputation in the name Budweiser amongst potential purchasers of beer in the UK due to the spillover advertising from American magazines etc, nevertheless their beer was not available on the open market in the UK (as opposed to being available to US servicemen throughout US bases). The Court of

---

[2] *Alain Bernardin et Cie* v *Pavilion Properties Ltd* [1967] RPC 581 at 585–588 (Pennycuick J, Crazy Horse); *Anheuser-Busch Inc* v *Budejovicky Budvar NP* [1984] FSR 413 (CA, Budweiser beer); cf *Metric Resources Corp* v *Leasemetrix Ltd* [1979] FSR 571 (Megarry V-C) and *Esanda Ltd* v *Esanda Finance Ltd* [1984] FSR 96 (New Zealand HC, spillover reputation from Australia sufficient). Cf *British Broadcasting Corp* v *Talbot Motor Company Ltd* [1981] FSR 228.

[3] See *Landa* v *Greenberg* (1908) 24 TLR 441 (Eve J, pen name 'Aunt Naomi' protected); *Hines* v *Winnick* (1947) 64 RPC 113 (Vaisey J, Dr Crock and his Crackpots); *Marengo* v *Daily Sketch & Sunday Graphic Ltd* (1948) 65 RPC 242 (HL, 'Kem' the pseudonym of a cartoonist).

[4] *Henry Faulder & Co Ltd* v *Rushton* (1903) 20 RPC 477 (CA, Silverpan jam); *Norman Kark Publications Ltd* v *Odhams Press Ltd* [1962] RPC 163 (Wilberforce J); *Cadbury-Schweppes Pty Ltd* v *The Pub Squash Co Ltd* [1981] RPC 486 (PC); cf *Elida Gibbs Ltd* v *Colgate-Palmolive Ltd* [1983] FSR 95 (Goulding J, where the defendant, despite pre-empting the plaintiff, had no bona fide intention of trading in the UK and quia timet relief was granted—probably wrongly decided).

Appeal in refusing relief held that at the time the defendant entered the UK market, the plaintiffs would not suffer any damage to their business or goodwill. In the light of this decision and the Advocaat formulation (which was applied in the Budweiser case), a number of the earlier cases as to the extent a plaintiff has to establish a trading activity here must be examined with care.

A foreign plaintiff having no place of business in this country may establish a sufficient reputation in this country by the sale of his goods either direct to customers or through an agent. Thus in *Panhard et Levassor SA* v *Panhard Levassor Motor Co Ltd* (1901) 18 RPC 405: the plaintiff was a manufacturer of cars in France without any place of business in this country and had sold cars to a number of people in this country either directly from Paris or through an importer. Farwell J held that the plaintiff had a reputation in this country sufficient to prevent a rival company (and its directors) from using its name, there being a UK market for such cars.

Similarly in *Poiret* v *Jules Poiret Ltd* (1920) 37 RPC 177 the plaintiff Paul Poiret established in Paris a substantial reputation as a costumier and designer of dresses and as a theatrical costumier. He had no place of business in England but had exhibited dresses in London and had many customers here, selling by himself or through an agent. During the war the defendant Alexander Nash set up in business in London as a costumier, dressmaker and theatrical costumier under the name Jules Poiret, which resulted in confusion with private customers and in the press. An injunction was granted by Younger J restraining the defendant from using the name Poiret with or without the name Jules in connection with the business of a costumier or dress designer.

This case was followed in *Sheraton Corp of America* v *Sheraton Motels Ltd* [1964] RPC 202 where an interlocutory injunction was granted by Buckley J restraining the defendant from advertising any hotel under the name Sheraton. Although the plaintiff had no hotel of that name in this country, the plaintiff owned a number of hotels in the United States of America and other countries which were called 'Sheraton Hotels' and there was evidence that bookings for such hotels were being taken at an office kept by the plaintiff in this country. Oliver LJ in the Budweiser case described this case as the 'high water mark' of such cases.[5]

---

[5] See also *Globelegance BV* v *Sarkissian* [1974] RPC 603 (Templeman J, where the plaintiff's international reputation in ladies' wear and sale of men's ties in London was sufficient to prevent the defendant opening a menswear shop in London as 'Valentino'); *C & A Modes* v *C & A Waterford Ltd* [1978] FSR (Ireland HC, SC).

By contrast, in *Alain Bernadin et Cie* v *Pavilion Properties Ltd* [1967] RPC 581[6] Pennycuick J refused to grant an interlocutory injunction restraining the defendant from setting up an establishment in London called the 'Crazy Horse Saloon' on the ground that the plaintiff had failed to establish a reputation in this country by user over here despite the evidence of confusion amongst members of the public. In this case the plaintiff was the owner of the 'Crazy Horse Saloon' in Paris and had circulated publicity material in this country. However, the plaintiff had no office in this country and therefore took no bookings here and on this ground the Court distinguished the *Sheraton Corp of America* v *Sheraton Motels Ltd.*

2 Fancy name

If the name is a fancy one which is coined by the trader and has no meaning when applied to the article, it will readily become distinctive of his goods as opposed to the goods of some other trader. Examples of fancy names are Eureka Shirts, Amami toilet preparations, Avro aeroplanes.[7] It is plain that not only will a fancy or invented name become a trade name far more readily than a descriptive name but also there is far less excuse for imitating such a fancy name. As Lord Herschell stated in *Reddaway* v *Banham* (1896) 13 RPC 218 at 228 'where the trade mark is a word or device never in use before, and meaningless, except as indicating by whom the goods in connection with which it is used were made, there could be no conceivable legitimate use of it by another person. His only object in employing it in connection with goods of his manufacture must be to deceive.'

---

[6] Followed in *Amway Corp* v *Eurway International Ltd* [1974] RPC 82 (Brightman J) and in *The Athletes Foot Marketing Associates Inc* v *Cobra Sports Ltd* [1980] RPC 343 (Walton J, where the plaintiff who was a well known franchiser in USA of 'The Athlete's Foot' as shoe shops and was preparing to franchise a company in UK failed to secure interlocutory injunction to restrain the defendants opening a shop called 'Athlete's Foot Bargain Basement'); criticised in *C & A Modes* v *C & A (Waterford) Ltd* [1978] FSR 126 (Ireland HC, SC); *Baskin-Robbins Ice Cream Co* v *Gutman* [1976] FST 545 (Graham J) and in *Maxim's Ltd* v *Dye* [1977] FSR 364 (Graham J); see also *Ten-Ichi Co Ltd* v *Jan Car Ltd* [1990] FSR 151 (H K, Sears J) where the defendant's restaurant in Hong Kong was identical in name and style to a chain of restaurants of the plaintiffs in Japan and the plaintiffs were intending to open a restaurant in Hong Kong.

[7] *Ford* v *Foster* (1872) 7 Ch App 611; *Prichard & Constance (Wholesale) Ltd* v *Amata Ltd* (1924) 42 RPC 63 (Romer J); *A V Roe & Co Ltd* v *Aircraft Disposal Co Ltd* (1920) 37 RPC 249 (Peterson J).

3 Descriptive name[11]

Owing to the obvious reluctance of the courts to accept that a descriptive name is a trade name and to allow a trader to monopolise ordinary English words for his wares, the plaintiff who is claiming that such a word has become his trade name has a difficult burden to discharge. Every trader for instance has a right to call a certain kind of beverage 'malted milk'[8] or a certain weave of cloth 'cellular',[9] for such names are descriptive of a certain kind of article and do not denote an article made or sold by a particular trader. However as Lord Herschell said in *Reddaway* v *Banham* (1896) 13 RPC 218 at 228, 'the name of a person, or words forming part of the common stock of language, may become so far associated with the goods of a particular maker that it is capable of proof that the use of them by themselves, without explanation or qualification by another manufacturer, would deceive a purchaser into the belief that he was getting the goods of A, when he was really getting the goods of B. In a case of this description, the mere proof by the plaintiff that the defendant was using a name, word, or device which he had adopted to distinguish his goods would not entitle him to any relief. He could only obtain it by proving, further, that the defendant was using it under such circumstances or in such manner as to put off his goods as the goods of the plaintiff. If he could succeed in proving this, I think he would, on well-established principles, be entitled to an injunction.'

Such considerations apply equally to businesses or services. See for example *Park Court Hotel Ltd* v *Trans-World Hotels Ltd* [1972] RPC 27 (Ungoed-Thomas J), which concerned the use of the name 'International' in relation to an hotel.

4 Whether name is descriptive or fancy may depend on what article it is applied to

In *McCain International Ltd* v *Country Fair Foods Ltd* [1981] RPC 69 (CA, the 'Oven Chip' case: see p 32), Templeman LJ observed that the true distinction between a descriptive name and a fancy name is that between a name which is descriptive of the product and a name which is distinctive of the manufacturer.

A good illustration of when a name is descriptive and when it is fancy was given by Neville J, in the case of *Henry Thorne & Co Ltd* v *Sandow*

---

[8]   *Horlick's Malted Milk Co* v *Summerskill* (1917) 34 RPC 63 (HL).
[9]   *Cellular Clothing Co* v *Maxton* (1899) 16 RPC 397 (HL).

(1912) 29 RPC 440 at 451. The plaintiff had for some years sold and advertised his cocoa as 'Health Cocoa' and although the judge held the name had become distinctive of the plaintiff in certain parts of England no injunction was granted. Neville J stated 'supposing a person had introduced a fishing rod on the market and called it a "Health Fishing Rod" . . . the connection between the word used to denote the fishing rod and its ordinary meaning is so slight that I could imagine a case in which the Court might come to the conclusion that the word "Health" had become distinctive of a make of fishing rods, and that other persons ought not to be entitled to use a word, which they were exceedingly unlikely to introduce for themselves unless they wanted to interfere with the trade of the owner of the trade mark . . . But, when it comes to the same word used in connection with an article of diet, I think we are confronted by a totally different set of circumstances, and I must say, not to put it too high, that it seems to me that a person who sought to prove that throughout the United Kingdom — as I think he would have to prove — the word "Health", in connection with an article of diet, was only descriptive of his particular manufacture, would have an exceedingly difficult task before him.'[10]

5   Secondary meaning may be acquired by descriptive word

To prove that a descriptive name is a trade name to which the plaintiff has an exclusive right it is necessary to show that words which are primarily descriptive have through usage become associated exclusively with the plaintiff(s) and thus distinguish their goods or business from other similar goods or businesses.[11] In *Reddaway v Banham* (1896) 13 RPC 218 (HL),

---

[10]   See also, eg, *Saville Perfumery Ltd* v *June Perfect Ltd* (1941) 58 RPC 147 (Bennet J, 'June' applied to soap); *Treasure Cot Co Ltd* v *Hamleys Bros Ltd* (1950) 67 RPC 89 (Harman J, 'Treasure Cot' applied to babies, and dolls' cots).

[11]   Cf under the Trade Marks Act 1938, the ability to register a trade mark in Part B of the register. Section 10(2)(a) of the Trade Marks Act 1938 empowered the tribunal to have regard to the extent to which a name or word is 'inherently capable of distinguishing' the applicant's goods. The House of Lords held that even though a name or word is 100 per cent factually capable of distinguishing an applicant's goods (see s 10(2)(b)), nevertheless certain names or words are too descriptive to be inherently capable of distinguishing such goods and thus are unregistrable (*Re York Trailer Holdings Ltd* [1982] FSR 111 ('York' for trailers held unregistrable); cf *Re Blue Paraffin Trade Mark* [1977] RPC 473 (CA, 'Blue Paraffin' for paraffin coloured with blue dye registrable). Cf position under the Trade Marks Act 1994, s 1(1) the requirement is that the trade mark must be capable of distinguishing goods or services.

camel hair was prima facie descriptive of the material of which belting was made; but it had acquired a secondary meaning in the trade which connoted that it was made by Reddaway. As Lord Halsbury said, 'the more simple the phraseology, the more like it is to a mere description of the article sold, the greater becomes the difficulty of proof.'[12] It has been held to be particularly so in the case of a natural product (for example Whitstable Oysters) coming from and described by reference to a particular district.[13] When it is so established the descriptive name ceases to be common property, and becomes the property of one particular trader.

In *Burberrys* v *Cording & Co Ltd* (1909) 26 RPC 693 at 709, 704, 701 Parker J said:

> It is only rarely that an English word primarily descriptive and which has become the name of a particular article of commerce, can be so distinctive of the goods of a particular manufacturer that the Court will restrain its use as calculated to deceive where there has been no actual deception, and no intention to take any fraudulent advantage of another by using the word. It is, of course, a truism to state that unfair dealing of any sort ought to be restrained by Courts of Justice, but there is another principle and one equally important, namely, that everybody dealing in an article of commerce is entitled to use any words which are or have become current in the English language as denoting or describing that article provided he can do so without deceiving the public to another's injury.

> Upon the facts, as I have found them, the word "Slip-on" is and has always been used by the plaintiffs, primarily as a word describing the article, and ... the word does in fact describe the article in the minds of both the trade and the public. The word has never been used by the plaintiffs primarily as a word distinctive of goods of their own manufacture. If it has come to distinguish their goods from those of others, it has done so by acquiring a secondary meaning without losing its descriptive character. Though I do not agree with the

---

[12] See also *Cellular Clothing Company* v *Maxton* (1899) 16 RPC 397 at 405 (HL) where Lord Halsbury states 'where you are dealing with a name which is properly descriptive of the article, the burden is very great to show that by reason of your using that name, descriptive of the article you are selling, you are affecting to sell the goods of somebody else'.

[13] Cf *Montgomery* v *Thompson* (1891) 8 RPC 361 (HL, Stone Ales, defendant prevented from marketing ale or beer not made by the plaintiff as 'Stone Ales' or 'Stone Ale' even though the same was brewed at Stone); *Worcester Royal Porcelain Co Ltd* v *Locke & Co Ltd* (1902) 19 RPC 479 (Byrne J, Worcester China and porcelain).

argument that a word cannot be at the same time both descriptive and distinctive, I think the fact that it retains its *prima facie* descriptive signification increases the difficulty of proving that it is distinctive of the goods of any particular manufacturer. If a word is *prima facie* the name of or description of an article, evidence that it is also generally associated with the name of a particular manufacturer is, in my opinion, by no means conclusive that it has become a distinctive word which cannot be used of the same article when made by others without risk of deception.

It is important for this purpose to consider whether the word or name is *prima facie* in the nature of a fancy word or name, or whether it is *prima facie* descriptive of the article in respect of which it is used. It is also important for the same purpose to consider its history, the nature of its use by the person who seeks the injunction, and the extent to which it is or has been used by others. If the word or name is *prima facie* descriptive or be in general use, the difficulty of establishing the probability of deception is greatly increased. Again, if the person who seeks the injunction has not used the word or name simply for the purpose of distinguishing his own goods from the goods of others, but primarily for the purpose of denoting or describing the particular kind of article to which he has applied it, and only secondarily, if at all, for the purposes of distinguishing his own goods, it will be more difficult for him to establish the probability of deception.

In *Office Cleaning Services Ltd* v *Westminster Window and General Cleaners Ltd* (1946) 63 RPC 39[14] it was held by the House of Lords that where the name of a business consists of words descriptive of that business

---

[14] Applied in *Deane* v *Schofield* [1962] RPC 179 (Plowman J, The Under Six Club — The Over Six Club); *Industrial Furnaces* v *Reaves* [1970] RPC 605 (Graham J, Industrial Furnaces—Reaves Industrial Furnaces); *Park Court Hotel Ltd* v *Transworld-Hotels Ltd* [1972] RPC 27 (Ungoed-Thomas J, Hotel International-London International Hotel); cf distinguished in *Southern Music Publishing Co Ltd* v *Southern Songs Ltd* [1966] RPC 137 (Buckley J, 'Southern' held to be distinctive of plaintiff's music publishing business); *Pickwick International Inc (GB) Ltd* v *Multiple Sound Distributors Ltd* [1972] RRPCK 786 (Megarry J, Top of the Pops—Pick of the Pops for gramophone records, interlocutory injunction granted). Cf *Furniture Ltd* v *Harris* (1989) FSR 536 (Browne-Wilkinson V-C): the plaintiffs were trading under the style 'Furniture Land', selling branded furniture, the defendants were trading under the style 'Furniture City'—there was no triable issue; *County Sound plc* v *Ocean Sound Ltd* [1991] FSR 367 (CA) 'The Gold AM' radio programme. The plaintiffs had not acquired a secondary meaning in a name which was descriptive of the content of the programme, ie Gold, Golden.

which have not acquired a secondary meaning, a slight difference between the plaintiff's and defendant's title will, in the absence of fraud, be a sufficient distinction. In that case the difference between 'Office Cleaning Services' and 'Office Cleaning Association' was held to be sufficient, it being observed that 'where a trader adopts words in common use for his trade name some risk of confusion is inevitable. But that risk must be run unless the first user is allowed unfairly to monopolise.'

In *William Stevens Ltd* v *Cassell* (1913) 30 RPC 199[15] Neville J in refusing relief to the publishers of a magazine called 'The Magazine of Fiction' said: 'It is undoubtedly a matter of importance to protect a trader from any unfair attempt to take advantage of his reputation, but it is, I think, equally important to protect all His Majesty's subjects in their right to use the King's English, and the law will not recognise a monopoly of English words of common import.'

In *Reckitt & Colman Products Ltd* v *Borden Inc* [1990] RPC 341, a get-up case, it was found as a fact that the marketing of lemon juice in a yellow natural size lemon-shaped squeeze pack had acquired a secondary significance—it indicated not merely lemon juice, but specifically the plaintiff's Jif lemon juice. Lord Oliver at 414 states 'In the end, the question comes down not as to whether the respondents are entitled to a monopoly in the sale of lemon juice in natural size lemon-shaped containers, but as to whether the appellants, in deliberately adopting, out of all the many possible shapes of container, a container having the most immediately striking feature of the respondent's get-up, have taken sufficient steps to distinguish their product from that of the respondent's.'

6 Words both descriptive and distinctive

As Fletcher Moulton LJ stated in *Joseph Crosfield & Sons Ltd's Application* (1909) 26 RPC 837 at 857 (CA) (in relation to the registrability of the word 'Perfection' as a trade mark) 'descriptive names may be distinctive and vice versa. No class of words are more directly and intentionally distinctive than proper names, and yet originally they were usually, if not invariably, descriptive in all languages. They still are so among savage peoples, and although among civilised nations the original significations of proper names are not remembered, or regarded, we see that the natural tendency to use descriptive words as names still exists since nick-names—the only names that are now invented—are usually

---

[15] See also *D C Thomson & Co Ltd* v *Kent Messenger Ltd* [1975] RPC 191 (Megarry J, Sunday Post objected to a use of South East Sunday Post; papers held not confusingly similar; Sunday Post not a fancy word) and Chapter 5, pp 88 et seq.

descriptive. There is therefore no natural or necessary incompatibility between distinctiveness and descriptiveness in the case of words as trade marks ... the question whether a word is or is capable of becoming distinctive of the goods of a particular maker is a question of fact ...'

In *Havana Cigar & Tobacco Factories Ltd* v *Oddenino*[16] Russell J found that the words 'a Corona cigar' originally meant a cigar of the Corona brand but that the use for many years of the words 'Coronas' or 'Corona' as a size name for various brands had attached to the words 'a Corona cigar' a further meaning, namely, a cigar of a certain size and shape, but not necessarily of the Corona brand; and that the words 'a Corona cigar' used as a size name, denoted to many people other features beyond mere shape and size. 'This descriptive meaning has not destroyed or supplanted the original meaning,' he said. 'To the majority of people the words "a Corona cigar" mean a cigar of the "La Corona" brand; but there is no doubt that to a large number of persons the words do not indicate brand, but size and shape.' An injunction was granted restraining the defendant, his servants and agents 'from selling or supplying in response to any order for "some cigars—Coronas," or "Corona cigars," or a "Corona cigar," or "Coronas", or "a Corona", cigars or a cigar not of the Corona brand, unless it be first clearly ascertained that the customer giving the order does not require cigars or a cigar of the Corona brand and no other brand'.

In *Cellular Clothing Co Ltd* v *G White & Co Ltd* (1952) 70 RPC 9, an action which turned on the evidence of certain trap orders, Harman J held that a concession by the plaintiff that some members of the public used the word 'Aertex' as the description of a type of cellular fabric was fatal to the plaintiff's action for passing off based on such trap order.

The name 'Daimler' as applied to motor cars was originally merely descriptive of the system on which the cars worked but later when the system was obsolete became a trade name for cars made by the plaintiff firm.[17]

7 Different meaning to trade and to public

Sometimes a word means more or less to the trade than to the public. In such cases the public is more important, since 'persons in the trade, in their dealings *inter se*, know exactly what they want to describe and how to

---

[16] (1923) 40 RPC 229 (Russell J); (1924) 41 RPC 47 (CA); followed in *Goddard* v *The Watford Co-op Society* (1924) 41 RPC 218 (Astbury J); considered and distinguished in *John Jacques & Son Ltd* v *Chess* (1940) 57 RPC 77 (CA).

[17] *Daimler Motor Co (1904) Ltd* v *London Daimler Co Ltd* (1907) 24 RPC 379 (CA).

describe it'.[18] So where a fancy name 'Eureka' as a designation for a particular kind of shirt was in general use in price lists which circulated between manufacturers and retail dealers, this was held not to prejudice the right of the inventor to the exclusive use of the name as a trade mark in the sale of the article to the public,[19] and the fact that 'gramophone' meant to the trade instruments made by a certain maker, although to the public generally it meant merely a particular type of instrument, was held not to entitle the maker to protect the name as referring exclusively to instruments of his own manufacture.[20]

8   Trade name which has become publici juris

A plaintiff may lose his right to protect a name which he has allowed rivals to use to such an extent that it has become publici juris or which he himself has used on goods in a descriptive way. A trade mark or name may by general use cease to denote goods made by a certain trader and become descriptive of a certain type of article[21]—thus the mark or name in question may come to describe a particular process relating to goods of a certain type[22] or to describe a type of article used for a particular purpose.[23]

In *Ford* v *Foster*[24] it was argued that 'Eureka' had ceased to apply solely to the plaintiff's goods and had come to be a term applicable to a special cut of shirt. Mellish LJ said 'I think that the test must be whether the use of it by other persons is still calculated to deceive the public, whether it may still have the effect of inducing the public to buy the goods not made by the original owner of the trade mark as if they were his goods. If the mark has come to be so public and in such universal use that nobody can be deceived by the use of it, and can be induced from the use of it to believe that he is

---

[18] *Havana Cigar & Tobacco Factories Ltd* v *Oddenino* (1923) 40 RPC 229 at 241 (Russell J); see also *Unicorn Products Ltd* v *Roban Jig & Tool Co (UK) Ltd* [1976] FSR 169 (Whitford J, injunction refused where 'Bullet' darts had no reputation in minds of the public even though a substantial reputation with the trade).

[19] *Ford* v *Foster* (1872) 7 Ch App 611.

[20] *Re Gramaphone Co's Application* (1910) 28 RPC 689 (Parker J).

[21] *Havana Cigar & Tobacco Factories Ltd* v *Oddenino* (1923) 40 RPC 229 (Russell J); (1924) 41 RPC 47 (CA).

[22] *Liebig's Extract of Meat Co* v *Hanbury* (1867) 17 LT 298 (Wood V-C, Liebig's Extract).

[23] *G H Gledhill & Sons Ltd* v *British Perforated Toilet Paper Co* (1911) 28 RPC 714 (CA, Gledhill Rolls).

[24] (1872) 7 Ch App 611 at 628, cited by Lindley L J in *Reddaway* v *Bentham Hemp Spinning Co* (1892) 9 RPC 506 (CA); see also *Treasure Cot Co Ltd* v *Hamleys Bros* (1950) 67 RPC 89 (Harman J).

buying the goods of the original trader, it appears to me, however hard to some extent it may appear on the trader, yet practically, as the right to a trade mark is simply a right to prevent the trader from being cheated by other persons' goods being sold as his goods through the fraudulent use of the trade mark, the right to the trade mark must be gone'.

Thus every trader has a right to call a certain kind of cleaner a 'vacuum cleaner'[25] or floor covering 'linoleum'[26] and in *G H Gledhill & Sons Ltd* v *British Perforated Toilet Paper Co* (1911) 28 RPC 714 (CA) it was held that though the name 'Gledhill's Coils' had originally meant coils made by the plaintiff, it had subsequently lost its distinctive character and had come to mean any coils that could be used in a Gledhill till.

Where a trade mark or name was originally distinctive, the onus is on the defendant to prove that it has lost its distinctive character[27] and that the use of the mark or name no longer is capable of deceiving the public as to the origin of the goods.[28] In *Argyllshire Weavers Ltd* v *A Macaulay Tweeds Ltd* [1964] RPC 477 (Court of Session) it was held that the mark 'Harris Tweed' had not lost its distinctive character because of its surreptitious use on machine made cloth.

9 Name of new or patented article is generally descriptive[29]

Where goods are the subject of Letters Patent[30] or a registered design[31] or their manufacture involves a secret process[32] then anyone will be entitled to use the name which describes such goods when the patent or design has expired or the secret process becomes known, provided that such use of the

---

[25] *British Vacuum Cleaner Co Ltd* v *New Vacuum Cleaner Co Ltd* (1907) 24 RPC 641 (Parker J).

[26] *Linoleum Manufacturing Co* v *Nairn* (1878) 7 Ch D 834 (Fry J).

[27] *Powell* v *The Birmingham Vinegar Brewery Co Ltd* (1896) 13 RPC 235 at 253 (CA); *Jaegar* v *Jaegar & Co Ltd* (1927) 44 RPC 83 (Romer J); 437 (CA).

[28] *Ford* v *Foster* (1872) 7 Ch App 611 at 628; *Treasure Cot Co Ltd* v *Hamleys Bros Ltd* (1950) 67 RPC 89 at 90 (Harman J).

[29] See also Chapter 5, pp 81–84.

[30] *Cheavin* v *Walker* (1877) 5 Ch D 850 (CA): *Linoleum Manufacturing Co* v *Nairn* (1878) 7 Ch D 834 (Fry J, linoleum); *Bowden Wire Ltd* v *Bowden Brake Co* (1913) 30 RPC 609 (Warrington J, Bowden Control descriptive of system of controlling motor cycles by means of Bowden Wire); cf *Re Cheseborough's Trade Mark* (1901) 18 RPC 191 (Buckley J); (1902) 19 RPC 342 (CA) (Vaseline: where articles only subject to a foreign patent).

[31] *Winser & Co Ltd* v *Armstrong & Co* (1898) 16 RPC 167 (Byrne J).

[32] *Siegert* v *Findlater* (1878) 7 Ch D 801 at 813 (Fry J, the 'Angostura Bitters' case where deception was proved and an injunction granted); *Massam* v *Thorley's Cattle Food Co* (1880) 14 Ch D 748 at 755 (CA).

name is fair[33] and does not deceive anyone as to the origin of the goods in question. In *Singer Machine Manufacturers Co* v *Wilson* (1877) 3 App Cas 376 (HL) it was held that 'Singer' machines meant machines manufactured by the Singer Manufacturing Company and not merely machines of a certain design and that 'Singer Systems' did not mean anything to the ordinary purchaser of such machines. However, in *Singer Manufacturing Co* v *Loog* (1882) 8 App Cas 15 (HL) it was held that rival traders had a right to advertise their machines as made on the 'Singer System' making it quite clear that their machines were not made by the Singer Manufacturing Company.

In *Cellular Clothing Co* v *Maxton*[34] Lord Davey said 'where a man produces, or invents, if you please, a new article, and attaches a descriptive name to it, a name which, as the article has not been produced before, has of course not been used in connection with the article, and secures for himself either the legal monopoly or a monopoly in fact of the sale of the article for a certain time, the evidence of persons who come forward and say that the name in question suggests to their minds and is associated by them with the plaintiff's goods alone, is of a very slender character, for this very simple reason because the plaintiff was the only maker of the goods during the time that his monopoly lasted, and therefore there was nothing to compare with it, and anybody who wanted the goods had no shop to go to, and no merchant or manufacturer to report to except the plaintiff.'

In *Fels* v *Christopher Thomas & Bros Ltd* (1903) 21 RPC 85 it was held that 'Naptha Soap' meant to the public soap with naptha in it and not necessarily the soap of the plaintiff who had first introduced it into this country and sold it in large quantities. Likewise 'Liebig's Extract' or 'Baron Liebig's Extract of Meat' have been held to be descriptive of a well known process and are therefore free for all to use and any maker of it may print a portrait of the Baron on the wrapper.[35] Similarly in *Linoleum Manufacturing Co* v *Nairn* (1878) 7 Ch D 834 it was held by Fry J that 'linoleum' was merely descriptive of a process on the ground that where the inventor of a new substance gives it a name and having taken out a patent for the invention has, during the continuance of the patent, alone made and sold the substance by that name, he is not entitled to the sole use of that name after the expiration of the patent. Also in *Winser & Co Ltd* v

---

[33] *Singer Manufacturing Co* v *Loog* (1882) 8 App Cas 15 (HL); see also *Daimler Motor Co (1904) Ltd* v *London Daimler Co Ltd* (1907) 24 RPC 379 (CA, Daimler originally descriptive of system latterly distinctive of car).

[34] (1899) 16 RPC 397 at 409 (HL). See also *Parsons Bros & Co* v *John Gillespie & Co* (1897) 15 RPC 57 (PC, flaked Oatmeal).

[35] *Liebig's Extract of Meat Co Ltd* v *Hanbury* (1867) 17 LT 298 (Wood V-C); *Liebig's Extract of Meat Co Ltd* v *Anderson* (1886) 55 LT 206 (Chitty J).

Armstrong & Co (1898) 16 RPC 167, the name 'Winser Interceptors' for sewer interceptors was held by Byrne J to be the name of a certain type of interceptor which previously had been the subject of a registered design and not to denote an interceptor supplied by the plaintiff.

In *McCain International Ltd* v *Country Fair Foods Limited* [1981] RPC 69 the Court of Appeal stated that where a person introduces a new product to the market, gives it a name descriptive of the product and has a monopoly, whether legal or de facto, in that product he cannot claim a monopoly in that name. He can only require that other persons who make the same product distinguish their products by appropriate means. The plaintiff introduced onto the UK market a novel product—chips cooked in the oven or baked under the grill and sold them under the name 'McCain Oven Chips'. It was held that 'Country Fair Oven Chips' and 'Birds Eye Oven Chips' sufficiently differentiated the defendant's products.

In *My Kinda Town Ltd* v *Soll* [1983] RPC 407 the plaintiff opened a restaurant in London under the name 'The Chicago Pizza Pie Factory' specialising in a particular kind of pizza called the Chicago pizza. The defendant also opened up a restaurant in London called 'LS Grunts Chicago Pizza Company'. Despite evidence of confusion between the two restaurants, the Court of Appeal in refusing to grant an injunction held that as the words 'Chicago pizza' were descriptive of a new kind of pizza, the impression that the ordinary member of the public would get from the use of such words in the defendant's name was that both businesses sold the same commodity.

In contrast to the foregoing, in *Island Trading Company* v *Anchor Brewing Company* [1989] RPC 287a Knox J restrained the defendants from selling keg beer (as opposed to beer in bottles) under their trade mark 'Anchor Steam Beer' as it would be likely to be confused with the plaintiff's Newquay Real Steam Beer. However, the cases referred to above do not appear to have been cited and this case can only be explained on the special facts that as the defendants had not sold any substantial quantities of keg beer it would not harm them from being so injuncted until trial.

However, persons other than the plaintiff will be prevented from using the name of an article which is the subject of a secret process as they do not know how to produce it and the public will therefore not get the article they expect to get.[36] Thus in *Powell* v *The Birmingham Vinegar Brewery Co Ltd* (1897) 14 RPC 720 (HL)[37] the defendant's sauce, though very similar, was

---

[36] *Lecouturier* v *Rey* (1910) 27 RPC 268 (HL); *Goddard* v *The Watford Co-op Society* (1924) 41 RPC 218 (Astbury J); and see also footnote 32 above.

[37] Cf *Native Guano Co* v *Sewage Manure Co* (1889) 8 RPC 125 (HL) considered by Lord Diplock in *Erven Warnink BV* v *J Townend & Sons (Hull) Ltd* [1980] RPC 31 at 96, 97 (HL).

not the real sauce made by the plaintiff, so that the defendant was restrained from selling it as 'Yorkshire Relish' and in *Siegert* v *Findlater* (1878) 7 Ch D 801 (Fry J) a defendant was restrained from selling his article as 'Angostura Bitters' because he did not know the plaintiff's secret and could not make an article identical with that of the plaintiff. Furthermore, as Harman LJ said in *E Hoffman-La Roche & Co AG* v *DDSA Pharmaceuticals Ltd* [1972] RPC 1 at 21 (CA), 'in a get-up it is quite different: it is not a description, it is a mark, just as if here they had said "Roche's product" and because the public has always had CDP in a green and black form . . . it seems to me that it is a perfectly natural assumption for a member of the public to make, that all the green and black capsules emanated from the same manufacturer.'

10 Area of reputation[38]

Where a plaintiff can only prove a reputation and goodwill in his trade mark, name or get-up within a limited geographical area questions arise as to how far the courts will protect such goodwill outside the limited area. In *Ewing* v *Buttercup Margarine Company Ltd* [1917] 2 Ch 1 the plaintiff was trading in dairy products in Scotland and the North of England under the name 'Buttercup Dairy Company' but proposed to expand further south, whilst the defendant had its office in Westminster and intended to sell margarine to the wholesale trade. The Court of Appeal in restraining the defendant from using the name 'Buttercup Margarine Company Ltd' stated that a defendant may be calculated to deceive and cause the plaintiff damage *either* by diverting customers from the plaintiff to the defendant *or* occasioning a confusion between the two businesses by suggesting they are connected. In *Brestian* v *Try* [1958] RPC 161 the plaintiff carried on business as ladies' hairdressers under the name 'Charles of London' with branches in London, Wembley and Brighton. The defendant who had adopted the same name as a ladies' hairdresser in Tunbridge Wells was restrained from

---

[38] As regards instances of limited injunctions see *The Clock Ltd* v *Clock House Hotel Ltd* (1936) 53 RPC 269 (CA, where the injunction was limited to restraining the defendant from using the words complained of on the defendants' premises); *A Levey* v *Henderson-Kenton Holdings Ltd* [1974] RPC 617 (Foster J, plaintiff's strong local residual goodwill as 'Kentons department stores' in Newcastle protected where defendants' well-known furniture and furnishings retailers in South restrained from using Kentons in Newcastle).

using such name. There was some evidence of confusion that the defendant's shop was another branch of the plaintiffs. Jenkins LJ in considering (at 170) the defendants' contention that the plaintiffs could not succeed as they had not established any reputation and goodwill in the Tunbridge Wells area said 'But the matter cannot be decided by a mere allocation of goodwill by areas. The question in cases of this sort must surely be whether, given a proprietory interest in the goodwill attached to a name, that name is being used by an interloper in circumstances in which such use is calculated to cause confusion or deception. Distance may no doubt in some cases reduce and sometimes even remove the likelihood of confusion or deception but that must be a question of fact . . . Moreover, reasonable scope for the expansion of the plaintiff's business by the opening of new branches should be allowed, and conversely the possibility of expansion by the defendant should be taken into account.'

In *Henry Faulder & Co Ltd* v *Rushton Ltd* (1903) 20 RPC 477 (CA) the plaintiff was a jam manufacturer in Stockport and had for some years used the word 'Silverpan' as the name of their jams. The defendant traded at Wigan and Chorley and started using the word 'Silverpan' to describe the defendant's jams. The plaintiff company, although they had advertised their goods at Wigan and were known at Chorley, had no very substantial trade or reputation there. The defendant relied on the fact that the plaintiff had little or no reputation in the word 'Silverpan' in the district where the defendant sold the defendant's goods, but nevertheless an injunction was granted. Romer LJ said at 493, 494, 'I will take the first question which had to be decided, and that may be stated as follows—at the time when the defendants first commenced to use the term "Silverpan" had that term acquired in the markets of Lancashire, and in other markets, the meaning of the plaintiffs' jams, that is to say, of jams manufactured and sold by the plaintiffs? As I have said, I think that on the evidence it had. Of course, I do not mean that in every town in which there was a market for jams you could find a majority of the inhabitants who knew about this jam; still less do I suppose that a majority of inhabitants of the districts in which this jam was chiefly sold, as a whole knew the jam intimately, or possibly at all; but I think that in the markets I have referred to a substantial number of persons who were interested in the question, and whom, from their position, one would expect to have known about the jam, did so know the plaintiffs' jam; and I certainly think, upon the evidence, that all who knew the phrase at all, as applied to jam, before the acts of the defendants which are complained of, identified the term as meaning the plaintiff's goods'.

Vaughan Williams LJ said, at 492, 'It is not only necessary that there

35

should be proof of the identification of this word "Silverpan" with the plaintiffs' firm, but it is necessary to show that that identification is recognised within the district in which the defendants, whose user of the word is complained of, carry on business. But this does not mean that there must be proof that the word "Silverpan" is recognised by every one in the district. In my judgment it is sufficient if there is, as there seems to be in this case, a user in the district of the name of "Silverpan" exclusively in connection with the plaintiffs' firm coupled with a large user of the word "Silverpan" exclusively by *Faulders* throughout a large portion of Lancashire, and especially that portion of Lancashire which is immediately contiguous to the Wigan district'.

In *Chelsea Man Menswear Ltd* v *Chelsea Girl Ltd* [1987] RPC 189 the plaintiffs traded as wholesalers in menswear under the label 'Chelsea Man' with shops in Coventry, Leicester and London called 'Nickelby'. The defendants were a very substantial chain store trading throughout the UK in women's clothing under the name 'Chelsea Girl' and had decided to extend their business to menswear by opening a chain of shops under the name 'Chelsea Man' either next door to or in the same premises as their existing shops. It was argued that a nationwide injunction was not justified but that it should be limited to the areas in which the plaintiffs' shops were located. In dismissing the appeal Slade LJ stated (at 204) 'the establishment of ring fences in the drafting of the injunction would afford even less satisfactory protection of the plaintiffs against two other forms of likely damage in relation to customers or potential customers, that is to say other than actual diversion of custom. The evidence shows clearly enough that a substantial number of the men entering into a shop of the defendants'... on seeing goods marked with the "Chelsea Man" label, would recognise that label and assume that the goods emanated either from the Nickelby business or the plaintiffs... it also establishes that a substantial number of such persons would be likely (*a*) to regard the quality of the goods which he saw as inferior... and/or (*b*) to regard the defendants' business as connected with that of the plaintiffs.' Nourse LJ stated (at 208) 'the Court must always provide for the reasonable protection of the plaintiff and no more, while paying due regard to the practical workings of any injunction which it grants.'

By way of example of a case where the courts have refused to restrain a defendant trading in a different part of the UK to the plaintiff, in *S Chivers*

& *Sons* v *S Chivers & Co Ltd* (1900) 17 RPC 429[39] the plaintiff produced
and sold 'Chivers' jam and jelly at Histon, Cambridgeshire, whilst the
defendant made and sold jelly at Cardiff as 'Cardiff Jelly' with the label
indicating the makers were 'S Chivers & Co Ltd'. Farwell J suggested that
in order to protect a trade name in a descriptive word the plaintiff must
show that it had attained a secondary meaning that was 'locally universal'
at least over the area in which the defendant traded and that 'the
universality really must be co-extensive at any rate with England and
Wales'. However this is plainly an overstatement and inconsistent with the
statement of Lord Shand in *Cellular Clothing Co* v *Maxton*,[40] 'supposing a
plaintiff were able to prove that in a number of the southern counties of
England his goods had been sold under that name, and if it could therefore
be held that in these counties by its universal use the word had acquired a
secondary signification, that would surely never entitle the plaintiff to have
an injunction in every part of England.'

11 Time necessary to acquire goodwill[41]

It is not possible to say how long it is necessary for a name or get-up to be
used before the trader acquires a reputation or goodwill sufficient to bring
a passing-off action. The time required will depend on how distinctive the
particular name or mark is and to what goods or business such name or
mark is applied.

In *Powell* v *The Birmingham Vinegar Brewery Co Ltd* (1897) 14 RPC 720
(HL) the plaintiff's sauce had been on the market for over twenty five years
whereas in *McAndrew* v *Bassett* (1864) 33 LJ Ch 561 (Wood V-C) the
plaintiff's product had only been on the market six weeks and in the case
of 'Mr Chippy' the plaintiff's mobile fish and chip van had been operating

---

[39] See also *Merchant Banking Co of London* v *Merchants Joint Stock Bank* (1878) 9
Ch D 560 (Jessell M R) and *George Outram & Co Ltd* v *London Evening
Newspapers Co Ltd* (1911) 28 RPC 308 (Warrington J); where injunctions were
refused because of the plaintiff's area of trade did not overlap that of the
defendant; *Evans* v *Eradicure Ltd* [1972] RPC 808 (Goff J, where interlocutory
injunction refused—rival businesses operated in different areas, one business
expanded westwards and the other eastwards with eventual clash of interests
and resulting likelihood of confusion; see also *Henry Thorne & Co Ltd* v *Sandow*
(1912) 29 RPC 440 at 453 (Neville J, Health Cocoa unknown in London, no
injunction); *The Ridgway Co* v *Hutchinson* (1923) 40 RPC 335 (Sargant J, small
and trifling sales of 'Adventure' magazines in UK amongst Americans,
injunction refused).
[40] (1899) 16 RPC 397 at 408 (HL); see judgment in Court of Session 15 RPC 581.
[41] See also p 18 above.

in the Isle of Wight for only three weeks.[42] Indeed in *BBC* v *Talbot Motor Co Ltd* [1981] FSR 228[43] the plaintiff's 'CARFAX' scheme for a car radio for traffic information had at the date of seeking interlocutory relief not been launched, yet the Court restrained the defendant from using such name for a vehicle spare parts service—the plaintiff's scheme having received advanced publicity.

On the other hand, one month was held not to be sufficient time for the plaintiff to establish that a symbol consisting of a heart and male and female biological symbols had become exclusively associated with the plaintiff's business of arranging introductions between members of the opposite sex by means of a computer,[44] and in the case of a periodical called 'The Licensed Victuallers' Mirror' three days was held to be an insufficient time to acquire a sufficient reputation to prevent a paper from using the same name.[45] Six months' use of the name 'The Gold AM' for a radio programme was held insufficient for the plaintiff to have acquired a secondary meaning in such a descriptive name.[46]

In each case it is a pure question of fact whether the plaintiff has proved that his goods or business are known to a sufficient part of the trade or public under or by a certain mark, name or get-up.

12 Right to the bona fide use of defendant's own name[47]

It was argued in *Parker-Knoll Ltd* v *Knoll International Ltd* [1962] RPC 265 that a person has an absolute right to use his own name provided he does so honestly. That proposition so far as it applies to the use of one's own name upon or in connection with the goods themselves was rejected by the majority of the House of Lords (Lord Denning dissenting). Lord Morris (at 279) stated 'it follows that someone may, even by using his own name and using it innocently, make a representation that is untrue, that is a representation that goods which in fact are his are the goods of someone else . . .' Lord Hodson, (at 284) with reference to *Joseph Rodgers & Sons*

---

42 *Stannard* v *Reay* [1967] RPC 589 (Buckley J, interlocutory injunction granted).
43 See also *W H Allen & Co* v *Brown Watson Ltd* [1965] RPC 191 (Pennycuick J, title of unpublished book 'My Life and Loves' by Frank Harris due to advanced publicity was held distinctive of the plaintiff); *Elida Gibbs Ltd* v *Colgate-Palmolive Ltd* [1983] FSR 95 (Goulding J, where quia timet relief was granted against the defendant who had pre-empted the plaintiff's advertising campaign using a 'tree theme' for toothpaste).
44 *Compatibility Research Ltd* v *Computer Psyche Ltd* [1967] RPC 201 (Stamp J).
45 *Licensed Victuallers' Newspaper Co* v *Bingham* (1888) 38 Ch D 139 (CA).
46 *County Sound plc* v *Ocean Sound Ltd* [1991] FSR 367 (CA).
47 See also Chapter 5, p 92 and Chapter 7, pp 112–115.

Ltd v *W N Rodgers & Company*,[48] stated 'He [Romer J] said "It is the law of this land that no man is entitled to carry on his business in such a way as to represent that it is the business of another, or is in any way connected with the business of another; that is the first proposition. The second proposition is that no man is entitled so to describe or mark his goods as to represent that the goods are the goods of another. To the first proposition there is, I myself think, an exception: a man, in my opinion, is entitled to carry on his business in his own name so long as he does not do anything more than to cause confusion with the business of another, and so long as he does it honestly. It is an exception to the rule which has of necessity been established . . . To the second rule, to which I have referred, I think there is no exception at all; that is, that a man is not entitled so to describe his goods so as to lead to the belief that they are the goods of somebody else. It is not necessary that there should be exception to that".' Lord Hodson continued 'The statement of Romer J, in *Rodgers'* case notes the distinction which is drawn between trading under a name and passing-off of goods by the use of a name. The distinction noticed by Romer J was accepted as correct by Viscount Simonds in *Marengo* v *Daily Sketch and Sunday Graphic Ltd*.' Lord Devlin (at 291) also approved of Romer J's second proposition.

13 Trade name which plaintiff has ceased using

If the trade mark, name or get-up in dispute is no longer in use, the plaintiff can only maintain an action for passing off if he is able to establish that there is some residual goodwill in such mark or name.[49] Mere intention not to abandon on the part of the plaintiff is not enough.[50] Nor can a name be protected by someone to whom the right to use it purports to have been

---

48 (1924) 41 RPC 277 at 291.
49 See *Norman Kark Publications Ltd* v *Odhams Press Ltd* [1962] RPC 163 (Wilberforce J). See also *Ad-Lib Club Ltd* v *Granville* [1972] RPC 673 (Pennycuick J, club closed for five years, sufficient residual goodwill); *Berkeley Hotel Co Ltd* v *Berkeley International (Mayfair) Ltd* [1972] RPC 237 (Pennycuick J); *A Levey* v *Henderson-Kenton (Holdings) Ltd* [1974] RPC 617 (Foster J); cf *Star Industrial Co Ltd* v *Yap Kwee Kor* [1976] FSR 256 (PC, once a company abandons all or part of its former business it will cease to have any proprietary right entitled to protection); *Thorneloe* v *Hill* (1894) 11 RPC 61 (Bristow V-C); *Beazley* v *Soares* (1882) 22 Ch D 660 (Pearson J).
50 *Norman Kark Publications Ltd* v *Odhams Press Ltd* [1962] RPC 163 (Wilberforce J).

transferred unless transferred with the goodwill of the business,[51] for the right to use a trade name at common law passes with the goodwill of the business.[52]

14 Assignment of trade name

Where the trade name together with the goodwill attached to it are sold, generally speaking the successor in title will be able to stop the vendor or a third party from using the same[52] including preventing the vendor from soliciting his former customers.[53] However, the goodwill (and hence the trade name) may not as a practical reality be transferable because the same attaches to the transferor.

Thus where the goodwill relates to an individual artist or designer such goodwill may remain with the individual rather than original company. In *Franke* v *Chappell* (1887) 57 LT (NS) 141 (Chitty J) the plaintiff who had promoted and organised 'Richter concerts' conducted by Herr Richter was unable to restrain the defendant from similarly advertising and organising a series of 'Richter concerts' being concerts conducted by the well-known conductor. This case should be contrasted with *Bentley Motors (1931) Ltd* v *Lagonda Ltd* (1946) 64 RPC 33 (Roxburgh J) where it was held that 'Bentley' cars signified cars made and marketed by the successive Bentley motor car companies and *not* the designer thereof, one Walter Owen Bentley.[54]

Similarly where the trade name denotes goods of a particular manufacture, eg 'Gold Flake' cigarettes, a purported transfer of the goodwill and trade marks to another company who are merely importers of the goods in question will not provide that company with the necessary reputation to found a passing off action, the goodwill remaining de facto vested with the makers of the cigarettes—see *Imperial Tobacco Co of India Ltd* v *Bonnan* (1924) 41 RPC 441 (PC); see, too, *Lacteosote Ltd* v *Alberman* (1927) 44 RPC 211 (Clauson J) where a purported assignment of a

---

[51] *Thorneloe* v *Hill* (1894) 11 RPC 61 (Bristow V-C); see also *Pinto* v *Badman* (1891) 8 RPC 181 (HL).

[52] *Levy* v *Walker* (1879) 10 Ch D 436 (CA); *Leather Cloth Co* v *American Leather Cloth Co* (1865) LR 11 HL Cas 523; see also *R J Reuter Co Ltd* v *Mulhens* (1953) 70 RPC 235 (CA, assignment of goodwill in '4711 Eau de Cologne' by Custodian of Enemy Property); cf registered trade marks which may be assigned in gross as may unregistered marks if assigned with registered marks—see s 22 of the Trade Marks Act 1938.

[53] *Trego* v *Hunt* [1896] AC 7 (HL).

[54] See also *The Birmingham Vinegar Brewery Co* v *The Liverpool Vinegar Co* [1888] WN 139 (North J, Holbrook's Worcester Sauce).

registered trade mark by the French producer to the UK importer without the goodwill of the French business was held to be contrary to s 22 of the Trade Marks Act 1905. So also where the trade mark attaches to a particular building such as a shop, hotel or factory and where the business has been moved (or is sold but the vendor retains such premises), then the new owner of the premises (or the vendor of the business) may be entitled to continue to use the name in question unless there is an express covenant to the contrary—see Chapter 8, pp 131–133.

15 Licensing of trade name[55]

The bare licensing of a trade name without maintaining some active trade connection will render the name deceptive and therefore no longer distinctive of the licensor's business[56] so that the licensor will not be able to protect his (assumed) goodwill, nor will the licensee have acquired any rights in respect of third parties—see *Star Industrial Co Ltd* v *Yap Kwee Kor* [1976] FSR 256 (PC).

In *Re Bostitch Trade Mark* [1963] RPC 183[57] a registered trade mark case, an American company had allowed a British company to use the trade mark in dispute for the manufacture here of machinery to the American company's designs and with their know-how. It was held by Lloyd-Jacob J that there was a sufficient connection in the course of trade for the American company's mark not to have become deceptive (contrary to s 11 of the Trade Marks Act 1938). It is considered that the Bostitch test should apply whether the mark is registered or not.

However, an important question which arises as a consequence of the licensing of a trade mark or name is who owns the goodwill in the name. In the case of a registered trade mark there were provisions under the Trade Marks Act 1938 for registered user agreements which if complied

---

[55] See also Chapter 8, pp 133–135.

[56] *Bowden Wire Ltd* v *Bowden Brake Co Ltd* (1914) 31 RPC 385 (Warrington J).

[57] A case where there was no registered usership agreement; see s 28 of the Trade Marks Act 1938 whereby since 1938 the proprietor of a registered trade mark is deemed to be the user of the mark where the proprietor and the user comply with the registered user conditions of this section; see also the *Re American Greetings Corp's Application* [1984] FSR 199 (HL, where registration was refused because it would constitute 'trafficking in the trade mark' contrary to s 28(6)); see also *J H Coles Pty Ltd* v *Need* (1933) 50 RPC 379 (PC, where an Australian company who had licensed the use of its trade names for a particular locality to a retail shop for the purpose of selling goods supplied by the company was held to be able to restrain the shop from using such names on termination of the agreement).

with ensured that use by the registered user was deemed to be use by the proprietor (whether under the Trade Marks Act 1938 or at common law).[58] Under such provisions a registered usership agreement was only valid if the proprietor exercised quality control over the licensed goods. Trafficking in a trade mark was forbidden as being contrary to the public interest, so that at all times the goodwill in the business coincided with the use of the trade mark, as is the case at common law.

Under the Trade Marks Act 1994 there are no such limitations on the licensing (or assignment) of the registered trade marks so that for the future bare licensing of a registered trade mark will be permissible. However, both under the 1994 Act and at common law such licensing may lead to the name or mark becoming deceptive, so that some control over the use of the mark is both necessary and appropriate.

16   False description will not be protected

No protection will be given in respect of a trade mark or name which falsely describes the goods or business with which it is associated.

In *Leather Cloth Co* v *American Leather Cloth Co* (1865) LR 11 HL Cas 523 Lord Cranworth said 'so in cases of bottles or casks or wine stamped as being the growth of a celebrated vineyard . . . no protection would be given to the sellers of such goods if they were not really the produce of the places from which they purported to come.'

A maker of cigars who falsely represented to the public that his German cigars had been made in Havana was held not entitled to the protection of the Court,[59] and a plaintiff who made false representations as to the nature of the bile beans which the plaintiff sold failed to obtain an injunction owing to such false representations.[60]

However, as Goulding J stated in the Advocaat case [1980] RPC 31 at 51 a collateral misrepresentation by the plaintiff is not an automatic bar to relief, where it was unsuccessfully argued that as many people considered advocaat to be a concoction of eggs, sugar and brandy, when it was in truth a concoction of eggs, sugar and brandewijn, no equitable relief should be granted. Goulding J stated 'reputation and goodwill are, in my opinion, built up, in a trade like this, by the taste, strength and other sensible

---

[58]   See s 28(2) of the Trade Marks Act 1938.

[59]   *Newman* v *Pinto* (1887) 4 RPC 508 (CA, fraudulent get-up of boxes used for selling cigars, Bowen L J said 'an elaborate concatenation of pictorial lies'); see also *Re Fuente's Trade Marks* [1891] 2 Ch 166 (Romer J).

[60]   *Bile Bean Manufacturing Co* v *Davidson* (1905) 22 RPC 553 (Court of Session—OH); (1906) 23 RPC 725 (Court of Session—IH); see also *Perry* v *Truefitt* (1842) 6 Beav 66, 'Perry's Medicated Mexican Balm' a false description, injunction refused.

qualities of the goods, and not to any great extent by a belief regarding their constituents . . . the public will buy because they like the product, even if it does not contain brandy.'

Furthermore, mere puffing of the value of one's goods will not disentitle the plaintiff to relief if such statements do not deceive nor will mis-statements of so trifling a character as not to mislead purchasers.[61]

If the misrepresentation has been abandoned before the action the plaintiff may obtain relief,[62] and it seems that a misrepresentation which has been adopted after the action was brought does not bar the plaintiff's right.[63]

17   Plaintiff need not establish his actual identity nor that he alone is entitled to the mark or name

It is enough for the plaintiff to establish that a substantial proportion of the relevant public or trade know that when the trade mark, name, get-up or device in dispute is applied to certain goods it means that those goods come from a particular source. It is not necessary for the plaintiff to establish that the name of the source is known to such persons. As Lord Herschell said in *Powell* v *The Birmingham Brewery Co Ltd* (1897) 14 RPC 720 at 730 (HL)[64] 'I think the fallacy of the appellants' argument rests on this: that it is assumed that one trader cannot be passing off his goods as the manufacture of another unless it be shown that the persons purchasing the goods know of the manufacturer by name, and have in their mind when they purchase the goods that they are made by a particular individual. It seems to me that one man may quite well pass off his goods as the goods of another if he passes them off to people who will accept them as the

---

61   *Holloway* v *Holloway* (1850) 13 Beav 209 (Langdale MR); *Metzler* v *Wood* (1878) 8 Ch D 606 (CA); *Hogg* v *Kirby* (1803) 8 Ves 215 (LC); see also *Ford* v *Foster* (1872) 7 Ch App 611 (plaintiff sold Eureka shirts not debarred from protection because he falsely described himself as patentee which was a collateral matter). Cf *Johnson* v *Puffer & Co* (1930) 47 RPC 95 (Bennett J, the plaintiff affixed the legend 'Registered 321,009' to his mark and was thereby disentitled to an interlocutory injunction).
62   *Benedictus* v *Sullivan* (1894) 12 RPC 25 (Chitty J).
63   *Siegert* v *Findlater* (1878) 7 Ch D 801 at 811 (Fry J), applying *Ford* v *Foster* (1872) 7 Ch App 611.
64   See also *Lever* v *Goodwin* (1887) 4 RPC 492 at 504; 506 (CA); *William Edge & Sons Ltd* v *William Nicholls & Son Ltd* (1911) 28 RPC 582 (HL, a get-up case); *T Oertli AG* v *E J Bowman (London) Ltd* [1957] RPC 388 at 397 (CA); [1959] RPC 1 at 4 (HL); and *F Hoffman-La Roche & Co AG* v *DD SA Pharmaceuticals Ltd* [1969] FSR 410 (CA).

manufacture of another, though they do not know that other by name at all. In the present case it seems to me that 'Yorkshire Relish' meant the manufacture of a particular person.'

The source may be a particular manufacturer,[64] or a particular merchant,[65] or even a number of manufacturers or producers.[66] Thus the plaintiff may be one of several who are entitled to the goodwill or reputation in the trade mark, name, get-up or device in dispute.[66] Nor need all those persons entitled to use the trade mark or name be joined as co-plaintiffs.[67]

However, in passing off of the classical type the fact that the name may properly be used by others than the plaintiff, may make his case harder to prove.[68] In *Jamieson & Co v Jamieson* (1898) 15 RPC 169, at 163 (CA)[69] Vaughan Williams LJ said 'it is no part of my duty here to say, where there are two persons who are proved to have got their goods denoted by one name, that there might not be a case of fraudulent deception by using this name, in respect of which one of this group might sue, even though there were other persons in the group whose goods were denoted by the same name; but, although it is no part of my duty to draw any such hard and fast line, I do say, and say without hesitation, that the moment it is admitted that the goods of more traders than one are denoted by the same name, you have gone a long way towards disposing of the assertion that the particular name is understood in the trade to denote the goods of the plaintiff, and you have gone a long way to negative the suggested case of deception charged against the defendant by reason of his user of this name.'

---

[65] *A W Gamage Ltd v H E Randall Ltd* (1899) 16 RPC 185 at 197 (CA).

[66] *Dent v Turpin* (1861) 2 John & H 139 (Wood V-C); *Joseph Rogers & Sons Ltd v F M Hearnshaw* (1906) 23 RPC 349 (Buckley J); *Parker & Son (Reading) Ltd v Parker* [1965] RPC 323 (Plowman J). See also *J Bollinger v The Costa Brava Wine Co Ltd* [1960] RPC 16 at 25; [1961] RPC 116 at 120, (Danckwerts J, Champagne case); *Vine Products Ltd v Mackenzie & Co Ltd* [1969] RPC 1 (Cross J, Sherry case); and *Erven Warnink BV v J Townsend & Sons (Hull) Ltd* [1980] RPC 31 (HL, Advocaat case).

[67] *Southorn v Reynolds* (1865) 12 LT (NS) 75 (Wood V-C); Lord Watson in *Powell v The Birmingham Vinegar Brewery Co Ltd* (1897) 14 RPC 720 at 726 (HL) and see Note 56 above.

[68] *The Whitstable Oyster Fishery Co v The Hayling Fisheries Ltd* (1900) 17 RPC 461 Buckley J; (1901) 18 RPC 434 (CA); *Findlater, Mackie Todd & Co Ltd v Henry Newman & Co* (1902) 19 RPC 235 at 242 (Kekewich J).

[69] See also *Claudius Ash, Sons & Co Ltd v Invicta Manufacturing Co Ltd* (1912) 29 RPC 465 (HL); and *Joseph Rodgers & Sons Ltd v W N Rodgers & Co* (1924) 41 RPC 277 at 283 (Romer J).

18 Foreign plaintiff's reputation in this country not affected by foreign law

Where a foreign plaintiff has acquired a reputation and goodwill in this country, it is beyond the power of a foreign court or foreign legislation to prevent him from relying here on that reputation.

In *Lecouturier* v *Rey* (1910) 27 RPC 268 (HL)[70] the monks of the Grande Chartreuse were expelled from France in 1901 and their commercial business of selling liqueurs was transferred to a liquidator together with the 'customers and goodwill attached to the business'. The monks continued to produce their liqueurs in Spain and the liquidator started without knowing all the secrets of how to produce the liqueurs to produce them at the Grande Chartreuse monastery in France. It was held that the monks were entitled to restrain the liquidator from passing off liqueurs as those produced by them.

---

[70] Cf *R J Reuter Co Ltd* v *Mulhens* (1953) 70 RPC 235 (CA, '4711' Eau de Cologne where the goodwill in the former German business of the defendant was transferred by the Custodian of Enemy Property to the plaintiff).

Chapter 3

Probability of Deception

The misrepresentation giving rise to deception is most commonly as to the source of origin of the offending goods or business, namely that such goods or business are the plaintiff's or are in some way connected with the plaintiff. In addition there may be a misrepresentation as to the quality, composition or class of the goods (*Erven Warnink BV v J Townend & Sons (Hull) Ltd* [1980] RPC 31 (HL). See also *AG Spalding & Bros v AW Gamage Ltd* (1915) 32 RPC 273 (HL); and *Revlon Inc v Cripps & Lee Ltd* [1980] FSR 85 at 92, 112 (CA).

It is not necessary to prove that deception has actually occurred, the probability or likelihood of deception is the ground on which the court usually acts. Obviously if evidence of actual confusion can be obtained it becomes very difficult for a defendant to argue that no deception is likely to arise in the future. However, isolated instances of confusion do not necessarily give a right to relief.

Unlike infringement of a registered trade mark, mere confusion is not sufficient to found a passing off action. As Lord Devlin stated in *Parker-Knoll Ltd v Knoll International Ltd* [1962] RPC 265 at 289 'it is an action based on false representation and that axiom leads to three comments . . . the first is that the falsity of a representation does not depend (at any rate in the absence of fraud) on the meaning which the maker of the representation intended or believed it to have or upon the construction which the court itself puts upon it, but upon the way in which it would be reasonably understood by the persons to whom it is addressed . . . the second comment is that a false representation is one that is likely to deceive and not merely to confuse . . .'

The proof required to establish a probability of deception is that there would be a likelihood of deception in the mind of a substantial number of persons such as the ordinary purchaser or user (of the goods or services in question), purchasing with ordinary caution. In arriving at a decision the court must not surrender in favour of any witness its own independent judgment (see the *Parker-Knoll Ltd* case at 279 and 285 per Lord Morris and Lord Hodson).

46

1 The persons likely to be deceived

In considering the persons likely to be deceived the Court does not take notice of fools or idiots[1] because generally they are indifferent to what they buy, however it will strive to protect the unwary,[2] and the reasonably cautious purchaser (*Seixo* v *Provezende* (1866) 1 Ch App 192 at 196). As Neville J stated in *Henry Thorne & Co Ltd* v *Sandow* (1912) 29 RPC 440, at 453,[3] 'you ought not to consider what mistakes merely ignorant and careless people may make; it is far more important that fair and honest trading should not unnecessarily be interfered with than that every fool in the country should be protected from the consequences of his own folly. Therefore I think you must deal with the ordinary man and woman who would take ordinary care in purchasing what goods they require, and, if desiring a particular brand, would take ordinary precautions to see that they get it.' Further, as Viscount Maugham said in *Saville Perfumery Ltd* v *June Perfect Ltd* (1941) 58 RPC 147, at 175 (HL), 'it is not a defence to prove that there are persons who purchase the goods of the defendant who are not misled, if it is established that there are a large number of persons who are. It is, for example, quite a common occurrence in these cases to find that retail traders are not misled while ordinary customers are deceived. Again, where the trade relates to goods largely sold to illiterate or badly educated persons, the plaintiff has often established his case although it has been proved that well-educated persons have not been and will not be deceived'.

In each case the class of the probable customers or purchasers must be considered (*Henry Thorne & Co Ltd* v *Sandow* (1912) 29 RPC 440: Neville J). The purchaser of a bag of washing blue may be less well

---

[1] *Singer Manufacturing Co* v *Wilson* (1876) 2 Ch D 434 at 447; *Singer Manufacturing Co* v *Loog* (1882) 8 App Cas 15 at 18 (HL); *Payton & Co Ltd* v *Snelling, Lampard & Co Ltd* (1899) 17 RPC 48 at 57 (CA): (1900) 17 RPC 628 at 640 (HL); *Norman Kark Publications Ltd* v *Odham Press Ltd* [1962] RPC 163 (Wilberforce J); *Morning Star Co-op Society Ltd* v *Express Newspapers Ltd* [1979] FSR 113 (Foster J, 'moron in a hurry'); *Taittinger* v *Allbey Ltd* [1993] FSR 641 (CA).

[2] *Johnston* v *Orr Ewing* (1882) 7 App Cas 219 (HL); *Singer Manufacturing Co* v *Loog* (1882) 8 App Cas 15 at 18 (HL); (Lord Selborne LC); *Wotherspoon* v *Currie* (1872) LR 5 HL 508; cf *Dunlop Pneumatic Tyre Co Ltd* v *Dunlop Motor Co* (1907) 24 RPC 572 (HL).

[3] See also Romer LJ in *Payton & Co Ltd* v *Snelling, Lampard & Co* (1900) 17 RPC 48 at 57 (CA); *Hendriks* v *Montagu* (1881) 17 Ch D 638 at 646 (CA); *Schweppes Ltd* v *Gibbens* (1905) 22 RPC 601 (HL); and *Saville Perfumery Ltd* v *June Perfect Ltd* (1941) 58 RPC 147 (HL).

educated and more easily deceived[4] than the purchaser of a 'Dunhill' pipe—the latter would not be deceived by superficial similarities to some other pipe.[5] Foreigners might be misled where English people would not (*Johnston* v *Orr Ewing* (1882) 7 App Cas 219 (HL). In *Willcox* v *Pearson* (1901) 18 TLR 220, at 222, Swinfen Eady J said 'in cases of newspapers, it must always be borne in mind that they are intended for people who can read, and that, where the titles of two papers are different and the papers themselves are not similar in appearance, one paper is not really likely to be mistaken for another, except possibly momentarily'.

2 Fraud need not be proved

It is not necessary to prove fraud,[6] but if it can be proved that the defendant intended to pass off, the court will readily assume that there is a probability or likelihood of his intention succeeding, even where the likelihood of deception might otherwise seem to be slight.[7] In *Lloyd's* v *Lloyd's Southampton Ltd* (1912) 29 RPC 433, at 439 (CA), Cozens Hardy LJ said 'If I find that a man, taking a particular name under which to trade, is a knave, I give him credit for not being also a fool, and I assume that there is a reasonable probability that his knavish purpose will succeed.'

In *Claudius Ash, Son & Co Ltd* v *Invicta Manufacturing Co Ltd* (1912) 29 RPC 465, at 475 (HL), Lord Loreburn stated 'it is said in this case that the defendants intended to deceive—not that the goods were calculated even innocently to deceive—but that there was a fraudulent intention on the part of the defendants. That is a material fact which would be weighed duly and to which no doubt great weight would be attached by any Court if it were established, because no Court would be astute when they discovered an intention to deceive, in coming to the conclusion that a dishonest

---

[4] *William Edge & Sons Ltd* v *William Niccols & Sons Ltd* (1911) 28 RPC 582 at 593 (HL); see also *J Bollinger* v *The Costa Brava Wine Co Ltd* [1961] RPC 116 at 127 (Danckwerts J); *Saville Perfumery Ltd* v *June Perfect Ltd* (1941) 58 RPC 147 at 176 (HL); and *Lever* v *Goodwin* (1887) 4 RPC 492 at 505 (CA).

[5] *Dunhill* v *Bartlett & Bickley* (1932) 29 RPC 426 (Russell J); see also *Aquascutum* v *Cohen & Wilks* (1909) 26 RPC 651 (Joyce J); *Claudius Ash Sons & Co Ltd* v *Invicta Manufacturing Co Ltd* (1912) 29 RPC 465 (HL).

[6] See Chapter 1, p 2.

[7] See *Slazenger & Sons* v *Feltham & Co* (1889) 6 RPC 531 at 538 (CA) per Lindley LJ; *Reddaway* v *Banham* (1896) 13 RPC 218 (HL, where it was found by the jury that the defendant had endeavoured to pass off the defendant's belting as the plaintiff's); and *Parker-Knoll Ltd* v *Knoll International Ltd* [1962] RPC 265 at 278 (HL).

defendant had been unsuccessful in his fraudulent design. When once you establish the intent to deceive, it is only a short step to proving that the intent has been successful, but still it is a step even though it be a short step.'[8]

In *Parker-Knoll Ltd* v *Knoll International Ltd* [1962] RPC at 290 Lord Devlin stated that while proof of intent to deceive is unnecessary to the proof of falsity of a representation, it is not immaterial. The materiality is said to lie in the fact that where the object is to deceive 'the court will be very much more ready to infer that its object has been achieved. . . . It is not easy to see why the defendant's own estimate of the effect of his misrepresentation should be worth more than anybody else's. It seems probable that the rule is steeped in history rather than in logic and that it is the attenuated remains of the doctrine, which prevailed until the intervention of equity, that fraud was an essential element in the tort. It is a wholesome rule which I for one have no wish to disturb. I doubt if it is useful to try to formulate it more precisely than was done by Russell LJ in the present case when he said "where the evidence points to a fraudulent approach on the defendants' part it is a simple matter for the court to find that the hopes or expectations of the defendants will be realised."'

Thus, mere imitation of the plaintiff's device or trading style does not give rise to a right of action if there is no probability of deception.[9]

Where fraud has been shown and the defendant has been found to be attempting to get the benefit of the plaintiff's reputation, the Court will restrain the defendant from using a name, mark or get-up which may be confused with that of the plaintiff even where the defendant's goods or business to which such name etc, has been applied differ from that of the

---

[8] See also Lord Esher MR in *Reddaway* v *Banham* (1895) 12 RPC 83 at 89 (CA) and *Saxlehner* v *Appollinaris Co* (1897) 14 RPC 645 at 654 (Kekewich J).

[9] *Lever Bros Ltd* v *Bedingfield* (1898) 16 RPC 3 (CA); *Dunhill* v *Bartlett & Bickley* (1932) 39 RPC 426 at 438 (Russell J); *Laraine Day Ltd* v *Kennedy* (1953) 70 RPC 19 (Roxburgh J, as shop fronts not confusingly similar, defendant's motive irrelevant); *Gordon Fraser Gallery Ltd* v *Tatt* [1966] RPC 505 (Buckley J, imitation of artistic style not sufficient if little likelihood public would buy defendant's cards under the impression they were the plaintiff's); *Cadbury Schweppes (Pty) Ltd* v *The Pub Squash Co Ltd* [1981] RPC 486 (PC, copying of plaintiff's advertising campaign not enough); *My Kinda Town* v *Soll* [1983] RPC 407 (Copying of restaurant decor not enough); *Scott Ltd* v *Nice Pak Products Ltd* [1989] FSR 100 (CA). Copying of rectangular tub and blue colour for baby wipes was blunted by the absence of evidence of confusion from the USA, where the products had been sold side by side since 1981.

plaintiff. Thus in *Dunlop Pneumatic Tyre Co Ltd* v *Dunlop Lubricant Co*,[10] the plaintiff manufactured and marketed tyres for cycles and other accessories such as pumps, inflators etc, and the name 'Dunlop' had become identified with such goods. The defendant carried on a business of selling oils and lubricants for cycles and other accessories (but not the same class of accessories as the plaintiff) under a trading style similar to that of the plaintiff. It was held that the defendant was trying to get the benefit of the plaintiff's reputation, and that although the plaintiff did not sell oils or lubricants, the plaintiff might wish to do so, and an injunction was granted. Romer J said: 'It appears to me it would be wrong to allow him [the defendant] to carry on business under that name, and to describe the goods as he does as "Dunlop" goods, for that is the chief word that he uses on the covers of his goods, with regard to his burning oil and his graphite, which he sells. The word "Dunlop" is put in a very prominent way, and I am satisfied that he does that with a view of inducing customers to believe that those goods, if they are not the goods of the plaintiffs, are goods used in some way with their sanction, or connected in some way with them, so as to get the benefit of the plaintiffs' name. It appears to me that the plaintiffs are entitled to say that the word "Dunlop" ought not to be allowed to be used under those circumstances, with those objects, by the defendant; that it would injure them in their business very considerably if it is not stopped. They themselves are sellers of cycle accessories, though, as a matter of fact, up to the present time they have not sold burning oil or lubricants. But they may do so, and in the meantime it appears to me that they are entitled to come into Court and say that a name substantially identical with theirs ought not to be allowed to be used by the defendant in the way in which he is using it.'

If the plaintiff intends to rely at the trial on the fraud of the defendant he should plead it,[11] but even if it is not pleaded a Court is not excluded

---

[10] (1898) 16 RPC 12. See also *Eastman Photographic Co Ltd* v *The John Griffiths Cycle Corp Ltd* (1898) 15 RPC 105 (Romer J, plaintiff manufacturers of 'Kodak' cameras restrained defendant from using name 'Kodak' in respect of cycles); *Valentine Meat Juice Co* v *Valentine Extract Co Ltd* (1900) 17 RPC 673 (CA); *Harrods Ltd* v *R Harrod Ltd* (1923) 41 RPC 74 (CA, defendant a moneylender, plaintiff although operating a bank was not permitted by memorandum to act as moneylenders); *Legal & General Assurance Society Ltd* v *Daniel* [1968] RPC 253 (CA); *Lloyd's* v *Lloyd's (Southampton) Ltd* (1912) 29 RPC 438 (CA, defendant was ship broker, not Lloyds' agent); and *Montgomery* v *Thompson* (1891) 8 RPC 361 (HL, 'Stone Ale' fraudulently made by defendant at Stone).

[11] See *Claudius Ash, Sons & Co Ltd* v *Invicta Manufacturing Co Ltd* (1911) 28 RPC 252 (Warrington J); 597 (CA); (1912) 29 RPC 465 (HL); see also *HP Bulmer Ltd* v *J Bollinger SA* [1978] RPC 79 (CA) and Ord 18, r 12 of the Rules of the Supreme Court.

from considering whether fraud in fact exists (*John Walker & Sons Ltd* v *Henry Ost & Co Ltd* [1970] RPC 489 Foster J); *Midland Counties Dairy Ltd* v *Midland Dairies Ltd* (1948) 65 RPC 429 (CA)).

3 Where fraud absent a field of activity sufficiently closely allied to the plaintiff must be shown

It is difficult to establish actual deception or a likelihood of deception if the rival trader is not a competitor so that there is no common field of activity and therefore no diversion of custom, or if the rival goods are so dissimilar that no one would mistake the defendant's goods as or for the plaintiff's. In such cases it is necessary to establish that a substantial number of people are likely to assume there is a connection or association between the plaintiff's business or goods and the defendant's.

In *Ewing* v *Buttercup Margarine Co Ltd* (1917) 2 Ch 1 at 10–12, in answer to the defendants' contention that there can be no deception because they (the defendants) are wholesale people, while the plaintiff, trading as 'Buttercup Dairy Company', is a retailer, Lord Cozens-Hardy observed: 'I should be very sorry indeed if the jurisdiction of the Court should be regarded as so limited. No doubt mere confusion due to some acts of the defendant would not be a cause of action ... but I know of no authority, and I can see no principle, which withholds us from preventing injury to the plaintiff in his business as a trader by a confusion which will lead people to conclude that the defendants are really connected in some way with the plaintiff or are carrying on a branch of the plaintiff's business'.[12]

In *HP Bulmer Ltd* v *J Bollinger SA* [1978] RPC 79,[13] a case in which it was unsuccessfully contended that 'Champagne Cider' and 'Champagne Perry' were being passed off as being connected with the producers of champagne, the Court of Appeal rejected an argument that there could be no passing off of such cider or perry by being mistakenly associated or connected with the producers of champagne (as opposed to being mistakenly assumed to be genuine champagne). However, (at 117) Goff LJ stated: 'not every kind of connection claimed will amount to passing off;

---

[12] Cf Trade Marks Act 1994 s 10(3), where infringement of a registered trade mark is extended to include the case where the mark in question has a reputation in the UK and the defendant's use of its mark takes unfair advantage of, or is detrimental to, the distinctive character or the repute of the trade mark.

[13] See also *Fortnum & Mason plc* v *Fortnum Ltd* [1994] FSR 438 (Harman J), where no injunction granted against a defendant wholesaler in the importation and export of cheap plastic goods.

for example if one says that one's goods are very suitable to be used in connection with the plaintiff's . . . It is sufficient in my view if what is done represents the defendant's goods to be connected with the plaintiff's in such a way as would lead people to accept them on the faith of the plaintiff's reputation. Thus for example it would be sufficient if they were taken to be made under licence, or under some trading arrangement which would give the plaintiff some control over them . . .' Buckley LJ (at 100) considered it safer 'to concentrate upon the question whether the misrepresentation has damaged or is likely to damage the plaintiff's goodwill'.

Thus, for there to be a misrepresentation the plaintiff and defendant need not compete in the same line of business. It is enough that the goods or business of the defendant are sufficiently similar to the plaintiff's that a substantial proportion of the relevant trade or public will think that the goods in question come from a common source,[14] or are of the same quality or class or otherwise connected with the plaintiff's, or that the businesses in question are the same or under common control or have been amalgamated,[15] or that the defendant's business is an extension, branch or agency or has some other connection with the plaintiff's business.[16]

In *Derek McCulloch v Lewis A May (Produce Distributors) Ltd* (1947) 65 RPC 58 it was held by Wynn-Parry J that the plaintiff, a well-known broadcaster on Children's Hour (BBC) and known as 'Uncle Mac' had no cause of action for passing off in respect of the defendants' 'Uncle Mac's Puffed Wheat', there being no common field of activity in which the plaintiff and defendant were engaged. This case has been criticised as being

---

[14] See Chapter 5, pp 84, 85 for examples. See also *Unitex Ltd v Union Texturing Co Ltd* [1973] RPC 119 (CA, defendant plasterers, plaintiff manufacturer of a range of building materials; no interlocutory injunction, no real risk of damage).

[15] *North Cheshire & Manchester Brewery Co Ltd v Manchester Brewery Co* [1899] AC 83 (HL); see also Chapter 7, pp 118, 119.

[16] See, eg, *Ames Crosta Ltd v Pionex International Ltd* [1977] FSR 46 (Walton J, importation and sale of protective clothing sufficiently allied to plaintiff's Pionex Division engaged in the control of industrial pollution for people to think the plaintiff had expanded plaintiff's business); cf *Society of Motor Manufacturers and Traders Ltd v Motor Manufacturers and Traders' Mutual Insurance Co Ltd* (1925) 42 RPC 307; (CA, relief refused, plaintiff a trade protection society, no similarity with defendant's insurance business, no charge of fraud); *Newsweek Inc v BBC* [1979] RPC 441 (CA, Newsweek TV programme would not be associated with Newsweek magazine); *Miss World (Jersey) Ltd v James Street Productions Ltd* [1981] FSR 309 (CA, Miss Alternative World as a title for a film not connected with organisers of Miss World beauty contest); see also Chapter 7, pp 120, 121.

too narrowly decided,[17] but as was stated by Oliver J in *Lyngstad* v *Anabas Products Ltd* [1977] FSR 62, at 67, that criticism was based on a misconception of what Wynn-Parry J was saying: 'The expression "common field of activity" is not a term of art but merely a convenient shorthand term for indicating . . . the need for a real possibility of confusion which is the basis of the action.'

In *Lego System AS* v *Lego M Lemelstrich Ltd* [1983] FSR 155 the defendant was restrained from using the name LEGO in respect of irrigation equipment, particularly for gardens, in view of the evidence of the likely confusion (a business connection) with the plaintiff's well-known toy building bricks and construction sets. There was no evidence of fraudulent intention, but importance was attached to the distinctiveness of the name and its familiarity as a household name. Falconer J, while stating that whether or not the acts complained of amount to a misrepresentation must be a question of fact, stated 'of course, that is not to say that the proximity of a defendant's field of activity to that of the plaintiff will not be relevant to whether the defendant's acts complained of amount to a misrepresentation in any particular case'.

4 Comparison of defendant's name, mark or get-up with plaintiff's

Whether the plaintiff's and defendant's name, mark or get-up are so alike as to be likely to deceive is a question of fact for the Court to decide upon the evidence in each case.[18] The Court will have regard to the nature of the goods or business to which the mark or device is applied, the persons who purchase such goods or deal with the business and the impression that the mark or device will make on such persons. In comparing the marks or devices in dispute, and the impression they make, it is useful to consider whether they suggest the same idea,[19] as well as considering them visually and orally. Lord Maugham in *Aristoc Ltd* v *Rysta Ltd* (1945) 62 RPC 65, a registered trade mark case, said (at 72) 'the answer to the question whether the sound of one word resembles too nearly the sound of another . . . must nearly always depend on first impression, for obviously a person who is

---

[17] See *Henderson* v *Radio Corp Pty Ltd* [1969] RPC 218 (New South Wales Full HC, professional ballroom dancers held entitled to prevent use of their names and pictorial images in respect of a record of dance music); see also *Totalizator Agency Board* v *Turf News Pty Ltd* [1972] RPC 579 (Supreme Court of Victoria).
[18] See Chapter 10, p 161 as to the kind of evidence which is admissible.
[19] *Orr Ewing & Co* v *Johnston & Co* (1880) 13 Ch D 434 at 451 (CA); affirmed (1882) 7 App Cas 219.

familiar with both words will neither be deceived or confused. It is the person who only knows the one word and has perhaps an imperfect recollection of it who is likely to be deceived or confused. Little assistance, therefore, is to be obtained from a meticulous comparison of the two words, letter by letter and syllable by syllable, pronounced with the clarity to be expected from a teacher of elocution. The Court must be careful to make allowance for imperfect recollection and the effect of careless pronunciation and speech on the part not only of the person seeking to buy under the trade description, but also of the shop assistant ministering to that person's wants'. Likelihood of deception is not disproved by showing that a careful person knowing both the plaintiff's and defendant's goods or business would not be confused. The impression that a mark or device will make will also depend on whether the mark or device is descriptive, whether it is a local or geographical name, and whether it contains elements which are common to the trade.

5   Descriptive names

Where a trader adopts a name or mark which is descriptive of his business or goods, the Court will accept small differences as sufficient to avoid any likelihood of deception even though a certain amount of confusion may be inevitable. In *Office Cleaning Services Ltd* v *Westminster Window and General Cleaners Ltd* (1946) 63 RPC 39 (HL),[20] the plaintiff had traded under the style 'Office Cleaning Services' for some 12 years before the defendant started to trade as 'Office Cleaning Association'. In refusing an injunction Lord Simonds stated (at 43) 'so long as descriptive words are used by two traders as part of their respective trade names, it is possible that some members of the public will be confused whatever the differentiating words may be . . . It comes in the end, I think, to no more than this, that where a trader adopts words in common use for his trade name, some risk of confusion is inevitable. But that risk must be run unless the first user is allowed unfairly to monopolise the words. The Court will accept comparatively small differences as sufficient to avert confusion. A greater degree of discrimination may fairly be expected from the public where a trade name consists wholly or in part of words descriptive of the articles to be sold or the services to be rendered'.

---

[20] See also *General Radio Co* v *General Radio Co (Westminster) Ltd* [1957] RPC 471 (Roxburgh J); cf *Music Corp of America* v *Music Corp (GB) Ltd* (1947) 64 RPC 41 at 44 (Wynn-Parry J, where the plaintiff's name was held not to be descriptive) and *Midland Counties Dairy Ltd* v *Midland Dairies Ltd* (1948) 65 RPC 429 (CA). See also Chapter 5, pp 76 et seq and cases referred to.

6   Geographical names

Similar considerations apply to local or geographical names where the goods or business of the defendant are connected with the place which forms part of the name in dispute. In *Bach & Jackson Ltd* v *Cowan* [1969] RPC 156 the defendant was restrained from calling his hotel located opposite the plaintiffs' hotel 'The Pembridge Hotel' or 'Pembridge Hotel' on the evidence that the plaintiffs' hotel whose full name was 'Pembridge Gardens Hotel' was known as 'The Pembridge' of 'The Pembridge Hotel'. Plowman J in the course of his judgment applied the dictum of Romer LJ in *The Clock Ltd* v *The Clock House Hotel Ltd* (1936) 53 RPC 269 at 275 namely 'the principle is this, that no man is entitled to carry on his business in such a way or by such a name as to lead to the belief that he is carrying on the business of another man or to lead him to believe that the business which he is carrying on has any connection with the business carried on by another man', and cited with approval the following passage from *Kerly on Trade Marks*: 'In the case of trade names which are prima facie geographically descriptive, a special order has sometimes to be made in order to avoid any interference with the honest and proper use of them by persons other than the owner of the trade name.'[21] In *Arthur Smith (S & B Foundry Sands) Ltd* v *George Fieldhouse Ltd* [1961] RPC 110 (an interlocutory application) the plaintiff alone quarried foundry sand in Brereton (in the County of Chester), the defendant sold sand quarried several miles away as 'Brereton Sand'. Pennycuick J held that if a plaintiff is able to establish:

(i)   that he produces the substance in a given place,
(ii) that no one else produces the substance in that place,
(iii) that the defendant is selling the substance with the name of that place as a description, and
(iv) that there is likely to be deception of the public,

then he has satisfied the necessary requirements for success in a passing off action. The injunction granted was qualified so as not to prevent the

---

[21] *Kerly's Law of Trade Marks* (9th ed) para 758, (now 11th ed, paras 16–48). Examples of such special orders are: *Bewlay & Co Ltd* v *Hughes* (1898) 15 RPC 290 (North J, where the defendant, although restrained from using the name 'Dindigul' in connection with the sale of cigars not of the plaintiff's merchandise, was not prevented from describing cigars made of 'Digidul' tobacco (a place in India) as being so made); *J Bollinger* v *The Costa Brava Wine Co* [1961] RPC 116 at 127 (Danckwerts J, Champagne case); *Vine Products* v *Mackenzie Ltd* [1969] RPC 1 at 23 (Cross J, Sherry case) and *John Walker & Sons Ltd* v *Henry Ost & Co Ltd* [1970] RPC 489 (Foster J, Whiskey case).

defendant from selling sand quarried in the parish of Brereton in the County of Chester or any other parish bearing the name of Brereton (there being another Brereton near Rugeley in the County of Stafford).

An example of the honest and proper use of a geographical trade name is the case of *The Whitstable Oyster Fishery Co* v *The Hayling Fisheries Ltd* (1901) 18 RPC 434 (CA),[22] where 'Whitstable', applied to oysters, was descriptive of the place where the oysters reached maturity and the defendant was held entitled to describe the defendant's oysters by such name. However, if the plaintiff's name, albeit geographical, has acquired a secondary meaning, the defendant will be restrained from using such name even though his goods or business are connected with the place of the plaintiff's name. Thus, for example, in *Wotherspoon* v *Currie* (1872) LR 5 HL 508,[23] the plaintiff had for some years manufactured starch at Glenfield. Subsequently he left Glenfield and manufactured his starch elsewhere, but continued to call it 'Glenfield Starch'. The defendant started to manufacture starch at Glenfield and called it 'Glenfield Starch'. An injunction was granted restraining the defendant from so describing his starch or otherwise using the word 'Glenfield'. Lord Westbury said (at 521) 'I take it to be clear from the evidence, that, long antecedently to the operations of the respondent the word "Glenfield" had acquired a secondary signification or meaning in connection with a particular manufacture—in short, it had become the trade denomination of the starch made by the appellants. It was wholly taken out of its ordinary meaning, and in connection with starch had acquired that peculiar secondary signification to which I have referred. The word "Glenfield" therefore, as a denomination of starch, had become the property of the appellants. It was their right and title in connection with the starch.'

Where a geographical name is applied to a product naturally produced from a particular place by more than one person associated with the place

---

[22] See also *Rugby Portland Cement Co Ltd* v *Rugby and Newbold Portland Cement Co Ltd* (1891) 8 RPC 241 (Vaughan Williams J, Rugby Cement); *Grand Hotel Co of Caledonia Springs* v *Wilson* (1903) 21 RPC 117 (PC, Caledonian Water); *Hopton Wood Stone Firms Ltd* v *Gething* (1910) 27 RPC 605 (Parker J, Hopton Wood Stone); and *A Baily & Co Ltd* v *Clark, Son & Morland Ltd* (1938) 55 RPC 253 (HL, Glastonburys, a registered trade mark case).

[23] See also *McAndrew* v *Bassett* (1864) 33 LJ Ch 561 (Wood V-C, Anatolia Liquorice); *Seixo* v *Provezende* (1866) 1 Ch App 192 (Seixo Wines); *Bewlay & Co Ltd* v *Hughes* (1898) 15 RPC 290 (North J, Dindigul Cigars); *Montgomery* v *Thompson* (1891) 8 RPC 361 (HL, Stone Ales); *Worcester Royal Porcelain Co Ltd* v *Locke & Co Ltd* (1902) 19 RPC 479 (Byrne J, Worcester China & Porcelain); *Hunter & Palmer* v *Reading Biscuit Co Ltd* (1893) 10 RPC 277 (Chitty J, Reading Biscuits); and *Banbury Buildings Ltd* v *Sectional Concrete Buildings Ltd* [1970] RPC 463 (Pennycuick J, Banbury).

it would seem that a plaintiff could not prevent some other persons associated with the place using such name (*Arthur Smith (S & B Foundry Sands) Ltd* v *George Fieldhouse Ltd* [1961] RPC 110).[24] In *McAndrew* v *Bassett* (1864) 33 LJ Ch 561 (Anatolia liquorice) Page-Wood V-C stated (at 565) 'It is not like the case which I put myself, of there being some district which is the only district from which a well-known wine such as "Burgundy" is imported, and the first importer calls it "Burgundy"; although he may have stamped "Burgundy" on his corks for twenty years, he could not prevent anybody else from calling a wine produced in Burgundy by the name of the place from whence it was imported.'

However, where the defendant has no connection with the geographical name by which the plaintiff's goods or business are known he will be restrained from using such name in a manner likely to cause deception.[25]

7 Elements common to the trade

Where part of the plaintiff's name or get-up consists of some word or device which is common to the trade, the Court in comparing the plaintiff's name or get-up will pay more attention to those parts of the name which are not common, but does not disregard the parts which are common to the trade as the name or get-up must be considered as a whole (see *Coca-Cola Co of Canada Ltd* v *Pepsi Cola Co of Canada Ltd* (1942) 59 RPC 127 (PC), a registered trade mark case). This is particularly so where the reputation or goodwill relied upon by the plaintiff resides in some particular get-up of his goods.[26]

---

[24] See footnotes 21 and 22, above.
[25] See, eg, *Braham* v *Beachim* (1878) 7 Ch D 848 (Fry J) and subsequent proceedings (1878) Sebastian's Digest 633 (The Radstock Colliery Proprietors); *Arthur Smith (S & B Foundry Sands) Ltd* v *George Fieldhouse Ltd* [1961] RPC 110 (Pennycuick J, Brereton foundry sand); *J Bollinger* v *The Costa Brava Wine Co Ltd* [1960] RPC 16 (Danckwerts J); [1961] RPC 116 (Danckwerts J, Champagne); *Vine Products Ltd* v *Mackenzie & Co Ltd* [1969] RPC 1 (Cross J, Sherry).
[26] See *Payton & Co Ltd* v *Snelling, Lampard & Co Ltd* (1900) 17 RPC 48 (CA); (1900) 17 RPC 628; *FW Hampshire & Co (1927) Ltd* v *General Kaputire Syndicate Ltd* (1930) 47 RPC 437 (Clauson J held packaging common to trade); *Tetrosyl Ltd* v *Silver Paint & Lacquer Co Ltd* [1980] FSR 68 (CA, interlocutory injunction refused, get-up common to trade); and see Chapter 6, pp 96 et seq.

8 Where goods described as 'the same as', 'similar to' or 'better than' plaintiff's

A passing off action may lie where goods not of the plaintiff's are misrepresented as being the same as, or identical to, the plaintiff's but it is less clear whether a defendant would be liable by falsely describing his goods as 'similar to' the plaintiff's.[27] Certainty as far as interlocutory relief is concerned, any statement of comparison of the defendant's goods with the plaintiff's goods will raise questions as to the freedom of speech and unless obviously false, a court will refuse injunctive relief.[28]

In *Ciba-Geigy plc* v *Parke Davis & Co Ltd* [1994] FSR 8 at 12 the defendant's drug was stated to alter everything one would expect from the plaintiff's product with crucial difference, the price. Aldous J at 12–13 observed that such an alleged misrepresentation (as the same as or identical to the plaintiff's drug) 'can only found an action for passing off upon the extended principles set out by Lord Diplock in the *Warnink* case which have evolved to meet trading needs since *Reddaway* v *Banham* was decided.' No interim relief was sought in respect of such misrepresentation.

A statement that his goods are superior to those of another trader generally will not give rise to a passing off action,[29] nor will such an action lie against a trader who describes his foods for infants as far more nutritious and healthful than any other.[30] It is not so clear as to when a trader can use the trade name of another together with such words as

---

[27] See *Magnolia Metal Co* v *Tandem Smelting Syndicate Ltd* (1898) 15 RPC 701 (Ridley J); (1900) 17 RPC 477 at 485 (HL did not express a view as to whether there was a cause of action where defendant falsely represented the defendant's metal as the 'the same as' the plaintiff's 'magnolia metal'); *Burberrys* v *Raper and Pulleyn* (1906) 23 RPC 170 (Warrington J, injunction granted coats 'identical with Burberrys'); *Broad & Co Ltd* v *Cast Iron Drainage Co Ltd* [1970] FSR 363 (Graham J interlocutory injunction, drainage covers 'similar to' plaintiff's); *Combe International Ltd* v *Scholl (UK) Ltd* [1980] RPC 1 (Fox J, interlocutory injunction granted restraining defendant from representing the defendant's shoe insoles as 'substantially the same as' plaintiff's insoles—defendant's insoles held to be inferior to plaintiff's).

[28] See Chapter 9 p 142.

[29] *Hubbuck & Sons Ltd* v *Wilkinson Heywood & Clerk Ltd* [1899] 1 QB 86 (CA); cf *Ciba-Geigy plc* v *Parke Davis & Co Ltd* [1984] FSR 8 at 20–21.

[30] *White* v *Mellin* [1895] AC 154 (HL); see also Chapter 1, 16–19. See also *Consorzio del Prosciutto di Parma* v *Marks & Spencer plc* [1991] RPC 351 (CA): the courts would not entertain disputes about subjective quality such as flavour, only differences of kind, eg it is no longer Parma ham.

'type', 'quality', 'model', 'system', 'pattern', to describe his goods,[31] or when he can use another's trade name to indicate that his goods are suitable for use with that other's goods, for example as accessories to such goods. The general rule appears to be that if the trade name is being fairly used to describe the trader's goods then it will not constitute passing off (*Singer Manufacturing Co v Wilson* (1875) 2 Ch D 434 at 447 (CA); (1877) 3 App Cas 376 (HL)).

In *Singer Manufacturing Co v Wilson* it was held that Singer machines meant machines made by the Singer Manufacturing Company and not merely machines of a certain design, and that there was nothing known to ordinary purchasers as the 'Singer System'. But in *Singer Manufacturing Co v Loog* (1882) 8 App Cas 15 it was held that rival traders had a right to advertise their machines as made on the 'Singer System', making it quite clear that their machines were not made by the Singer Manufacturing Company. In *AV Roe & Co Ltd v Aircraft Disposal Co Ltd* (1920) 37 RPC 249 (Peterson J), an injunction was granted to prevent any aeroplanes other than those made by the plaintiffs, from being sold as 'Avro', but the defendant was not prevented from selling aeroplanes of other makers as 'Avro type', or 'type Avro'. Where, however, the plaintiff claimed that 'Armstrong Oilers' meant oilers made by the plaintiff and tried to prevent the defendant from selling oilers of the defendant's own make as 'Armstrong Type Oilers', an injunction was refused on the ground that the customers knew that the defendant's goods were not those of the plaintiff and that therefore there was no passing off (*Armstrong Oiler Co Ltd v Patent Axlebox & Foundry Co Ltd* (1910) 27 RPC 362: Joyce J).[31]

As regards accessories it has been contended that expressions such as 'Kodak Film', 'No 1 Brownie Film', 'No 3 Folding Pocket Kodak Film', are mere descriptions of films to fit the Kodak Company's cameras, and that other makers than the Kodak Company may so describe their own products. But it was held that such descriptions applied solely to goods made by the Kodak Company (*Kodak Ltd v London Stereoscopic & Photographic Co Ltd* (1903) 20 RPC 337: Eady J). It sometimes happens, however, that the makers have acquired a trade name in a certain article

---

[31] In the following the plaintiff succeeded: *Vacuum Oil Co Ltd v Gooch & Tarrant* (1909) 27 RPC 76 (Neville J, Vacuum quality); *Bechstein v Barker & Barker* (1910) 27 RPC 484 (Eve J, Bechstein Model); *J B Stone & Co Ltd v Steelace Manufacturing Co Ltd* (1929) 46 RPC 406 (CA, Alligator pattern). Cf with the following in which the plaintiff failed: *Singer Manufacturing Co v Loog* (1882) 8 App Cas 15 (HL, Singer system); *Armstrong Oiler Co Ltd v Patent Axlebox & Foundry Co Ltd* (1910) 27 RPC 362 (Joyce J, Armstrong type oilers); and *AV Roe & Co Ltd v Aircraft Disposal Co Ltd* (1920) 37 RPC 249 (Peterson J, Avro type).

but not in the accessories used with it. Thus in the case of 'Neostyle Duplicators' the makers were held to have established an exclusive right in connection with their duplicating machines, but that they had never had any exclusive right to the word in connection with accessories for use with the duplicators (*Neostyle Manufacturing Co Ltd* v *Ellam's Duplicator Co* (1903) 21 RPC 185 (Byrne J); (1904) 21 RPC 569 (CA)).

It is also possible for names of accessories which were once trade names to become words which merely describe their suitability for use with a certain article. 'Gledhill's coils' were found to have meant until 1902 coils manufactured by Gledhill for use in Gledhill's cash tills. But some years later they had lost the exclusive reference to Gledhill's manufacture, and acquired a secondary meaning which meant coils for use in Gledhill's cash tills without reference to any particular manufacturer (*GH Gledhill & Sons Ltd* v *British Perforated Toilet Paper Co* (1911) 28 RPC 714: CA).

It is important to bear in mind that even if no passing off action lies in the above types of cases an action for infringement of registered trade mark may do so. However s 10(6) of the Trade Marks Act 1994 provides a defence where use is honestly made for the purposes of identifying goods or services of the proprietor (or a licensee).

Chapter 4

Damage or Injury to Goodwill

There must be some likelihood of damage or injury to the goodwill of the plaintiff's business or trade[1] resulting from the defendant's misrepresentation and mere inconvenience or annoyance to a plaintiff or his business is not enough (*Day* v *Brownrigg* (1878) 10 Ch D 294 (CA); *Street* v *Union Bank of Spain & England* (1885) 30 Ch D 156 (Pearson J); *Treasure Cot Co Ltd* v *Hamleys Bros Ltd* (1950) 69 RPC 89 (Harman J)).

However, where once evidence of deception or likely deception is established some injury to the plaintiff's goodwill or business will readily be presumed. In *AG Spalding & Bros* v *AW Gamage Ltd* (1915) 32 RPC 273, at 287 (HL), Lord Parker stated:[2]

> It is sufficient to say that the misrepresentation being established, and being in its nature calculated to produce damage, the plaintiffs are *prima facie* entitled both to an injunction and to an inquiry as to damage, the inquiry, of course, being at their own risk in respect of costs.

This should be contrasted with *Erven Warnink BV* v *J Townend & Sons (Hull) Ltd* [1980] RPC 31 at 106 (HL), the Advocaat case, where Lord Fraser's formulation of the tort of passing off (agreed to by three of the other law lords) requires the plaintiff to establish he has suffered or is really

---

[1] *Merchant Banking Co of London* v *Merchants Joint Stock Bank* (1878) 9 Ch D 560 Jessell MR;. see also Chapter 1.

[2] See also 32 RPC at 283, 284 (Lord Parker); and *Draper* v *Trist and Tristbestos Brake Linings Ltd* (1939) 56 RPC 429 (CA held that the Court will infer damage without proof of special damage; Lord Goddard stated at 442: 'The law assumes, or presumes, that if the goodwill of a man's business has been interfered with by the passing off of goods, damage results therefrom. He [the plaintiff] need not wait to show that damage has resulted . . .') considered in *Procea Products Ltd* v *Evans & Sons Ltd* (1951) 68 RPC 210, at 219, 220 (Roxburgh J). See also *John Hayter Motor Underwriting Agencies Ltd* v *RBHS Agencies Ltd* [1977] FSR 285 (CA).

likely to suffer substantial damage to the goodwill. This difference in approach may be due to the different facts of the two cases—the Advocaat case relating to the deceptive naming of a product and its consequential impact on the plaintiff's goodwill, in contrast to the typical classical case of passing off which automatically results in consequential diversion of custom. At first instance, Goulding J in the Advocaat case stated (at 52), 'in this class of case there are, as Buckley LJ pointed out in the *Bulmer* case, two types of damage to be considered: direct loss of sales through the defendants' illegitimate competition, and a more gradual damage to the plaintiffs' business through depreciation of the reputation that their goods enjoy . . . damage of the second type can rarely be susceptible of positive proof.'

Damage or injury to goodwill may take a number of forms depending on the character of the misrepresentation, the most frequent case being a diversion of custom from the plaintiff to the defendant. In addition, where two businesses are confused in the public mind as being connected with each other, the resultant injury that may be suffered will depend on the type of business in question. Thus, as Warrington LJ stated in *Ewing* v *Buttercup Margarine Coy Ltd* [1917] 2 Ch 1 at 13–14 'The quality of goods I sell, the kind of business I do, the credit or otherwise which I enjoy are all things which may injure the other man who is assumed wrongly to be associated with me.'

In *Lego System AS* v *Lego M Lemelstrich Ltd* [1983] FSR 155 at 194, where the defendant was proposing to market garden sprays and sprinklers made of coloured plastic material under the LEGO mark, there was no likelihood of diversion of custom. However, Falconer J having found that the plaintiff's reputation in the mark LEGO was wide enough to extend to goods such as garden sprinklers made of coloured plastics material, stated:

The plaintiffs now have the potentiality of using the mark and the attractive force of its reputation themselves to market their own goods in the garden equipment field or to license or franchise another trader to use it in that field . . . obviously, the possibility of licensing or franchising another trader to use LEGO in the gardening equipment area would be lost if the defendants are allowed to continue using LEGO in this country in relation to their products. The effect, therefore, of the defendants continuing to use LEGO in this country in relation to their products would be to destroy that part of the plaintiff's reputation in their mark LEGO and goodwill attached to it which extends to such goods.[3]

In *Taittinger* v *Allbev Ltd* [1993] FSR 614 at 667–670, the Court of Appeal in deciding that the term 'elderflower champagne' for a non-alcoholic beverage in a champagne-style bottle was likely to cause deception resulting in a likelihood of damage to the plaintiff, held that the relevant damage was that damage which was the reasonably foreseeable consequence of the misrepresentation, irrespective of any intention to injure. Referring to the Advocaat and Sherry cases they identified as relevant damage the blurring or erosion of the name champagne, which will inevitably result in a depreciation or debasement of the reputation in such name.

By way of contrast in two other cases the Court of Appeal has held that despite evidence of confusion or the likelihood of confusion, no real damage was likely to be suffered to the plaintiff's goodwill. In *Anheuser-Busch Inc* v *Budejovicky Budvar NP* [1984] FSR 413 (Budweiser beer) it was held that as the plaintiff had not established a sufficient trading activity in this country by the relevant date, they had no goodwill to be injured. In *Stringfellow* v *McCain Foods (GB) Ltd* [1984] RPC 501 there was no evidence of damage suffered to the plaintiff's nightclub as a result of the defendants sales of 'Stringfellows' chips—such as falling off of attendance or membership. The Court of Appeal held that a court should not readily infer the likelihood of damage to the plaintiffs especially against an innocent defendant in a different line of business. The onus in such a case lay on the plaintiffs to show that damage to their business reputation was likely to result and that it would cause more than minimal loss. The evidence did not show that the plaintiff would have been able to exploit merchandising rights in the name 'Stringfellows' but for the defendant's actions.

In a number of cases where interlocutory relief has been sought,

---

[3]   See also *Henderson* v *Radio Corp Pty Ltd* [1969] RPC 218 at 236, a case cited in the Lego case where the full High Court of New South Wales held appropriation of the professional or business reputation of the plaintiff without permission is an injury in itself 'no less than the appropriation of his goods or money. The professional recommendation [of the plaintiffs] was and still is theirs, to withhold or bestow at will, but [the defendant] has wrongfully deprived them of their right to do so and of the payment or reward on which, if they had been minded to give their approval to the defendant's record, they could have insisted'; followed in *Associated Newspapers Plc* v *Insert Media Ltd* [1991] FSR 380 which held that where it is established that there is a clear intention to exploit a plaintiff's goodwill, there is no need for clear evidence as to the damage likely to be suffered distinguishing *Stringfellow* v *McCain Foods (GB) Ltd* [1984] RPC 501.

particularly before *American Cyanamid Co* v *Ethicon Ltd* [1975] RPC 513 (HL), the courts have frequently refused to grant relief where there is no real or tangible risk of damage pending the trial of the action even where confusion between the names had been established.[4] This may frequently arise where there is no competing business and hence no diversion of custom, damage being to the reputation and thus the goodwill of the plaintiff's business.[5] In *Borthwick* v *Evening Post* (1899) 37 Ch D 449 where the plaintiff had long been proprietor of 'The Morning Post', a morning newspaper and the defendant started an evening newspaper called 'The Evening Post', the Court of Appeal held that no interlocutory injunction should be granted because even if the public were to be deceived into supposing there was some connection between the two papers, there was no evidence that such a supposition would cause any injury to the plaintiff's finances or reputation. On the other hand in *Walter* v *Ashton* [1902] 2 Ch 282[6] an interlocutory injunction was granted restraining the defendant from representing that the cycles offered by him for sale were offered for sale by the plaintiff who was the proprietor of *The Times* or from representing that he was carrying on business as a department of *The Times* or in any way holding out *The Times* to be the owners of or connected with his business. The defendant had previously conducted a successful sales campaign selling 'Daily Express' bicycles with the co-operation of that paper and was seeking to launch a new campaign selling '*The Times*' bicycles but without their involvement. Byrne J held that the plaintiff was exposed to some risk and liability, a risk even of being exposed to litigation, had steps not been taken to discount the name of the newspaper from the advertisements and circulars issued by the defendant.

---

4   *Marathon Oil Co* v *Marathon Shipping Co Ltd* [1968] RPC 443 (Stamp J, defendant shipping agent in the dry cargo market not competitor of plaintiff's oil business); *Unitex Ltd* v *Union Texturing Company Ltd* [1973] RPC 119 (CA, defendant reputable plasterer, no likely damage to plaintiff's business, suppliers to building trade); *John Hayter Motor Underwriting Agencies Ltd* v *RBHS Agencies Ltd* [1977] FSR 285 (CA, underwriters at Lloyds, no loss of business); see also Chapter 9 as regards the granting of interlocutory relief.

5   See *Erven Warnink BV* v *J Townend & Sons (Hull) Ltd* [1980] RPC 31 at 93 (HL). See also, eg, *Lyons Maid Ltd* v *Trebor Ltd* [1967] RPC 222 (Buckley J, 'Zoom' bubble gum even if confused with plaintiffs' 'ZOOM' ice lollipops, no damage would result). But note *BBC* v *Talbot Motor Co Ltd* [1981] FSR 228 (Megarry V-C, where injury to goodwill rather than the precise way it was inflicted was all that was considered necessary).

6   See also *Eatman Photographic Materials Co Ltd* v *John Griffiths Cycle Corp Ltd* (1898) 15 RPC 105 (Romer J, Kodak Cycle case); *Dunlop Pneumatic Tyre Co Ltd* v *Dunlop Lubricant Co* (1898) 16 RPC 12 (Romer J); *John Dickinson Ltd* v *Apsley Press Ltd* (1937) 54 RPC 219, 226 (Crossman J); and *Annabel's (Berkeley Sq) Ltd* v *Shock* [1972] RPC 838 (CA). See also Chapter 5, pp 84 et seq.

Where the name in dispute is generally descriptive, likelihood of confusion without a real risk of injury to the plaintiff's goodwill is not sufficient. Thus in *Rubber and Technical Press Ltd* v *Maclaren & Sons Ltd* [1961] RPC 264 Cross J refused to grant to the publishers of 'Rubber and Plastics Age' an interlocutory injunction to restrain the defendant using the title 'Rubber and Plastics Weekly', holding that there was very likely to be a certain amount of confusion in the addresses of the publishers but that for there to be passing off the confusion must go beyond that and lead to loss of goodwill and custom. See also *Office Cleaning Services Ltd* v *Westminster Window and General Cleaners Ltd* (1946) 63 RPC 39 (HL, final injunction refused, some confusion inevitable).

Where the plaintiff does not trade (being a professional or charitable body) the plaintiff's reputation will still be protected if injury is likely to result thereto by reason of the defendant's misrepresentations.[7] Thus in *British Medical Association* v *Marsh* (1931) 48 RPC 565 a drug store was restrained from using as part of its name the letters 'BMA' so as to represent it was in any way connected with the plaintiffs. After reviewing all the earlier cases Maugham J stated at 574:

> I think, therefore, the professional cases are far from establishing the view which some people have held that *Clark* v *Freeman* is an authority for the proposition that a professional man has no remedy if a tradesman chooses to put forward some quack remedy or article of that kind as having been prescribed or been sold for the benefit of or the approval of the medical man in question. What is necessary in such a case to prove is, either positive injury, or in a *quia timet* action, a reasonable probability of injury; and if that is done, I for my part, see no reason why such an action should not succeed.

---

[7] See *Society of Accountants and Auditors* v *Goodway* (1907) 24 RPC 159 (Warrington J); *British Legion* v *British Legion Club* (1931) 48 RPC 555 (Farwell J); and *Dr Barnardo's Homes* v *Barnardo Amalgamated Industries Ltd* (1949) 66 RPC 103 (Vaisey J). See also Chapter 7, pp 110 et seq.

Chapter 5

Use of Trade Marks on Goods

A very frequent means whereby one trader passes off his goods as the goods of another, is by imitating the trade name of the goods of his competitor. Generally speaking, the trade name is the name which may be a word or a phrase, by which the trader chooses to identify and promote his goods. However, a trader's goods may be referred to by the public or trade by some other name and thereby acquire a trade name other than that chosen by the trader.

In *Anglo-Swiss Condensed Milk Co v Metcalfe* (1886) 3 RPC 28 (Kay J)[1] the plaintiff was a producer of condensed milk and other articles which were marketed as 'Milk Maid' brand, bearing a label depicting a figure representing a milk maid. A large number of people referred to and knew the plaintiff's produce as 'Dairy Maid' brand and the Court granted the plaintiff an injunction restraining the defendant from using the name 'Dairy Maid' in relation to condensed milk and other articles produced by the plaintiff.

1 More than one trade name for same goods may be protected

In a case where goods of a trader are known by two names, it is no defence to an action for passing off under one name, that they are widely known under a different name. Both names are entitled to protection. In *Orr Ewing & Co v Johnston & Co* (1880) 13 Ch D 447, Fry J said 'if goods are sold in the market by a particular maker as A and B, in my judgment no

---

[1] See also *Edge & Sons Ltd v Gallon & Son* (1900) 17 RPC 557 (HL, defendant's blue called 'Oval Blue' but customers often ask for it as 'Dolly Blue'); *Hodgson and Simpson v Kynoch Ltd* (1898) 15 RPC 465 (Romer J, Lion Soap); and *White Hudson & Co Ltd v Asian Organisation Ltd* [1965] RPC 45 (PC, plaintiff's cough sweets wrapped in orange coloured wrappers printed with the word 'Hacks', known in Singapore as 'red paper cough sweets').

rival manufacturer has the right to appropriate to himself either of the names A or B'.

In *Worcester Royal Porcelain Co Ltd* v *Locke & Co Ltd* (1902) 19 RPC 479, the plaintiff and the plaintiff's successors had used the names 'Worcester', 'Royal Worcester' and 'Grainger's Worcester China' to designate china and porcelain manufactured by them. In restraining the defendant from using the name 'Worcester' in relation to china and porcelain, it was held by Byrne J that the plaintiff was not disentitled to such relief by reason of the fact that some of the plaintiff's goods were described as 'Royal Worcester' or 'Grainger's Worcester China'.

2 Right to trade name of foreign origin

Where a person by agreement with a person abroad sells or manufactures and sells goods in this country under a trade name originating from that other person and the agreement comes to an end, it is a question of fact who is entitled to the goodwill in such name. In *Aktiebolaget Manus* v *RJ Fullwood and Bland Ltd* (1949) 66 RPC 71 (CA),[2] the plaintiff, a Swedish firm, was the manufacturer of milking machines sold under the name 'Manus' and the defendant and the defendant's predecessors in title were the sole importers of such machines in this country. By an agreement with the plaintiff in 1940 the defendant was permitted to manufacture the machines in this country provided the defendant sold such machines under the name 'Manus'. After the plaintiff's patents relating to the machines expired, the defendants asserted rights to the name 'Manus'. It was held that the reputation in the name 'Manus' belonged to the plaintiff and that the plaintiff was entitled to restrain the defendant from using the name. In this case it was proved that before the licence was granted to the defendant, 'Manus' milking machines were known in this country as coming from some foreign source.

In *Oertli AG* v *EJ Bowman (London) Ltd* [1959] RPC 1 (HL), the plaintiff Swiss company granted a licence to P Ltd, to manufacture certain patented mixing machines and to use the plaintiff's registered trade mark 'Turmix' for such machines. This licence was transferred to the defendant and was

---

[2] Explained in *T Oertli AG* v *EJ Bowman (London) Ltd* [1959] RPC 1 (HL). See also *Edison Storage Battery Co* v *Britannia Batteries Ltd* (1931) 48 RPC 350 (Bennett J, defendant, who was an importer of plaintiff's erstwhile patented storage batteries under names 'Edison accumulators' and 'Edison Storage Batteries' was restrained from using such names in relation to accumulators manufactured by a third party).

subsequently terminated for non-payment of royalties. The defendant continued to use the mark 'Turmix' but later sold mixing machines which the defendant claimed to be improvements, under the name 'Magimix'. It was held that at no time had the name 'Turmix' become identified in this country with the plaintiff and that the plaintiff therefore could not restrain the defendant from passing off the plaintiff's goods under such name. In this case it would appear that the Court was not satisfied that the name 'Turmix' had become identified with either party. See also *Goddard* v *Hyam & Goddard* (1917) 35 RPC 21 (Younger J).

In *Re Bostitch Trade Mark* [1963] RPC 183 a foreign manufacturer sold his goods (stapling machines) in the UK through a distributor until wartime conditions made it impractical, so the manufacturer assisted the distributor setting up manufacturing facilities here. Later a dispute arose, and the distributor contended that the 'Bostitch' mark had come to signify to the public goods of the distributor's manufacture. Lloyd-Jacob J held that by advertising themselves as distributors of the foreign manufacturer's goods the mark and the goodwill in the name 'Bostitch' in the minds of the purchasing public (even if not the trade) remained at all times as the foreign manufacturer's.

It would seem that where a person is merely the selling agent or distributor (sole or otherwise) of goods of a manufacturer which are marketed under the manufacturer's name, he will not acquire any right to the goodwill in such name and will not be able to maintain an action for passing-off against a third party.[3] However, if the distributor markets goods under his own name or get-up, or indeed the name of the manufacturer without any reference to the manufacturer, the manufacturer of such goods (not otherwise having any reputation in such name in this country) will not generally acquire any rights in such name or

3   *Dental Manufacturing Co Ltd* v *C De Trey & Co* (1912) 29 RPC 617 (CA). See also *Goodfellow* v *Prince* (1887) 35 Ch D 9 at 20 (CA); *Saxlehner* v *Apollinaris Co* (1897) 14 RPC 645 (Kekewich J); *Re Apollinaris Co's Trade Marks* (1891) 8 RPC 137 Kekewich J); *Imperial Tobacco Co of India Ltd* v *Bonnan* (1924) 41 RPC 441 PC); *The Roberts Numbering Machine Co* v *Davis* (1935) 53 RPC 79 (Luxmoore J); and *Suhner & Company AG* v *Suhner Ltd* [1967] RPC 336, (Plowman J, plaintiff Swiss company, manufacturer of electronic goods held to have goodwill in the UK); cf *Re Diehl Trade Mark* [1970] RPC 435 (Buckley J, where the importer was held to be entitled to the ownership of the Diehl trade mark as against the foreign manufacturer).

get-up and may be restrained by the distributor from selling such goods under a similar name.[4]

It seems also that, where A in the UK orders a certain article to be made for him abroad by B, and it is so made to his special order and imported by him into the UK, where he sells it under a name which comes to be associated with it, B cannot stop A from getting the very same article made in the UK or elsewhere and selling it under that name.[5] Where, however, the defendant had sold wine produced from the plaintiff's vineyard under the name of the vineyard joined with the name of the defendant's firm, and after the defendant had ceased business with the owner of the vineyard, continued to get wine elsewhere and to call it by the same name as the defendant had used before, it was held by Joyce J that the owner of the vineyard could restrain the defendant, although the defendant had been allowed to use the defendant's name in connection with the wine, since the use of the name by the defendant was a representation that the wine was substantially the produce of the plaintiff's vineyard (*Van Zeller v Mason, Cattley & Co* (1907) 25 RPC 37).

3   Honest concurrent user

In *Edge & Sons Ltd v Gallon & Son* (1900) 17 RPC 557 (HL)[6] the plaintiff sold the plaintiff's blue as 'Dolly' from 1888; the blue supplied by the defendant was manufactured by one Ripley under his mark which consisted of a washing tub, known variously as a 'Dolly' tub or a 'Peggy' tub. Ripley had used his mark since 1871 and it was held that concurrent use of the term 'Dolly' to denote Ripley's blue as well as the plaintiff's blue was proved and the plaintiff was not entitled to an injunction.

---

4   *J Defries & Sons Ltd v Electric and Ord Finance Accessories Co Ltd* (1906) 23 RPC 341 (Joyce J). See also *Freeman Bros v Sharpe Bros & Co Ltd* (1899) 16 RPC 205 (North J); *J Ullman & Co v Leuba* (1908) 25 RPC 673 (PC); *Sturtevant Engineering Co Ltd v Sturtevant Mill Co of USA Ltd* (1936) 53 RPC 430 (Farwell J, plaintiff company built up own goodwill in UK); and *Adrema Ltd v Adrema-Werke GmbH* [1958] RPC 323 (Danckwerts J, where UK company also made certain types of machinery with foreign suppliers' acquiescence).

5   *J Defries & Sons Ltd v Electric & Ordnance Accessories Co Ltd* (1906) 23 RPC 341 (per Joyce J). See also *CG Vokes Ltd v Evans & Marble Arch Motor Supplies Ltd* (1932) 49 RPC 140 (CA, where goods made by B in UK, exclusively for A, A can stop third party selling such goods not dealt with by A).

6   Cf *Goddard v The Watford Co-op Society* (1924) 41 RPC 218 (Astbury J); see also *Godfrey Phillips & Sons v Thomas Ogden & Co Ltd* (1895) 12 RPC 325 (Wills J); *Robert Bosch AG v RH Cook & Co* (1930) 47 RPC 462 (Maugham J).

It was clear in that case that the defendant's use of the disputed name was both honest and concurrent and should be contrasted with the case of *Poiret* v *Jules Poiret Ltd* (1920) 37 RPC 177, where the plaintiff, Paul Poiret, by the outbreak of the first world war had a considerable reputation both in Paris and in this country as a costumier, dressmaker and designer of ladies' dresses and as a theatrical costumier. On the outbreak of war the plaintiff was called up for military service and his premises were taken over by the French Government as a factory for making soldiers' shirts, and he did not resume his business until June 1919. The defendant Alexander Nash in February 1914 set up business in London as a costumier, dressmaker and theatrical costumier under the name 'Jules Poiret'. Subsequently in 1917 the defendant formed the defendant company and by the time the plaintiff resumed business he had built up a considerable reputation. It was held by Younger J that the defendant had taken the name of Poiret knowing of the plaintiff's reputation in Paris and in England with a view to getting the benefit of such reputation and an injunction was granted restraining the defendant from using the name Poiret with or without the name Jules. See also *JC Penney Co Inc* v *Penney's Ltd* [1975] FSR 367 in which the relevant date for deciding whether it was a case of shared reputation was held to be the defendant's first act of passing off.

In a case where a defendant is able to raise a defence of honest concurrent user, usually it is because the plaintiff's trade name, however well known, does not mean the plaintiff's goods only. Thus in *S Chivers & Sons* v *S Chivers & Co Ltd* (1900) 17 RPC 420, it was held by Farwell J that the plaintiff had not proved that 'Chivers' table jelly meant the plaintiff's table jelly and no one else's, and that the defendant did not describe the defendant's jelly in such a way as to lead persons to believe it was the plaintiff's jelly. In *Rolls Razor Ltd* v *Rolls Lighters Ltd* (1949) 66 RPC 299 (CA) the parties were trading honestly in different goods (razors and lighters respectively) and even though some confusion between the two businesses had occurred, the action failed. See also *Jamieson* v *Jamieson* (1898) 15 RPC 180 (CA); *Evans* v *Eradicure* [1972] RPC 808 (Goff J, expanding rival businesses); *City Link Travel Holdings Ltd* v *Lakin* [1979] FSR 653 (Whitford J, parcel delivery service); *Habib Bank Ltd* v *Habib Bank AG Zurich* [1982] RPC 1 (CA, shared reputation of banks in question).

Where there has been an honest and concurrent use of a trade name by two traders, but the use by one of the traders has practically ceased for some years and in the meantime the other trader has acquired a large sale of his goods and has established such a reputation in the market that the trade name has become associated solely with that other's goods, then the first trader may not afterwards revive the use of the trade name in his business in such a way as to pass off his goods as those of the other trader (*Daniel and Arter* v *Whitehouse and Britton* (1898) 15 RPC 134 (Barnes J, Brazilian Silver)).

4   Parallel imports of goods

In *Champagne Heidsiech et Cie Monopole SA* v *Buxton* (1930) 47 RPC 28 (Clauson J) the plaintiff's champagne was sold in England in bottles bearing similar labels to that used for the Continental market save for omission of the word 'Brut', but the champagne was of different quality catering for the different tastes of the two countries, although there was evidence that both qualities had been sold in England. An injunction was refused preventing the defendant from selling the 'French' quality in this country, it being held, inter alia, it was for the plaintiff to make clear the difference between the two qualities. A similar conclusion was reached in *Revlon Inc* v *Cripps & Lee Ltd* [1980] FSR 85 (CA). The facts were Revlon Inc disposed in the USA of large quantities of 'Revlon Flex' medicated shampoo and conditioner, a product which had not been marketed by Revlon International in the UK. The defendant imported and distributed quantities of the product to the British market—it being accepted that the goods in question were not sub-standard. The plaintiff's claim for an interlocutory injunction failed (both in respect of registered trade name and passing off). Buckley LJ found that no 'reasonably perspicacious member of the public would suppose that a bottle (of US origin) so labelled contained the same product as one labelled in the way in which the UK shampoo product is labelled'. It followed that no one would be mistaken into buying the imported medicated shampoo as or for the UK 'beauty' shampoo. It was also held it was the plaintiff's own actions which gave rise to their difficulties. See also *Imperial Tobacco Co of India Ltd* v *Bonnan* (1924) 41 RPC 441 (PC, importation of genuine 'Gold Flake' cigarettes into India not passing off despite presence of exclusive distributorship).

The Champagne and Revlon cases were distinguished in *Wilkinson Sword Ltd* v *Cripps & Lee Ltd* [1982] FSR 16 (Falconer J) where an application to strike out a statement of claim as disclosing no (reasonable) cause of action was refused. The statement of claim alleged that the importation of razor blades of the plaintiff's manufacture from the USA which though marketed abroad under the 'Wilkinson' trade marks were of inferior quality to similar blades manufactured and marketed by the plaintiff in the UK. This case was followed in *Colgate-Palmolive Ltd* v *Markwell Finance Ltd* [1989] RPC 497 (CA), where toothpaste originally produced and sold by a subsidiary company of Colgate US in Brazil found its way onto the UK market. It was held that marketing such toothpaste of an inferior quality to UK Colgate toothpaste without Colgate US's consent or licence constituted passing off not by reason of a misrepresentation as to origin, but as to the character and quality of the goods.

5 Impact of EC Law

In accordance with the provisions of Arts 30–36 and 85 of the Treaty of Rome the EC authorities have struck down numerous arrangements whereby markets in Member States of the EC have sought to be partitioned by use of trade marks. In *Centrafarm BV* v *Winthrop BV* [1974] 2 CMLR 480,[7] the European Court of Justice has stated that the holder of a trade mark in one Member State may not prevent the importation of goods from another Member State if they were marketed by him or with his consent. This concept, known as the doctrine of exhaustion of rights, was extended to cover a case where the trade marks in question were of common origin but had been assigned to different enterprises or even compulsorily acquired and resold (see *Van Zuylen Frères* v *Hag AG* [1974] 2 CMLR 127 (Hag No 1)).

However, in the subsequent case of CNL SUCAL v Hag GFAG (1990) 3 CMLR 571 (Hag No 2),[8] the European Court of Justice overruled its decision in Hag No 1. In Hag No 1 proceedings by Van Zuylen Frères, the Belgian entity that owned the 'Hag' marks in the Benelux countries, who were seeking to restrain the importation of 'Hag' coffee products from Germany into Luxembourg, failed on the ground that any such restraint would be in competition with the free movement of goods within the Common Market, and therefore contrary to Art 30. As the mark was of common origin no exception could be made under Art 36. Van Zuylen Frères' predecessors in title had acquired the 'Hag' mark in 1994 from the German company's Belgian subsidiary as a result of an expropriation order of enemy property after the war.

In Hag No 2, CNL SUCAL NV, who are the successors in title to Van

---

[7] See also *Dansk Supermarket* v *Imerco* [1981] 3 CMLR 590; [1981] ECR 181: reject china sold in Denmark as firsts, trade mark owner given consent to its sale in the UK on condition not exported to Denmark; held trade mark and copyright rights exhausted. However, such a ruling did not permit the contravention of Danish domestic law on fair marketing. See *Mantruck Services Ltd* v *Ballinlough Electrical Refrigeration Co Ltd* (1992) 1 CMLR 325 (Supreme Court of Ireland), exclusive distributor cannot restrain parallel importation; prima facie contrary to Art 85(1).

[8] (1990) ECR 3711; affirmed in *Re Compulsory Patent Licences: EC* v *UK* (1992) 2 CMLR 709.

Zuylen Frères, were successfully restrained by the German company from importing into Germany from Belgium decaffeinated coffee under the 'Hag' mark. The Court, in reversing its former decision, held that there was no contravention of Art 30. The essential function of a trade mark is to guarantee to the end consumer the origin of the product so that the consumer can distinguish such product from products of other origins. In the absence of any consent on the part of the proprietor of the trade mark to the putting into circulation in another Member State of the product bearing such mark (ie no exhaustion of rights), and the fact that the proprietor and CNL SUCAL NV were independent undertakings without any economic links (a factor no doubt connected with the first).

In the recent case of *IHT Internationale Heiztechnik GmbH* v *Ideal-Standard GmbH*[9] the Court has held that where a trade mark had been voluntarily assigned for one or several Member States to an undertaking which had no economic link with the assignor, the assignor could oppose the marketing in those Member States in which he had retained the trade mark, of products to which that mark has been affixed by the assignee. This decision effectively puts an end to the extension of the doctrine of exhaustion of rights to common origin cases. The Court distinguished imported products from a licensee or a subsidiary from the case of an assignment to an independent third party in that in the latter case the assignor (original proprietor) no longer had the means of controlling the quality of the products marketed by the assignee.

It was pointed out by the Court that where trade mark assignments within the Common Market were part of a market-sharing agreement, the prohibition under Art 85 against anti-competetive agreements applied, and any such assignment would be void (see, eg, *Grundig-Consten* (1964) CMLR 489).

The reasoning behind these decisions is that whilst Art 30 prohibits all qualitative restrictions and measures having equivalent effect on imports and exports between Member States, Art 36 exempts measures which are justified on grounds of the protection of industrial and commercial property. Furthermore, Art 222 provides that the Treaty shall in no way prejudice the rules in Member States governing the system of property ownership. As a compromise or balancing exercise between Arts 30 and 36, the European Court has drawn a distinction between the *existence* of the industrial property rights and the *exercise* of the same. Thus the Court has consistently held that the exercise of such rights in so far as any enforcement or exploitation thereof may affect trade between Member States can only be justified if such exercise is necessary for safeguarding

---

[9] Case C-9/93, reported in *The Times*, 7 July 1994.

what the Court refers to as 'the specific subject matter' of the property rights.

The Court has held on many occasions that the specific subject matter of a trade mark right is to grant the owner the right to use the mark for the first marketing of a product and in this way to protect him against competitors by selling products to which the mark has been improperly affixed. To determine the exact effect of this right, account must be taken of the essential function of the mark, viz to give the consumer or end user a guarantee of the identity of the origin of the marked product, by enabling him to distinguish that product without any possible confusion from other products of a different provenance.[10]

In *Terrapin (Overseas) Ltd* v *Terranova Industrie CA Kapferer & Co* [1976] 2 CMLR 482, the German owner of the mark 'Terranova' was held to be entitled to prevent the importation from Britain of 'Terrapin' prefabricated buildings. As the Court of Justice stated in that case, 'if . . . the principle of the free movement of goods were to prevail over the protection given by the respective national laws, the specific objective of industrial and commercial property rights would be undermined.' In *Deutsche Renault AG* v *Audi AG* the German owner of the mark 'Quattro' for cars was entitled to prevent the importation from France of 'Quadra' cars. The Court of Justice reiterated that in the absence of unity within the Community, the setting up of protective conditions and the criteria for judging the risk of confusion between two names is a matter for the national law and falls within the terms of Art 36. This article only admits derogation from the fundamental principle of the free movement of goods to the extent to which such derogation is justified for the purpose of safeguarding the specific subject matter of the industrial property right.

Justification under Art 36 on grounds of public policy cannot be extended to include considerations of consumer protection. However, such considerations may be taken into account in establishing whether national measures which apply to domestic and imported products are caught by Art 30. Thus in *Industrie Diensten Groep BV* v *JA Beele Handelmaatschappij BV* (1982) ECR 707[11] imitation cable ducts from Germany which were imported into Holland were found likely to be confused with those sold there by the plaintiffs. The European Court of Justice held that national laws prohibiting such imitation were permissible provided that there was no discrimination between domestic and imported products, on the gounds of the protection of consumers and promotion of

---

[10] See *Deutsche Renault AG* v *Audi AG* (1993) 66 CMLR 421.
[11] Cf *Kohl* v *Ringelhan & Rennett* [1985] 3 CMLR 340; [1986] FSR 8.

fair trading being in accordance with Art 10 bis of the Paris Convention for the Protection of Industrial Property.

Thus where goods are imported from one Member State to another under a name giving rise to confusion then where the rights in question have been acquired independently, they may lawfully be protected and the doctrine of exhaustion of rights has no application.[7] Nor does such doctrine apply where goods are imported from outside the EEC (*see EMI Records Ltd* v *CBS UK Ltd* [1976] 2 CMLR 235; *Revlon Inc* v *Cripps & Lee Ltd* [1980] FSR 85, CA). Furthermore such doctrine does not apply where the genuine goods have been tampered with (for example, repackaging or relabelling of drugs) because 'the guarantee of origin would in fact be jeopardised if it were permissible for a third party to affix the mark to the product, even to an original product' (see *Hoffman-La Roche & Co AG* v *Centrafarm* [1978] 3 CMLR 217; *Centrafarm BV* v *American Home Products Co* [1979] 1 CMLR 326[12] cf *Pfizer* v *Eurim-Pharm* (1982) 1 CMLR 406, where the parallel importer merely applied external packaging without interfering with the internal packaging or original trade mark). However, it has been left open for the national courts to determine whether in any particular case the enforcement of the trade mark rights is contrary to Art 36, being a disguised restriction on trade.

In *ICI Ltd* v *Berk Pharmaceuticals Ltd* [1981] FSR 1, it was sought to raise as a Euro defence that no relief should be granted restraining the defendant from selling pills of a confusingly similar get-up to those of the plaintiff because the plaintiff was alleged to be in breach of Art 86 of the Treaty of Rome (viz abuse of dominant position by charging excessive prices therefor). This argument was rejected by Megarry J, there being no nexus between the defendant's alleged misrepresentations as to get-up and the plaintiff's alleged breaches of Art 86.

In *Lansing Bagnall Ltd* v *Buccaneer Lift Parts Ltd* (1984) 1 CMLR 224 at 228, the Court of Appeal in refusing to strike out a defence of abuse of dominant position in a copyright action and distinguishing over the *ICI* v *Berk* case, stated (of that case) 'It is important for the Court to remind itself that the Vice Chancellor was not dealing with an industrial copyright case. He was dealing with a case of passing off. There is nothing in Art 86 of the Treaty of Rome which allows passing off. Passing off is essentially misrepresentation. It cannot be an abuse of a dominant position to stop someone passing off your goods.' This seems to be both good law and common sense.

However, in *IBM* v *Phoenix International (Computers) Ltd* [1994] RPC 251 Ferris J in considering a number of cases since *ICI* v *Berk*, including

---

[12] See also *Kerlane Trade Mark* (1993) 68(3) CMLR 190.

the *Lansing Bagnall* case, whilst striking out the Art 86 Euro defence in a trade mark and passing off action on the grounds of no nexus, was not prepared to consider passing off or trade mark cases as a different category from other intellectual property cases.

6 Loss of right to protection by labelling with another's name

A manufacturer may lose his right to protect a trade name by using that trade name on his goods in connection with someone else's name. Where a cigarette manufacturer of 'Eton' cigarettes sold some boxes of them with the name 'Eton', together with the name of some other person, stamped on them,[13] and where a manufacturer whose pencils were known as 'Spanish Graphite Pencils' had supplied some of his pencils to a trader and put the trader's name in front of the words 'Spanish Graphite',[14] it was held that the plaintiffs in both cases were not entitled to protect the trade name.

7 Classification of trade names

While each case must be decided on its own facts, often the facts of one case bear similarities to the facts of another case and it is useful to compare such cases.

The following lists of cases are intended to give some guidance as to when a defendant will be restrained.

7.1 Descriptive names

Injunction granted (where descriptive name has acquired some measure of distinctiveness of plaintiff's goods)

'Blue Orchid' brilliantine, which was blue and smelt of orchids, held distinctive (*Delavelle (GB) Ltd* v *Harry Stanley* (1946) 63 RPC 103: Evershed J).

'Burberry', defence that it meant a coat of a particular shape failed (*Burberrys* v *Raper and Pulleyn* (1906) 23 RPC 170: Warrington J; cf *Burberrys* v *Cording & Co Ltd* (1909) 26 RPC 693: Parker J).

'Camel Hair Belting', secondary meaning established (*Reddaway* v *Banham* (1986) 13 RPC 218 (HL)).

'Computervision' title of publication (*Computervision Corp* v *Computer*

---

[13] *Wood* v *Butler* (1886) 32 Ch D 247 (Pearson J); 257 (CA).
[14] *Wolff & Son* v *Nopitsch* (1900) 17 RPC 321 (Cozens-Hardy J).

Vision Ltd [1975] RPC 171: Plowman J, interlocutory injunction even though products not in competition).

'Crystal' applied to ball-point pen, made from plastic powder known to trade as crystal (*Biro-Swan Ltd* v *Tallon Ltd* [1961] RPC 326: Russell J).

'Goddard's Plate Powder' (*Goddard* v *Hyam & Goddard* (1917) 35 RPC 21 (Younger J) considered in *Goddard* v *The Watford Co-op Society* (1924) 41 RPC 218 (Astonbury J): Goddard's Plate Powder held to have acquired a secondary meaning).

'Iron-Ox Tablets' denoted plaintiff's remedy, not iron oxide as a drug (*Iron-Ox Remedy Co Ltd* v *Co-op Wholesale Society Ltd* (1907) 24 RPC 425: Parker J, defendant restrained from selling 'Iron Oxide Tablets' without better distinguishing from plaintiff's 'Iron-Ox Tablets').

'June', injunction granted to restrain the use of the name 'June' on shampoo powder, lipstick and setting lotion (*Saville Perfumery Ltd* v *June Perfect Ltd* (1941) 58 RPC 147: HL, no injunction in respect of defendant's name).

'Maclean's Powder' so named to describe a formula of a Dr Maclean and originally known as a prescription both to medical circles and public, but had become identified with plaintiff's as plaintiff's product (*Macleans Ltd* v *JW Lightbown and Sons Ltd* (1937) 54 RPC 230: Farwell J, qualified injunction granted).

'Special Brew' beer (*Carlsberg* v *Tennent Caledonian Breweries Ltd* [1972] RPC 847: Court of Session, interim interdict).

'Steam' beer, plaintiffs Newquay Real Steam Beer, granted interlocutory injunction to restrain defendants, Anchor Steam Beer, from selling keg beer (as opposed to bottled beer) as steam beer, both made by similar steam process. *Island Trading Co* v *Anchor Brewing Co* [1989] RPC 87a (Knox J).

'Top of the Pops' records (*Pickwick International Inc (GB) Ltd* v *Multiple Sound Distributors Ltd* [1972] RPC 786, CA, interlocutory injunction 'Pick of the Pops' held confusingly similar).

'Top breeders recommend it' slogan for 'Pedigree Chum' dog food, defendants prevented from launching similar dog food called 'Top Breed'; *Mars GB Ltd* v *Country Petfoods Ltd* (13 Feb 1987 unreported, Mervyn Davies J).

'Treasure Cots' babies' cots, even though to a substantial number of people that term meant a cot of a particular type (*Treasure Cot Co Ltd* v *Hamley Bros Ltd* (1950) 67 RPC 89: Harman J, declaration granted in qualified form in respect of toy/dolls' cots as well as babies').

'Vapour Rub' not descriptive in Jamaica (*De Cordova* v *Vick Chemical Co* [1951] 68 RPC 103: PC, 'Karsote Vapour Rub' held not to be a sufficient distinction from 'Vapo Rub').

'What's New In . . .' magazine series of ten titles defendants prevented form using title What's New in Training' due to risk of confusion of plaintiff's advertisers (*Morgan Grampian plc* v *Training Personnel Ltd* [1992] FSR 262).

Injunction refused (where name descriptive of goods in question)

'Adventure' (title of US magazine) failed to stop 'Hutchinsons Adventure Story' magazine (*The Ridgway Co* v *Hutchinson* (1923) 40 RPC 335: Sargant J).

'Maidenhead Advertiser' failed to stop 'The New Advertiser' also in Maidenhead (*Baylis & Co (The Maidenhead Advertiser) Ltd* v *Darlenko Ltd* [1974] FSR 284: Plowman J).

'Athletics Weekly' failed to prevent 'Athletics Monthly' (*World Athletics and Sporting Publications Ltd* v *ACM Webb (Publishing) Co Ltd* [1981] FSR 27: CA, 'Can't unfairly monopolise word "athletics"').

'Bullet' darts descriptive of shape of dart to public even though not to trade (*Unicorn Products Ltd* v *Roban Jig & Tool Co (UK) Ltd* [1976] FSR 169: Whitford J).

'Castle Albums' no exclusive right to name for albums for photographs with pictorial borders of views of castles (*Schove* v *Schmincke* (1886) 33 Ch D 546: Chitty J, 'these terms are not exhaustively descriptive, few descriptions are, but they are descriptive so far as they go and serve to denote the difference between different sorts of album').

'Cellular cloth' descriptive of a certain weave of cloth (*Cellular Clothing Co* v *Maxton* (1899) 16 RPC 397, HL).

'Chequerboard' fencing not established as distinctive of the plaintiff (*T & C Associated Industries Ltd* v *Victoria Wagon Works Ltd* (1930) 48 RPC 148: Maugham J).

'Chicago Pizza' descriptive of a certain type of pizza (*Mykinda Town Ltd* v *Soll* [1983] RPC 407).

'Classic' greeting cards held not to designate the plaintiff's cards (*Sharp Ltd* v *Solomon Bros Ltd* (1915) 32 RPC 15: CA).

'Electromobile' descriptive of a car driven by electricity (*Electromobile Co Ltd* v *British Electromobile Co Ltd* (1908) 25 RPC 149: CA).

'Flaked Oatmeal' descriptive of a preparation of oats reduced to powder then steamed, rolled and flaked (*Parsons Bros & Co* v *John Gillespie and Co* (1897) 15 RPC 57: PC).

'Glassy mints' descriptive in Leicester of certain type of sweets (*Fox's Glacier Mints Ltd* v *Joblings* (1932) 49 RPC 352: Clauson J), oral trap orders for 'Glacier Mints' could have been mistaken for 'glassy mints'.

The 'Gourmet' monthly magazine could not prevent a similar monthly magazine the 'BBC Gourmet Good Food' (*Advance Magazine Publishing Inc* v *Redwood Publishing Ltd* [1993] FSR 449, Harman J).

'Gripe Water' held to describe a palliative for gripes, no secondary meaning (*Woodward Ltd* v *Boulton Marco Ltd* (1915) 32 RPC 173: Eve J).

'Guaranteed Corsets' name merely descriptive of terms of sale (*Symington & Co* v *Footman, Pretty & Co* (1887) 56 LT 696: Kay J).

'Haematogen' a general medicinal preparation known to doctors and pharmacists (*Hommel* v *Bauer & Co* (1904) 22 RPC 43: CA).

'Health' for a brand of cocoa, held to be commendatory only (*Henry Thorne & Co Ltd* v *Sandow* (1912) 29 RPC 440: Neville J).

'Linoleum' floor covering (*Linoleum Manufacturing Co* v *Nairn* (1878) 7 Ch D 834: Fry J).

'Malted Milk' descriptive of milk combined with malt (*Fels* v *Christopher Thomas & Bros Ltd* (1903) 21 RPC 85: CA).

'Newsweek' magazine failed to stop BBC using name as TV programme (*Newsweek Inc* v *BBC* [1979] RPC 441: CA).

'Nourishing stout' (*Raggett* v *Findlater* (1873) LR 17 Eq 29: V-C).

'Oval Blue' laundry blue not acquired secondary meaning (*Ripley* v *Griffiths* (1902) 19 RPC 590: Farwell J).

'Oven Chips' not acquired secondary meaning (*McCain International Ltd* v *Country Fair Foods Ltd* [1981] RPC 69, CA).

'Post Office Directory' no exclusive right (*Kelly* v *Byles* (1880) Ch D 682: Bacon V-C and CA).

'Prophylactic' descriptive of a particular shape and type of toothbrush (*Cordes* v *R Addis & Son* (1923) 40 RPC 133: Eve J).

'Rolls' for lighters indicated 'Rolls Royce' class (*Rolls Razor Ltd* v *Rolls Lighters* (1949) 66 RPC 299: CA).

'Rubber and Plastics Age' periodical failed to stop 'Rubber and Plastics Weekly' (*Rubber and Technical Press Ltd* v *Maclaren & Sons Ltd* [1961] RPC 264: Cross J, interlocutory injunction refused, held confusion must lead to loss of goodwill and custom).

'Slip On' held to relate to a particular kind of coat anyone may make or sell (*Burberrys* v *Cording & Co Ltd* (1909) 26 RPC 693: Parker J).

'Staunton' chessmen to distinguished chess players meant chessmen of a particular design and not necessarily the plaintiff's (*John Jacques & Son Ltd* v *Chess* (1940) 57 RPC 77: CA).

'Sunday Post' mainly distributed in North failed to stop 'South East Sunday Post' (*DC Thomson & Co Ltd* v *Kent Messenger Ltd* [1975] RPC 191: Megarry J, interlocutory injunction refused no likelihood of confusion; see also *Morning Star Co-Op Society Ltd* v *Express Newspapers Ltd* [1979] FSR 113: Foster J, interlocutory injunction refused 'Daily Star' not confused with 'Morning Star', only 'moron in a hurry').

'Top Model' hair spray not confusingly similar to 'Top Secret' hair spray (*Max Factor Hollywood & London (Sales) Ltd* v *Callinan Giles & Co Ltd* [1959] RPC 96: Vaisey J refused interlocutory injunction, no similarity of get-up).

'Universal' textile winding machines descriptive of type of machinery (*Universal Winding Co Ltd* v *George Hattersley & Sons Ltd* (1915) 32 RPC 479: Joyce J).

'Vacuum cleaner' a descriptive term (*British Vacuum Cleaner Co Ltd* v *New Vacuum Cleaner Co Ltd* (1907) 24 RPC 641: Parker J).

7.2   Geographical names (descriptive of origin)

Injunction granted

'Anatolia' liquorice distinctive of plaintiff's product and not a word common to all denoting place where liquorice root largely grown (*McAndrew* v *Bassett* (1864) 33 LJ Ch 561: Wood V-C).

'Apollinaris' mineral water (*Apollinaris Co Ltd* v *Norrish* (1875) 33 LT 242: Bacon V-C).

'Banbury Buildings' but defendant allowed to use name Banbury as bona fide part of address (*Banbury Buildings Ltd* v *Sectional Concrete Buildings Ltd* [1970] RPC 463: Pennycuick J).

'Brereton' sand, plaintiff only person to quarry sand in Brereton (Chester) (*Arthur Smith (S & B Foundry Sands) Ltd* v *George Fieldhouse Ltd* [1961] RPC 110: Pennycuick J, interlocutory injunction).

'Champagne' signifies a particular product produced in the Champagne district of France by the growers and shippers of that area and not a type of wine. The term 'Spanish Champagne' held to deceive a substantial portion of the public into thinking it to be genuine champagne (*J Bollinger* v *The Costa Brava Wine Co Ltd* [1960] RPC 16 (Danckwerts J) [1961] RPC 116 (Danckwerts J).

'Dindigul' cigars, but defendant not prevented from describing cigars which were in fact made of Dindigul tobacco as being so made (*Bewlay & Co Ltd* v *Hughes* (1898) 15 RPC 290: North J).

'Glenfield Starch', name acquired secondary meaning even though plaintiff no longer manufactured starch at Glenfield and defendant had started to do so (*Wotherspoon* v *Currie* (1872) LR 5 HL 508).

'Harris Tweed' means tweed handwoven in the Outer Hebrides produced from Scottish wool which is dyed, spun and finished in the Outer Islands (*Macaulay (Tweeds) Ltd* v *Hepworths Ltd* [1961] RPC 184 (Cross J); *Argyllshire Weavers Ltd* v *A Macaulay (Tweeds) Ltd* [1964] RPC 477: Court of Session).

'London Candles' in Morocco market (*Price Patent Candle Co Ltd* v *Ogston & Tennant Ltd* (1909) 26 RPC 797: Court of Session—OH).

'Reading biscuits' (*Huntley & Palmer* v *Reading Biscuit Co Ltd* (1893) 10 RPC 277: Chitty J, qualified interlocutory injunction).

'Scotch' whisky (*John Walker & Sons Ltd* v *Henry Ost & Co Ltd* [1970] RPC 489: Foster J).

'Seixo' wines, defendant whose conduct was not free from suspicion restrained from using the name 'Seixo' even though his wine was produced from a vineyard in the Seixo district, Oporto (*Seixo* v *Provezende* (1865) 1 Ch App 192: qualified injunction).

'Sherry' simpliciter means wines from Jerez in Spain but acquiescence/delay allowed defendant to use expressions such as 'Australian', 'Cyprus', 'South African' or 'British' sherry (*Vine Products Ltd* v *Mackenzie & Co Ltd* [1969] RPC 1: Cross J).

'Stone Ale', defendant who fraudulently set up brewery in Stone restrained from using such name; secondary meaning (*Montgomery* v *Thompson* (1891) 8 RPC 361: HL).

'Worcester' distinctive of plaintiff's china and porcelain even though some of the plaintiff's products were known as 'Royal Worcester' and 'Grainger's Worcester China' (*Worcester Royal Porcelain Co Ltd* v *Locke & Co Ltd* (1902) 19 RPC 479: Byrne J).

Injunction refused

'Caledonia Water' a natural product, difficulty of proving secondary meaning all the greater particularly where others use the name for water from same locality (*Grant Hotel Co of Caledonia Springs* v *Wilson* (1903) 21 RPC 117: PC).

'Hopton Wood', 'Hopton' stone did not mean a certain quality and seam exclusively quarried by the plaintiff (*Hopton Wood Stone Firms Ltd* v *Gething* (1910) 27 RPC 605: Parker J; cf the facts of the 'Brereton' sand case).

'Rugby' Portland cement did not mean the plaintiff's cement exclusively but applied to cement from the district of Rugby (*Rugby Portland Cement Co Ltd* v *Rugby and Newbold Portland Cement Co Ltd* (1891) 8 RPC 241: Vaughan Williams J).

'Whitstable Oysters' was not confined to the plaintiff's oyster beds but applied also to those of the defendant (*The Whitstable Oyster Fishery Co* v *The Hayling Fisheries Ltd* (1900) 17 RPC 461: Buckley J).

7.3 Article the subject of a patent, registered design or some secret process or formula[15]

Injunction granted

'Angostura Bitters', plaintiff's secret formulation not known to defendant (*Siegert* v *Findlater* (1878) 7 Ch D 801: Fry J).

---

[15] See Chapter 2, pp 31–34.

'Chartreuse' liqueurs made by monks' secret process protected even though business, goodwill and trade marks by French law became vested in defendant and monks no longer manufactured at La Grande Chartreuse in France (*Le Couturier* v *Rey* (1910) 27 RPC 268: HL).

'Daimler' originally descriptive of system but later when system became obsolete became distinctive of car (*Daimler Motor Co (1904) Ltd* v *London Daimler Co Ltd* (1907) 24 RPC 379: CA).

'Demon' tennis racquets with patented handles, defendant restrained from selling 'Demotic' tennis racquets (*Slazenger & Sons* v *Feltham & Co* (1889) 6 RPC 531: Kekewich J).

'Edison' accumulators and storage batteries (*Edison Storage Battery Co* v *Britannia Batteries Ltd* (1930) 48 RPC 350: Bennett J).

'Maclean's Powder' originally descriptive of a formula of Dr Maclean had become so identified with plaintiff that others must make it clear that a powder made up from a prescription of Dr Maclean was not the plaintiff's powder (*Macleans Ltd* v *JW Lightbown and Sons Ltd* (1937) 54 RPC 230: Farwell J).

'Procea' bread made to special formula containing certain of plaintiff's ingredients (*Procea Products Ltd* v *Evans & Sons Ltd* (1951) 68 RPC 210: Roxburgh J).

'Singer' machines meant plaintiff's machines not merely machines of a certain design (*Singer Machine Manufacturers* v *Wilson* (1877) 3 App Cas 376 (HL); *Singer Manufacturing Co* v *Spence & Co* (1893) 10 RPC 297: Romer J; *Singer Manufacturing Co* v *British Empire Manufacturing Co Ltd* (1903) 20 RPC 313: Kekewich J).

'Yorkshire Relish', defendant's sauce not the real sauce made by the plaintiff although very similar (*Powell* v *The Birmingham Vinegar Brewery Co* (1897) 14 RPC 720: HL).

Injunction refused

'Capstan' closets manufactured and sold as such by defendant after licence with plaintiff under a patent had expired (*Freeman Bros* v *Sharpe Bros & Co Ltd* (1899) 16 RPC 205: North J).

'James's blister', deceased inventor's nephew had discovered secret of how to make ointment (*James* v *James* (1872) LR 13 Eq 421: Romilly MR).

'Liebig's Extract' or 'Baron Liebig's Extract of Meat' descriptive of well known process free for all to use (*Liebig's Extract of Meat Co Ltd* v *Hanbury* (1867) 17 LT 298 (Wood V-C); *Liebig's Extract of Meat Co Ltd* v *Anderson* (1886) 55 LT 206: Chitty J; but this does not mean any manufacturer may represent his as 'the only genuine' brand of Liebig).

'Linoleum' floor covering, plaintiff held not entitled to the exclusive use of the word 'linoleum' on the expiration of his patents it being the only name for the new substance for this type of floor covering (*Linoleum Manufacturing Co* v *Nairn* (1878) 7 Ch D 834: Fry J).

'Native Guano' descriptive of a once patented process for manufacturing fertiliser from human excreta, plaintiff failed to prevent defendant from so calling his product (*Native Guano Co* v *Sewage Manure Co* (1889) 8 RPC 125: HL; considered in *Erven Warnink BV* v *J Townend & Sons (Hull) Ltd* [1980] RPC 90 at 97: HL).

'Staunton Chessman' descriptive as chessman of a particular design once the subject of a registered design (*John Jacques & Son Ltd* v *Chess* (1940) 57 RPC 77: CA).

'Universal Winding' machines descriptive of machines the subject of expired patents (*Universal Winding Co Ltd* v *George Hattersley & Sons Ltd* (1915) 32 RPC 479: Joyce J).

'Vacuum cleaner' where patentee gave such name to the patented article and it thus became descriptive of such articles in general (*British Vacuum Cleaner Company Ltd* v *New Vacuum Cleaner Co Ltd* (1907) 24 RPC 641 at 652: Parker J).

'Winser Interceptors' for sewer interceptors (once the subject of a registered design) was held to be the name of a type of interceptor and not to denote the plaintiff's (*Winser & Co Ltd* v *Armstrong & Co* (1898) 16 RPC 167: Byrne J).

7.4 Article which takes the name of its inventor, designer etc

Injunction granted

'Daimler' car (*Daimler Motor Co (1904) Ltd* v *London Daimler Co Ltd* (1907) 24 RPC 379: CA; cf *Daimler Motor Car Co Ltd* v *British Motor Traction Co Ltd* (1901) 18 RPC 465 (Buckley J) where six years earlier the word 'Daimler' meant a type or system of motor).

'Dorman' motor engines (*WH Dorman & Co* v *Henry Meadows Ltd* [1922] 2 Ch 332: Astbury J; see also *Bentley Motors (1931) Ltd* v *Lagonda Ltd* (1946) 64 RPC 33 (Roxburgh J) where it was held 'Bentley' denoted a car made and marketed by the plaintiff).

'Goddard's Plate Powder' (*Goddard* v *The Watford Co-op Society* (1924) 41 RPC 218: Astbury J).

'Holbrook's Worcester Sauce' (*Birmingham Vinegar Brewery Co* v *Liverpool Vinegar Co and Holbrook* [1888] WN 139: North J, sauce named after one Holbrook, plaintiff's traveller).

'Maclean's Powder' (*Macleans Ltd* v *JW Lightbown & Sons Ltd* (1937) 54 RPC 230: Farwell J).

'Singer' sewing machine (*Singer Machine Manufacturers* v *Wilson* (1877) 3 App Cas 376 (HL); *Singer Manufacturing Co* v *Spence & Co* (1893) 10

RPC 297 (Romer J); *Singer Manufacturing Co v British Empire Manufacturing Co Ltd* (1903) 20 RPC 313: Kekewich J).

'Thorley's Food for Cattle' (*Massam v Thorley's Cattle Food Co* (1880) 14 Ch D 748 at 754: CA).

Injunction refused

'Liebig's Extract' or 'Baron Liebig's Extract of Meat', descriptive of a well-known process so that any maker may use the name or print a portrait of the Baron on the wrapper (*Liebig's Extract of Meat Co Ltd v Hanbury* (1867) 17 LT 298 (Wood V-C); *Liebig's Extract of Meat Co Ltd v Anderson* (1886) 55 LT 206 (Chitty J); cf *Liebig's Extract of Meat Co Ltd v Chemists Co-op Society Ltd* (1896) 13 RPC 736 (CA), a get-up case, where wrappers held confusingly similar).

'Lieut. James's Blister', a horse blister ointment the recipe of which was discovered by the nephew of the inventor after the inventor's death. In an action by the inventor's successors in business it was held that the nephew was entitled to make and sell the ointment as 'Lieut. James's Blister' provided he did not represent he was the original inventor or the successor of the invention or that his was the only genuine preparation (*James v James* (1872) LR 13 Eq 421: Romer MR).

'Richter Concerts' meant concerts conducted by Herr Richter, not concerts organised by the plaintiff (*Franke v Chappell* (1887) 57 LT (NS) 141: Chitty J).

'Shorland' cycling shoe named and introduced by the plaintiff after a well-known cyclist called Frank Shorland with his permission, not distinctive of the plaintiff but descriptive of a type of shoe (*AW Gamage Ltd v HE Randall Ltd* (1899) 16 RPC 185: CA, motion for retrial refused).

'Staunton Chessmen' meant a particular shape of chessmen (*John Jacques & Son Ltd v Chess* (1940) 57 RPC 77: CA).

7.5 Where name in dispute is applied to different kinds of goods[16]

Injunction granted

'Dunhill' sunglasses, plaintiff's reputation in pipes (*Alfred Dunhill Ltd v Sunoptic SA* [1979] FSR 337: CA, personal defendant, a relative of the plaintiff Dunhills).

'Dunlop' oils and lubricant for cycles, plaintiff's reputation in tyres for cycles (*Dunlop Pneumatic Tyre Co Ltd v Dunlop Lubricant Co* (1898) 16 RPC 12: Romer J, defendant's fraudulent intent).

---

[16] See also Chapter 3, pp 51–53.

'Eagle' children's holiday camp, plaintiff's reputation as proprietors of the children's paper 'The Eagle' (*Hulton Press Ltd* v *White Eagle Youth Holiday Camp Ltd* (1951) 68 RPC 126: Wynn-Parry J).

'Elan' home computers, plaintiff's reputation *Elan Software (Eprans) (Elan Digital Systems Ltd* v *Elan Computers Ltd* (1984) FSR 373).

'Henderson' photograph on record album of dance music, plaintiff's professional dancers (*Henderson* v *Radio Corp Pty Ltd* [1969] RPC 218: New South Wales, Full HC).

'Kodak' cycles, plaintiff's reputation in photographic materials and cameras including bicycle cameras (*Eastman Photographic Materials Co Ltd* v *The John Griffiths Cycle Corp Ltd* (1898) 15 RPC 105: Romer J, fraudulent intention).

'Lego' irrigation equipment, plaintiff's reputation as children's building bricks and construction sets (*Lego System AS* v *Lego M Lemelstrich Ltd* [1983] FSR 155: Falconer J, final injunction).

'Marigold' toilet tissues, plaintiff's reputation in gloves and plastic pants for babies (*LRC International Ltd* v *Lilla Edets Sales Co Ltd* [1973] RPC 560: Whitford J).

'TAB' a weekly newspaper principally devoted to providing a race-tipping service, plaintiff a statutory body holding monopoly in Victoria, Australia of off course betting (*Totalizator Agency Board* v *Turf News Pty Ltd* [1972] RPC 579: Smith J, Supreme Court of Victoria).

'Times' cycles, plaintiff proprietor of *The Times* newspaper (*Walter* v *Ashton* [1902] 2 Ch 282: Byrne J).

'Treasure' in respect of dolls' cots, plaintiff's reputation in babies' cots (*Treasure Cot Co Ltd* v *Hamley Bros Ltd* (1950) 67 RPC 89 (Harman J).

'Valentine', 'Valentine Extract' for general food, plaintiff's reputation as a medicine (*Valentine Meat Juice Co* v *Valentine Extract Co Ltd* (1900) 17 RPC 673: CA).

'Warwick' motor tyres, plaintiff's reputation in tyres for cycles and motor cycles (*Warwick Tyre Co Ltd* v *New Motor & General Rubber Co Ltd* (1910) 27 RPC 161: Neville J; followed in *Carreras Ltd* v *Adolph Frankau & Co Ltd* [1964] RPC 210: Plowman J, cigarettes and pipes).

Injunction refused

'Abba' T-shirts etc, plaintiff was a pop group (*Lyngstad* v *Anabas Products Ltd* [1977] FSR 62: Oliver J).

'Granada' cars, plaintiff's reputation in TV, theatre and cinema (*Granada Group Ltd* v *Ford Motor Co Ltd* [1973] RPC 49: Graham J).

'Lucas' tyres, plaintiff's reputation in cycle and motor accessories (*Joseph Lucas Ltd* v *Fabry Automobile Co Ltd* (1905) 23 RPC 33: Warrington J).

'Newsweek' for TV programme, plaintiff publishers of American magazine (*Newsweek Inc* v *BBC* [1979] RPC 441: CA).

'Red Label' for cigarettes, plaintiff's reputation in whisky (*John Walker & Sons Ltd* v *Rothmans International Ltd* [1978] FSR 357: Brightman J).

'Rolls' lighters, plaintiff's reputation in razors (*Rolls Razor Ltd* v *Rolls Lighters Ltd* (1949) 66 RPC 299: Harman J).

'Stringfellows' oven chips not likely to be associated with a well known club of the same name (*Stringfellows* v *McCain Foods (GB) Ltd* [1984] RPC 501 (CA)).

'Wombles' skips, plaintiff's reputation in fictional characters (*Wombles Ltd* v *Wombles Skips Ltd* [1977] RPC 99: Walton J).

'Zoom' bubble gum, plaintiff's reputation in iced lollipops (*Lyons Maid Ltd* v *Trebor Ltd* (1967) RPC 222: Buckley J).

7.6 Plaintiff's goods of one class or quality passed off as another

Injunction granted

'British Maid' condensed milk, old and thus stale stock being passed off as or for plaintiff's standard milk (*Wilts United Dairies Ltd* v *Thomas Robinson Sons & Co Ltd* [1958] RPC 94: CA).

'Champagne' Continental quality restrained from being passed off as British quality (*Champagne Heidsieck et Cie* v *Scotto and Bishop* (1926) 43 RPC 101: Tomlin J, labels applied were forgeries); cf *Champagne Heidsieck et Cie* v *Buxton* (1930) 47 RPC 28; Clauson J, held no likelihood of deception).

'Colgate' toothpaste. Importation of toothpaste produced by the plaintiffs for the Brazilian market which was inferior to that sold by the plaintiffs in the UK (*Colgate-Palmolive Ltd* v *Markwell Finance Ltd* [1989] RPC 497).

'Gillette' safety razor blades, sale of second hand used or unusable blades as genuine blades (*Gillette Safety Razor Co & Gillette Safety Razor Ltd* v *Franks* (1924) 41 RPC 499: Astbury J; also *Gillette Safety Razor Co & Gillette Safety Razor Ltd* v *Diamond Edge Ltd* (1926) 43 RPC 310: Romer J).

Inserts of advertising material into the plaintiff's publications without their consent, causing the goods to be altered goods, was held to misrepresent to the recipient that the publisher would and did accept responsibility for the altered goods (*Associated Newspapers Group plc* v *Insert Media* [1991] FSR 380 (CA)).

'Jameson's' whisky, plaintiff's three year old whisky passed off for their seven year old whisky (*Jameson & Son Ltd* v *Clarke* (1902) 19 RPC 255: Chatterton V-C, injunction by consent).

'Morris' car, unused but secondhand car sold as 'new' (*Morris Motors Ltd* v *Lilley* [1959] 1 WLR 1184: Wynn-Parry J; *Morris Motors Ltd* v *Phelan*

[1960] RPC 209: Roxburgh J; see also *Vanden Plas* v *Cars & Caravans Bolton Ltd* [1965] FSR 93: Pennycuick J; cf *Standard Motor Co Ltd* v *Grantchester Garage Ltd* [1960] RPC 211: Buckley J, no injunction).

'Orb' footballs, plaintiff's discarded footballs passed off as plaintiff's 'new and improved' balls (*A G Spalding & Bros* v *A W Gamage Ltd* (1915) 32 RPC 273: HL).

'Swoppets' toys, plaintiff's unfinished rejects sold without explanation (*Britains Ltd* v *M Morris & Co (London) Ltd* [1961] RPC 217).

'Teachers' Highland Cream Whisky', plaintiff's inferior whisky sold as special quality (*Teacher* v *Levy* (1905) 23 RPC 117: Lloyd-Jacob J).

Various publications of the plaintiff had been tampered with by the defendant who had added to them an advertising supplement without making it clear that such publications had been altered (*Illustrated Newspapers Ltd* v *Publicity Services (London) Ltd* (1938) 55 RPC 172: Crossman J).

'Westinghouse Rectifiers' reassembled in an altered way (*Westinghouse Brake & Saxby Signal Co Ltd* v *The Varsity Eliminator Co Ltd* (1935) 52 RPC 295: Farwell J, Luxmoore J, form of injunction, default of defence).

Injunction refused

'Burgoyne's wine', defendant entitled to sell wine rejected by plaintiff as 'Burgoyne's Superior Australian Burgundy' (*Burgoyne & Co Ltd* v *Godfree & Co* (1904) 22 RPC 168: CA).

'Hunt, Roope's Grand Old Crusted Port' offered for sale by defendant in Price List stating 'usual credit price 60s per dozen now offered by us at 34s per dozen' held not to be passed off, as plaintiff had no established reputation in more expensive class of wine (*Hunt, Roope, Teage & Co* v *Ehrmann Bros* (1910) 27 RPC 512: Warrington J).

'Osram' and 'Mazda' electric light bulbs, defendant entitled to sell plaintiff's secondhand bulbs at reduced prices where customers expected to receive such secondhand goods (*General Electric Co Ltd* v *Pryce Stores* (1933) 50 RPC 232: Maugham J).

'Revlon Flex' medicated shampoo imported from USA held not to be inferior to other Revlon products sold in UK (*Revlon Inc* v *Cripps & Lee Ltd* [1980] FSR 85: CA; cf *Wilkinson Sword Ltd* v *Cripps & Lee Ltd* [1982] FSR 16: Falconer J, statement of claim held not to be demurrable).

7.7 Publications, books, papers and other creative works[17]

The owner and publisher of a publication (or producer of a film) may have a right to prevent a rival masquerading under the same or similar title

---

[17] As to rights of authors and journalists see Chapter 7, p 111.

provided that it can be established there is some probability that readers of the new publication (or viewers if it is a film) are likely to be deceived. Probability of deception depends to a large extent on the type of likely purchaser of the publication in question. Thus in *Willcox* v *Pearson* (1901) 18 TLR 220 the plaintiff, who was the proprietor of an evening paper circulating in Liverpool called 'The Evening Express' (often called 'The Express' for short), failed to restrain the circulation also in Liverpool of a morning paper called 'The North Express' which was dissimilar in appearance and contents. Swinfen Eady J said 'In cases of newspapers, it must always be borne in mind that they are intended for people who can read, and that, where the titles of two papers are different and the papers themselves are not similar in appearance, one paper is not likely to be mistaken for another except possibly momentarily'. (See also *DC Thomson & Co Ltd* v *Kent Messenger Ltd* [1975] RPC 191: Megarry J, Sunday Post failed to stop South East Sunday Post; and *Morning Star Co-op Society Ltd* v *Express Newspapers Ltd* [1979] FSR 113: Foster J, Morning Star failed to stop Daily Star—only a 'moron in a hurry' likely to be misled).

As was pointed out by Harman J in *Advance Magazine Publishing Inc* v *Redwood Publishing Ltd* [1993] FSR 449, magazines are generally sold in racks rather than over the counter, so that its visual impact to the would-be reader is of particular importance. In that case the style of the defendants title 'BBC Gourmet Good Food' was sufficiently different to the plaintiff's 'Gourmet' magazine.

The unauthorised insertion of advertising material into journals has been held by the Court of Appeal in *Associated Newspapers Group plc* v *Insert Media* [1991] FSR 380 to misrepresent to the reader that the publisher accepts responsibility for such insertion and a disclaimer to the effect that the publisher does not, would not be effective.

Injunction granted

'Anastasia', the plaintiff who was the producer of a film based on the play 'Anastasia' was entitled to prevent defendant advertising the defendant's film in such a way as to lead to the belief that the defendant's film was based on the play (*Twentieth Century Fox Film Corp* v *Gala Film Distributors Ltd* [1957] RPC 105: Roxburgh J).

'Bradshaw Railway Guide' was held entitled to stop an individual fraudulently carrying on business under the name Bradshaw's Publishing Company or publishing any publication the title of which contained the word 'Bradshaw' (*Blacklock & Co Ltd* v *Bradshaw's Publishing Co* (1926) 43 RPC 97: Lawrence J).

'The John Bull and Britannia' was entitled to stop a paper calling itself 'The True Britannia' and representing it as a continuation of 'The

Britannia', a paper which had been incorporated in the plaintiff's publication (*Prowett* v *Mortimer* (1856) 2 Jur (NS) 414: Stuart V-C).

'The Eagle' comic which also ran The Eagle Club was able to prevent the defendant from calling a children's holiday camp the 'White Eagle Youth Holiday Camp' (*Hulton Press Ltd* v *White Eagle Youth Holiday Camp Ltd* (1951) 68 RPC 126: Wynn-Parry J).

'Hemy's Royal Modern Tutor for the Pianoforte' was held to be too close to 'Hemy's New and Revised Edition of Jousse's Royal Standard Pianoforte Tutor', the word 'Hemy's' both on the outside of the book and on the title page being printed in much larger and more conspicuous type (*Metzler* v *Wood* (1878) 8 Ch D 606: CA).

'My Life and Loves' by Frank Harris, the plaintiff/publisher who had generated considerable advance publicity was able to restrain defendant from selling expurgated version under same title (*WH Allen & Co* v *Brown Watson* [1965] RPC 191: Pennycuick J).

'The New Car', the plaintiff who was the author and copyright owner of a theatrical sketch called 'The New Car' was able to restrain the defendant from passing off a talking film called 'His First Car' as being a film version of the plaintiff's sketch (*Samuelson* v *Producers Distributing Co Ltd* (1931) 48 RPC 580: CA, defendant sought to take advantage of the merits of the theatrical sketch including use of notices in the press; also deception likely because of the comedian's George Clarke's, appearance in both).[18]

The 'Surrey Comet' local newspaper was able to prevent the launch of the Sutton and Epsom Comet (*Knapp Drewett & Sons Ltd* v *Croydon Comet Ltd* (1986) unreported, Whitford J).

'What's New In . . .' magazine series able to restrain 'What's New In Training' (*Morgan Grampian plc* v *Training Personnel Ltd* [1992] FSR 262).

Injunction refused

'Adventure' (a US magazine) failed to stop a new magazine using the title 'Hutchinson's Adventure Story Magazine' (*The Ridgway Co* v *Hutchinson* (1923) 40 RPC 335: Sargant J).

---

18 See also *Raleigh* v *Kinematograph Trading Co Ltd* (1914) 31 RPC 143 (Eve J, plaintiff's title of play sought to be used for a film; case settled); cf *O'Gorman* v *Paramount Film Service Ltd* [1937] 2 All ER 113 (Clauson J, distinguishing the Samuelson case, where the author of a play 'Irish and Proud of It' failed to get an injunction to stop a film of the same title); also *Houghton* v *Film Booking Office Ltd* (1931) 48 RPC 329 (Bennett J, trustees of the will of an author of a play called 'The Younger Generation' failed to get an injunction to stop a film of the same title); and *Francis Day and Hunter Ltd* v *Twentieth Century Fox Corp Ltd* [1940] AC 112 (PC, appellant owner of the copyright in a song 'The Man who Broke the Bank at Monte Carlo' failed to stop film of same name).

'Maidenhead Advertiser' failed to stop 'The New Advertiser' (in Maidenhead), it being held 'Advertiser' was descriptive and 'New' sufficiently differentiated it (*Baylis & Co (The Maidenhead Advertiser) Ltd v Darlenko Ltd* [1974] FSR 284: Plowman J).

'Athletics Weekly' failed to stop 'Athletics Monthly', magazines would not be mistaken (*World Athletics and Sporting Publications Ltd v ACM Webb (Publishing) Co Ltd* [1981] FSR 27: CA).

'The Evening Express' failed to stop 'The North Express', both circulating in Liverpool, papers different in appearance and published at different time of day (*Willox v Pearson* (1901) 18 TLR 220: Swinfen Eady J).

'The Evening Times' published in Glasgow failed to stop 'The Evening Times' published in London (*George Outram & Co Ltd v London Evening Newspapers Co Ltd* (1911) 28 RPC 308: Warrington J).

'Everybody's Magazine' a shilling monthly, could not possibly be confused with a penny weekly called 'Everybody's Weekly' (*The Ridgway Co v Amalgamated Press Co* (1911) 29 RPC 130: Warrington J).

'Gordon Fraser' greeting cards with a distinctive style and colouring were imitated by the defendant but not likely to be bought by the public as or for a Gordon Fraser card (*Gordon Fraser Gallery Ltd v Tatt* [1966] RPC 505: Buckley J).

The 'Gourmet' monthly magazine failed to prevent the 'BBC Gourmet Good Food' magazine (*Advance Magazine Publishing Inc v Redwood Publishing Ltd* [1993] FSR 449 (Harman J).

'How to Appeal Against Your Rates' a book, plaintiff failed to prevent defendant using title of 'How to Appeal Against Your Rates Within the Metropolis': although confusion was established, title was held to be descriptive and had not acquired a secondary meaning (*Mathieson v Sir Isaac Pitman & Sons Ltd* (1930) 47 RPC 541: Maugham J).

'The Magazine of Fiction' failed to stop 'Cassell's Magazine of Fiction and Popular Literature' (*William Stevens Ltd v Cassell & Co Ltd* (1913) 30 RPC 199: Neville J).

'The Mail' failed to stop 'The Morning Mail', being different in appearance and published at a different time of the day (*Walter Emmott* (1885) 54 LJ Ch 1059: CA).

'Management To-day' failed to prevent publication of 'Security Management To-day' ableit there being a serious question to be tried, damage to the defendant being far greater than to the plaintiff (*Management Publications Ltd v Blenheim Exhibitions Group* [1991] FSR 550 (CA)).

'The Morning Post' failed to stop 'The Evening Post' (*Borthwick v The Evening Post* (1888) 37 Ch D 449: CA).

'The Morning Star' failed to stop 'The Daily Star' (*Morning Star Co-op Society Ltd v Express Newspapers Ltd* [1979] FSR 113: Graham J).

'Mothercare' failed to restrain publication of book under title 'Mother Care/Other Care' (*Mothercare* v *Penguin Books* [1988] RPC 113 (CA)).

'The Newcastle Daily Chronicle' (locally known as the 'Chronical') failed to stop 'The Sporting Chronicle and Prophetic Bell' the appearance and contents of the papers being dissimilar (*Cowen* v *Hulton* (1882) 46 LT (NS) 897: CA).

'Newsweek' magazine failed to stop the BBC using the name for a programme (*Newsweek Inc* v *BBC* [1979] RPC 441: CA).

'The Pet Library' failed to stop 'Ellson's Pet Library' (*The Pet Library (London) Ltd* v *Walter Ellson & Son Ltd* [1968] FSR 359: Megarry J).

'The Plumber and Decorator, Gas and Sanitary Engineering Journal' failed to stop 'The Plumbing and Decorating, Sanitary, Water and Gas Engineering Chronicle' (*Dale Reynolds & Co* v *General Newspaper Co* (1884) 1 TLR 177: Bacon V-C).

'Punch' failed to stop a weekly comic 'Punch and Judy' of similar size and appearance but being sold at a lower price (*Bradbury* v *Beeton* (1869) 39 LJ Ch 57: Malins V-C).

'Rubber & Plastics Age' trade journal failed to stop 'Rubber & Plastics Weekly' (*Rubber & Technical Press Ltd* v *Maclaren & Sons Ltd* [1961] RPC 264: Cross J, confusion not enough, must be loss of goodwill and custom).

'Sports Car & Lotus Owner' (popularly called 'Sports Car') failed to stop 'Sports Car Illustrated' (*Pearl Cooper Ltd* v *Richmond Hill Press* [1957] RPC 363: Upjohn J).

'Sunday Post' failed to stop 'South East Sunday Post' (*DC Thomson & Co Ltd* v *Kent Messenger Ltd* [1975] RPC 191: Megarry J).

The Tamworth Herald often referred to as 'The Herald' failed to prevent the Tamworth Herald and Post likely to be referred to as 'The Herald and Post'. Aldous J held there was no serious question to be tried as 'Herald' was commonly used by newspapers and confusion in the use of the name 'Tamworth' did not establish a misrepresentation (*Tamworth Herald Company Limited* v *Thompson Free Newspapers Ltd* [1991] FSR 337).

'To-Day' magazine (which had been amalgamated with Courier) failed to restrain the defendant using the title 'TODAY, the new JOHN BULL', it being held that even if the plaintiff had had a sufficient reputation in the name TO-DAY, the likelihood of confusion between the two publications was not sufficiently great, evidence as to embarrassment and inconvenience rather than taking of one publication for the other not being enough (*Norman Kark Publications Ltd* v *Odhams Press Ltd* [1962] RPC 163: Wilberforce J).

7.8 Right to bona fide use of defendant's name on goods[19]

Injunction granted

'Ballantyne, Stewart & Co Ltd' used on whisky labels restrained (*George Ballantine & Son Ltd* v *Ballantyne Stewart & Co Ltd* [1959] RPC 273: CA).

'Baume' watches held to be passed off by use of words 'Baume et Mercier, Geneva' on watches made by Baume et Mercier SA in Switzerland and imported by the defendant (*Baume & Co Ltd* v *AH Moore Ltd* [1958] RPC 226: CA).

'Dunhill' sunglasses and spectacle frames sold by the defendant by agreement with the great-grandson of the founder and son of the present chairman of the plaintiff company, restrained (*Alfred Dunhill Ltd* v *Sunoptic SA* [1979] FSR 337: CA).

'Goddards's Plate Powder', defendant retailer restrained from selling lesser-known product without clearly ascertaining that it was not the plaintiff's powder that was required (*Goddard* v *The Watford Co-op Society* (1924) 41 RPC 218: Astbury J).

'Knoll International' and 'Knoll' restrained even though use of own name on furniture was honest (*Parker-Knoll Ltd* v *Knoll International Ltd* [1962] RPC 265: HL).

'J Lyons' tea and cocoa named after defendant Joseph Lyons restrained (*J Lyons & Co Ltd* v *Lyons* (1931) 49 RPC 188; Mackinnon J).

'Teofani' cigarettes distinctive of plaintiff, defendant restrained from using his name on the packet (*Teofani & Co Ltd* v *Teofani* (1913) 30 RPC 446: CA).

'Wright's Baby Powder' restrained by producers of Wrights coal tar goods (*Wright, Layman & Umney Ltd* v *Wright* (1948) 65 RPC 185; affirmed (1949) 66 RPC 149: CA).

Injunction refused

'Brinsmead' piano distinctive of plaintiff but use of defendant's name 'Stanley Brinsmead' on cheaper pianos sold to a different class of people was held not to deceive (*John Brinsmead & Sons Ltd* v *Brinsmead* (1913) 30 RPC 489: CA); see also *Burgess* v *Burgess* (1853) 3 De GM & G 896: LJJ).

'Jamieson's' harness composition not distinctive of plaintiff's product, other manufacturers of same product using same name (*Jamieson & Co* v *Jamieson* (1898) 15 RPC 169: CA).

---

[19] See Chapter 2, pp 38–39 and Chapter 7, pp 112–115; cf Trade Marks Act 1938, s 8(*a*) and s 11(2)(*a*) of the Trade Marks Act 1994, where it is a defence in respect of the infringement of a registered trade mark.

Chapter 6

Imitation of Get-up of Goods

One of the most important ways in which a trader attracts customers and establishes a reputation in the market for his goods is the way he presents them to the customer, which is compendiously referred to as the 'get-up' of his goods. Thus the particular shape, size, colour or adornment of a trader's goods or the package in which such goods are sold may be distinctive of a trader and come to indicate his goods even if the goods are also known by some trade name.

The principle of law is the same as for other kinds of passing off. As stated by Lord Halsbury LC in *Powell* v *The Birmingham Vinegar Brewery Co* (1897) 14 RPC 720, at 727 (HL):

> The proposition of law is one which, I think, has been accepted by the highest judicial authority, and acted upon for a great number of years. It is that of Lord Justice Turner[1] who says, in terms 'No man can have any right to represent his goods as the goods of another person. In an application of this kind, it must be made out that the Defendant is selling his own goods as the goods of another'. That is the only question of law ... All the rest are questions of fact. The most obvious way in which a man would be infringing the rule laid down by Lord Justice Turner is if he were to say in terms, 'These are the goods manufactured by' a rival tradesman; and it seems to be assumed that, unless he says something equivalent to that, no action will lie. It appears to me that that is an entire delusion. By the course of trade, by the existence and technology of trade, and by the mode in which things are sold, a man may utter that same proposition, but in different words and without using the name of a rival tradesman at all. A familiar example, of course, is when, without using any name, by the identity of the form of the bottle or the form of the label, or the nature of the thing sold in the package, he is making the statement not in express words, but in one of those different forms in

---

[1] *Burgess* v *Burgess* (1853) 3 De GM & G 896 (LJJ).

which the statement can be made by something that he knows will be so understood by the public. In each case it comes to be a question whether or not there is the statement made; and if the statement is made, there can be no doubt of the legal conclusion that he must be restrained from representing that the goods that he makes are the goods of the rival tradesman. Then you get back to the proposition which I have read from Lord Justice Turner.

Generally speaking, only deliberate imitation or dishonesty can lead a trader to adopt a get-up for his goods which makes them liable to be confused with those of another (see, for example, *County Chemical Co Ltd v Frankenburg* (1904) 21 RPC 722 (Alverstone LCJ); and *Tavener Rutledge Ltd v Specters Ltd* [1959] RPC 83 (Danckwerts J); 355 (CA)). However even deliberate copying will not be sufficient if there is no probability of deception,[2] and a trader may honestly make use of those features of get-up which are common to the trade in which he is engaged. For instance mustard used to be commonly sold in tin boxes with yellow paper wrappers and red or black letters printed on them,[3] and the fact that one firm of tobacco manufacturers used a narrow red band round cigars to a greater extent than other manufacturers was held not to give them an exclusive right to use them as red bands were common to the cigar trade.[4]

If, however, the plaintiff invents for his goods a get-up that is not

---

[2] See *Lever Bros Ltd v Bedingfield* (1898) 15 RPC 453 (Kekewich J); (1898) 16 RPC 3 (CA); *De Long Hook & Eye Co Ltd v Newey Bros Ltd* (1911) 29 RPC 49 (Warrington J); *Laraine Day Ltd v Kennedy* (1952) 70 RPC 19 (Roxburgh J); *M Saper Ltd v Specters Ltd & Boxes Ltd* (1953) 70 RPC 173 (Harman J) and *Scott Ltd v Nice Pak Products Ltd* [1989] FSR 100 (CA).

[3] *Re Farrow's Trade Mark* (1890) 7 RPC 260, 264 (Stirling J).

[4] *Imperial Tobacco Co v Purnell & Co* (1904) 21 RPC 368 (Joyce J); 598 (CA). See also as examples of matters held common to trade: *Jamieson & Co v Jamieson* (1898) 15 RPC 169 (CA, boxes containing harness); *Packham & Co v Sturgess & Co* (1898) 15 RPC 669 (CA, bottles of sparkling lime wine); *Payton & Co Ltd v Snelling Lampard & Co* (1899) 17 RPC 48 (CA); (1900) 17 RPC 628 (HL, red, blue and green enamelled tins for French coffee); *F King & Co Ltd v Gillard & Co Ltd* (1905) 22 RPC 327 (CA, desiccated soup in paper packets and steel boxes); *JB Williams & Co v Bronnley & Co Ltd* (1909) 26 RPC 765 (CA, dome-topped maroon-coloured tins for shaving soap); *FW Hampshire & Co (1927) Ltd v General Kaputine Syndicate Ltd (1930)* 47 RPC 437 (Clauson J, packages for emollient preparation for chapped hands); *Roche Products Ltd v Berke Pharmaceuticals Ltd* [1973] RPC 473 (CA, white and yellow tablets for drug called 'Valium'); and *Tetrosyl Ltd v Silver Paint & Lacquer Co Ltd* [1980] FSR 68 (CA, plastic filler tubs). In *Boh Plantations Sdn Berhad v Gui Nee Chuan* [1975] FSR 541 (Appellate Division of Federal Court of Malaysia, 'common to the trade' was defined as being openly used by other traders).

common to the trade, for example by packing washing blue in oval shaped packets,[5] by packaging lemon juice in plastic yellow lemon-shaped containers,[6] by making his dusters of a certain shape, colour and size,[7] or by making cigars flat-ended or 'bull-nosed',[8] or mounting his goods for sale on certain kinds of show cards,[9] he is entitled to have his get-up protected when his get-up is sufficiently well known to be associated with his goods by the public.[10]

In cases of imitation of get-up, there is generally an imitation of several features, and it may be difficult to say how far the similarity is due to the custom of the trade and how far it is not.

'It is extremely difficult,' said Kekewich, J 'to define what are the limits of fair competition; but if competitors in a particular market do no more than follow the fashion of the market, and do not in any way seek to induce customers to buy their goods as being those of their rivals, I cannot judicially find fault with them because they adopt styles, shapes, sizes and colours which are common to the trade.'[11]

---

[5] *Ripley* v *Bandey* (1897) 14 RPC 591 (Kekewich J, injunction not given, owing to plaintiff's laches, case settled on appeal 14 RPC 944).
[6] *Reckitt & Coleman Products Ltd* v *Bowden Inc* [1990] RPC 341.
[7] *Jones* v *Hallworth* (1897) 14 RPC 225 (Kekewich J); see, however, *Jones Bros Ltd* v *Anglo American Optical Co* (1912) 29 RPC 1 (Swinfen-Eady J); 361 (CA)—where same plaintiff failed to obtain injunction in respect of same goods.
[8] *RJ Elliot & Co Ltd* v *Hodgson* (1902) 19 RPC 518 (Buckley J).
[9] *Parker and Smith* v *Satchwell* (1901) 18 RPC 299 (Farwell J, show cards for 'hair-coilers').
[10] *Shell-Mex & BP Ltd* v *Holmes* (1937) 54 RPC 287 (Luxmoore, J, pink paraffin). See also *Coca Cola Co* v *Barr* [1961] RPC 387 (Court of Session, shape of drink bottle); *John Haig & Co Ltd* v *Forth Blending Co Ltd* (1952) 69 RPC 323 (Court of Session); (1953) 70 RPC 259 (Court of Session, dimple bottles for whisky); cf *John Haig & Co Ltd* v *Brooks & Bohm (Wine Shippers) Ltd* (1955) 72 RPC 247 (Roxburgh J, defendant's bottles no depressions in them no likelihood of deception); *F Hoffman-La Roche & Co AG* v *DDSA Pharmaceuticals Ltd* [1972] RPC 1 (Pennycuick J, black and green drug capsules); *Roche Products Ltd* v *Inter-Continental Pharmaceuticals Ltd* [1965] RPC 374; cf *Roche Products Ltd* v *Berk Pharmaceuticals Ltd* [1973] RPC 473 (CA, white and yellow tablets for the drug valium); *Lee Kar Choo* v *Lee Lian Choo* (1967) 1 AC 602 (PC, tea labels); *New Way Packaged Products* v *S Lucking Ltd* [1960] RPC 147 (Cross J, suede cleaning material); *Tavener Rutledge Ltd* v *Specters Ltd* [1959] RPC 355 (CA, border-line case—tin boxes for sweets); *White Hudson & Co Ltd* v *Asian Organisation Ltd* [1965] RPC 45 (PC, red paper cough sweets); and *Sodastream Ltd* v *Thorn Cascade Ltd* [1982] RPC 459 (CA, grey coloured gas cylinders refilled with carbon dioxide).
[11] *Thomas Hubbuck & Son Ltd* v *William Brown, Sons & Co* (1900) 17 RPC 148 at 154 (Kekewich J, coat of arms on kegs of paint); see also *Alaska Packers' Association* v *Crooks & Co* (1901) 18 RPC 129 (Kekewich J).

1 How to decide whether imitation is legitimate[12]

In dealing with a case where the chief features imitated were features common to the trade, Lindley MR said in *Payton & Co Ltd v Snelling, Lampard & Co Ltd* (1899) 17 RPC 48, at 52 (CA):

> They [the plaintiffs] must make out that the defendants' goods are calculated to be mistaken for the plaintiffs', and, where, as in this case, the goods of the plaintiff and the goods of the defendant unquestionably resemble each other, but where the features in which they resemble each other are common to the trade, what has the plaintiff to make out? He must make out not that the defendant's are like his by reason of those features which are common to them and other people, but he must make out that the defendant's are like his by reason of something peculiar to him, and by reason of the defendant having adopted some mark, or device, or label, or something of that kind, which distinguishes the plaintiff's from other goods, which have, like his, the features common to the trade. Unless the plaintiff can bring his case up to that he fails. It appears to me that when once you get that clearly in your mind, when you eliminate those features which are common to the trade and ask yourselves, not whether the plaintiff's and the defendant's things are alike, but whether the defendant has copied that which distinguishes the plaintiff's, the conclusion must be different from that at which the learned judge arrived.

In that case the plaintiff complained of the defendant selling the defendant's coffee in circular enamel tins with different colours for the different sizes, but the Court of Appeal and the House of Lords, overruling Byrne J, gave judgment for the defendant. For it was a not unusual thing for such tins to be used in the trade.

But in eliminating the features common to the trade, it must be remembered that each similarity is cumulative, and that a number of imitations combined, even though they 'follow the fashion of the market' may amount to a passing off.

Thus in *Lever v Goodwin* (1887) 4 RPC 492 the plaintiff had for some time wrapped up tablets of soap in 12-ounce tablets labelled 'Sunlight, the Self-Washer Tablet', and wrapped in imitation parchment on which was printed spaced or broken letterpress, that is to say, letterpress some of which was in big type and some in small, and both big and small could be read either separately or in conjunction. The defendant sold 12-ounce

---

[12] See also p 107.

tablets of soap labelled 'Goodwins Self-Washing Tablet' wrapped in imitation parchment on which was printed spaced or broken letterpress with a somewhat different wording from that of the plaintiff and introducing the defendant's name several times in large letters. Chitty J and the Court of Appeal held that the plaintiff was entitled to an injunction.

In giving judgment, Cotton LJ said:

> Looking at the two tablets, one cannot but see that there is a very general resemblance between them, and especially a resemblance to people who cannot read. But [the defendants'] contention was this: "There is no trade-mark in 'Self-washing' or 'Self-washer,' there is no monopoly in this parchment paper; there is no monopoly in the spaced printing; then why should I be restrained in carrying on business from using those things as to which the plaintiffs cannot claim any monopoly whatever?" That was an obvious fallacy. There may be no monopoly at all in the individual things separated, but if the whole are so joined together as to attempt to pass off and to have the effect of passing off the defendants' soap as the plaintiffs', then, although the plaintiffs have no monopoly either in 'Self-washing' or 'Self-washer' or in the parchment paper, or in the spaced printing, yet if those things, in which they have no sole right, are so combined by the defendants as to pass off the defendants' goods as the plaintiffs', then the defendants have brought themselves within the old common law doctrine in respect of which equity will give to the aggrieved party an injunction in order to restrain the defendant from passing off his goods as those of the plaintiff.

It is clear, however, that where a trader seeks to monopolise a get-up composed of a number of elements common to the trade, he has a harder burden to discharge, and he will have to prove with great certainty that that particular get-up is associated with his goods, and that the imitation complained of will lead to the deception of purchasers. In *JB Williams Co v H Bronnley & Co Ltd* (1909) 26 RPC 481 at 486 Neville J, at first instance said:

> Of course I am not prepared to say that there may not be cases in which a trader may acquire by user an exclusive right of monopoly in respect of a combination of two or more matters which, by themselves, are absolutely common to the trade. There is no dispute here, I think, that the tin-lined box of this shape is common to the trade, and that the colouring of the box is also common to the trade. I think, as I said before, that it is also the fact that, until a few years before the commencement of this action, when boxes of such shape

and colour were put upon the market in more or less large quantities by the defendants, the plaintiffs were the only persons who used the combination in their get-up. In my opinion, the evidence which would be necessary to establish a monopoly in respect of such a thing as shape and colour—the shape and colour being individually common to the trade—would be something very different from the evidence which has been given in the present case . . . I do not think the mere use of a particular get-up, even for ten years or for more than ten years, by itself will ever give a man a right to a monopoly in such things as are common to the trade in which he deals.

If, however, he can prove sufficiently that the get-up is associated exclusively with his goods, and that its imitation will lead to deception, it seems that he is entitled to succeed. It will be no answer to say that features which in combination are distinctive are, when taken separately, common to the trade, and must therefore be eliminated in judging the similarity. The thing must be looked at as a whole, and if by a certain combination of trade features it has acquired a distinctive get-up among the purchasing public, it is entitled to protection.

In *Bryant & May Ltd* v *United Match Industries Ltd* (1932) 50 RPC 12, despite the fact that it was common to the trade to print labels in black upon a yellow background (as were both the plaintiff's and defendant's labels) and the defendant's matches were sold under the brand name 'Alpha', it was held by Chitty J that the design and adoption of the defendant's label was deliberate with the object of occasioning confusion with the plaintiff's label, and an injunction was granted accordingly.

2 Get-up may include features of article

Get-up is generally concerned with the way in which the article or goods are presented to the public and not with the inherent characteristics or qualities of such article or goods. In *Dunhill* v *Bartlett & Bickley*[13] Russell J stated 'apart from monopolies conferred by patents and apart from protection afforded by registration, it is open to anyone to adopt the ideas or devices of his neighbours and apply them to his own goods provided he

---

[13] (1922) 39 RPC 426 at 438 (red spot on defendant's pipes held not to cause confusion with plaintiffs' 'white spot pipes'); Design Copyright Act 1968 may also affect the position in that since its enactment there has no longer been any requirement to register the shape, configuration, pattern or ornament of a particular article in order to obtain protection therefor. Failure to register does not destroy protection under the Copyright, Designs and Patents Act 1988.

clearly distinguishes his goods from those of his neighbour.' To allow a plaintiff to obtain a monopoly in an article of a particular functional design would enable a trader to obtain an indefinite monopoly in that article which is something he would be unable to do by way of Letters Patent, Registered Design, copyright or registered trade mark.[14]

In *R J Elliot & Co Ltd* v *Hodgson* [1902] 19 RPC 518 an interim injunction was granted by Buckley J restraining the defendant from selling cigars made in the plaintiff's distinctive flat-ended shape without distinguishing such cigars from the plaintiff's cigars.[15]

In *JB Williams & Co* v *H Bronnley & Co Ltd*[16] Fletcher Moulton LJ said, 'the get-up of an article means a capricious addition to the article itself,—the colour, or shape, it may be, of the wrapper or anything of that kind; but I strongly object to look at anything, that has a value in use, as part of the get-up of the article. Anything which is in itself useful appears to me rightly to belong to the article itself.'

In *British American Glass Co Ltd* v *Winton Products (Blackpool) Ltd*[17] where the defendant imitated the plaintiff's ornamental dogs of a special design it was found that members of the public buying such an ornamental

---

14 See s 3(2) of the Trade Marks Act 1994, which excludes from registration shapes which result from the nature of the goods themselves, or which are necessary to obtain a technical result, or which give substantial value to the goods. See also *Coca-Kola T M* [1986] RPC 421: shape of bottle refused registration under the Trade Marks Act 1938 as not being a mark.

15 In *Cadbury Ltd* v *Ulmer Gmbh* [1988] FSR 385 Falconer J in a striking out application refused to follow this case. However, it was referred to by Lord Oliver in the *Jif Lemon* case ([1990] RPC at 411—see below). Cf *British American Glass Co Ltd* v *Winter Products (Blackpool) Ltd* [1962] RPC 230 (Pennycuick J), below.

16 (1909) 26 RPC 765, at 773 (CA). see also *Terrapin Ltd* v *Ariston Buildings Ltd* [1964] FSR 218 (CA); *Benchairs Ltd* v *Chair Centre Ltd* [1974] RPC 429 (Graham J at 435–436, shape of chairs the subject of a Registered Design, where words of Fletcher Moulton LJ were considered with a rider added—see p 83, 84); *George Hensher Ltd* v *Restawhile Upholstery (Lancs) Ltd* [1975] RPC 31 (Graham J, at 35–38, chairs and settees held not to be distinctive of plaintiffs); and *Jarman & Platt Ltd* v *I Barget Ltd* [1977] FSR 260 (CA furniture not distinctive of plaintiff even though theirs was the only furniture of this style on the market).

17 [1962] RPC 230. See also *Blundell* v *Sidney Margolis Ltd* (1951) 68 RPC 71 (Harman J, bubble gum in shape of false teeth not held to be distinctive of plaintiff); *Hawkins & Tipson Ltd* v *Fludes Carpets Ltd* (1957) RPC 8 (Danckwerts J, pattern of coir matting not distinctive of plaintiff); *Gordon Fraser Gallery Ltd* v *Tatt* [1966] RPC 505 (Buckley J, imitation of style of greeting cards no deception); and *Politechnika Ipari Szovetkezet* v *Dallas Print Transfers Ltd* [1982] FSR 529 (Dillon J, 'Rubik' cubes, not established that they emanated from one particular source).

trinket were only concerned with what it looked like and not by whom it was made and were not likely to be deceived that the defendant's dog (albeit identical) was the same as that made by the plaintiff. Pennycuick J in refusing an injunction said 'this is not really a passing off case as regards get-up in anyway at all. It is not a question of getting up; it is a question of the appearance of the actual articles sold.'

However, in *William Edge & Sons Ltd* v *William Niccolls & Sons*[18] the plaintiff company, who were manufacturers of washing blues and tints, had for a great number of years put these blues and tints on the market in a bag of cotton with a stick protruding, but having no name or label on the bag. They had largely advertised that their blues and tints always had a stick. The defendant also manufactured and sold blues and tints in quite a different shape and get-up until just before the action, when the defendant proceeded to put the defendant's goods on the market in the same form as the plaintiff's, but with a label attached, bearing the defendant's name conspiciously. An injunction was granted, by Swinfen Eady J, to restrain the defendant, but the Court of Appeal reversed his decision on the ground that the stick and all the other adjuncts of the article were objects of common utility, and that there was nothing distinctive in which the plaintiff could acquire a monopoly.

Cozens Hardy MR, in his judgment, said: 'If [a man] makes an article and relies solely on its necessary or useful component parts to distinguish his make from that of others, he is not entitled to complain because others, who make the same article, adopt the same shape and form, although they may thereby lead people to believe that their articles are those of the plaintiff: he has deliberately run the risk of such deception in order to try to obtain a monopoly to which he can never be entitled.' However, the House of Lords in allowing the appeal came to the conclusion, as a matter of fact, that the defendant had not sufficiently distinguished the defendant's goods from those of the plaintiff, having regard to the nature of the goods and the persons to whom they were sold.

Furthermore in *Benchairs Ltd* v *Chair Centre Ltd* [1974] RPC 429 Graham J stated, albeit obiter, 'I think there might be a case where an article itself is shaped in an unusual way not primarily for the purpose of giving some benefit in use or for any other practical purpose, but in order purely to give the article a distinctive appearance characteristic of the particular manufacture's goods. In such an event it seems to me possible that such manufacturer must be able in course of time to establish such a

---

[18] (1911) 28 RPC 53 at 65 (CA); 28 RPC 582 (HL). See also *RJ Elliott & Co Ltd* v *Hodgson* (1902) 19 RPC 518 (Buckley J, bull-nosed cigar held distinctive of plaintiff).

reputation in such distinctive appearance of the article itself as would give him a cause of action in passing off if his goods were copied, because in the circumstances assumed the putting of the copy on the market would amount to a representation that it emanated from the plaintiff. Such a possibility is no doubt remote but it is not impossible . . .' *William Edge & Sons Ltd* v *William Niccolls & Sons Ltd* was not referred to but Graham J's words are appropriate and in line with such authority.

In *Combe International Ltd* v *Scholl (UK) Ltd*[19] the plaintiff marketed a shoe insole called 'Odor-Eaters' containing activated charcoal. The defendant who was marketing a similar shoe insole (containing charcoal but not activated charcoal and therefore of inferior quality) was restrained from representing that the defendant's shoe insoles were 'substantially the same' as the plaintiff's—even though the respective trade marks and packaging were different. Fox J said at [1980] RPC 8 'the question is whether the defendants' article is offered in such a way as to lead the public to believe that it is the same at Combe's when in fact it is admittedly different'.

In *Reckitt & Colman Products Ltd* v *Borden Inc* [1990] RPC 341 the plaintiffs whose lemon juice was sold in plastic simulated lemon—shaped containers under the mark JIF succeeded in preventing the defendants from selling their lemon juice in lemon-shaped containers. The House of Lords held the defendants' label was not sufficient to distinguish to two products. Lord Oliver (at 410–411), in dismissing the argument that the lemon-shaped package is the very product itself and not the get-up of the product, on the facts of that case went on to state 'whether in fact the particular shape or configuration of the very object sold by a trader is incapable as a matter of law of protection in a case where it has become associated exclusively with his business is a proposition which is at least open to doubt'.

3 Use of similar promotional methods to promote similar goods

In *Masson Seeley & Co Ltd* v *Embossotype Manufacturing Co* (1924) 41 RPC 160, the defendant, using price lists, samples, instructions manuals

---

[19] [1980] RPC 1 (Fox J, interlocutory injunction granted); cf *British American Glass Co Ltd* v *Winton Products (Blackpool) Ltd* [1962] RPC 230, not referred to, where imitation of article was held by Pennycuick J not to constitute passing off (see p 99 above). See also *Masson Seeley & Co Ltd* v *Embossotype Manufacturing Co* (1924) 41 RPC 160 (Tomlin J, similar but inferior type marketed by the defendant using price lists, catalogues copied from the plaintiff); and *Kemtron Properties Pty Ltd* v *Jimmy's Co Ltd* [1979] FSR 86 (High Court of Hong Kong, defendant copied plaintiff's fan).

and catalogues copied extensively from the plaintiff, sought to sell to customers of the plaintiff a similar but inferior type used with a cutter-crush machine (used for producing embossed coloured lettering on cardboard). Tomlin J held that what the defendant company were doing 'was clearly calculated to deceive and produce the impression that they were selling the same goods as the Plaintiff company at a lower price'. But imitation of advertisements and the like is not actionable unless it leads to passing-off of the defendant's goods or business for the plaintiff's. So in *Wertheimer* v *Stewart, Cooper & Co* (1906) 23 RPC 481 where the plaintiff had devised a new and effective way of advertising his packets of garden seeds, and the defendant being struck with the excellence of the idea, adopted it, together with the language in which it was couched, almost unaltered, for the defendant's own seeds, the defendant was held by Kekewich J to be justified in so doing provided the defendant did not mislead the plaintiff's customers into buying the defendant's own goods in mistake for the plaintiff's. Likewise in *Cadbury-Schweppes Pty Ltd* v *The Pub Squash Co Ltd*[20] the defendant in Australia put on the market a lemon squash drink called 'Pub Squash' in yellow cans the same colour and size of those of the plaintiff's 'Solo' lemon squash, using a TV advertising theme (heroically masculine) and radio theme (nostalgic) very similar to that of the plaintiff, deliberately adopted by the defendant to take advantage of the plaintiff's advertising campaign. The Privy Council (Lord Scarman) endorsed Powell J's findings that the consuming public were not confused or misled by the get-up, the formula or the advertising of the defendant's product into thinking it was the plaintiff's squash, and that neither the TV theme nor the radio theme of the plaintiff had become the plaintiff's property in the sense that such themes distinguished the plaintiff's goods. In the course of his opinion Lord Scarman stated that the tort (of passing off) is:

> no longer anchored, as in its early nineteenth century formulation, to the name or trade mark of a product or business. It is wide enough to encompass other descriptive material, such as slogans or visual images, which radio, television or newspaper advertising campaigns can lead the market to associate with a plaintiff's product, provided

---

[20] [1981] RPC 429. See also *Bravingtons Ltd* v *Barrington Tennant* (1957) RPC 183 (Upjohn J doubted that the similarity of shops would deceive potential customers); *My Kinda Town Ltd* v *Soll* [1983] RPC 407 (CA, combination of name 'Chicago Pizza' and similar decor not sufficient to cause deception); cf *Elida Gibbs Ltd* v *Colgate-Palmolive Ltd* [1983] FSR 95 (Goulding J, where the defendant was restrained from adopting plaintiff's 'tree theme' advertising campaign).

always that such descriptive material has become part of the goodwill of the product. And the test is whether the product has derived from the advertising a distinctive character which the market recognises.

But competition must remain free; and competition is safeguarded by the necessity for the plaintiff to prove that he has built up an "intangible property right" in the advertised description of his product, or, in other words, that he has succeeded by such methods in giving his product a distinctive character accepted by the market. A defendant, however, does no wrong by entering a market created by another and there competing with its creator. The line may be difficult to draw; but, unless it is drawn, competition will be stifled.

4   Get-up must be associated with plaintiff's goods

In all cases a trader must prove that the get-up which is being imitated has become associated in the minds of the purchasing public with his goods[21] and no-one else's[22]. Without showing this, he has no more right to protection of get-up than he has to protection of trade name. 'It is a notion that runs through the minds of a great many persons in trade that if a trader once adopts a novel get-up he acquires some proprietary right in that get-up. Of course he does not do anything of the kind.'[23]

A more modern statement of the principle is to be found in *T Oertli* v *EJ Bowman (London) Ltd* [1957] RPC 388 at 397 (CA). Jenkins LJ said 'it is, of course, essential to the success of any claim in respect of passing off based on the use of a given mark or get-up that the plaintiff should be able to show that the disputed mark or get-up has become by use in this country distinctive of the plaintiff's goods so that the use in relation to any goods of the kind dealt in by the plaintiff or that mark or get-up will be understood by the trade and the public in this country as meaning that the goods are the plaintiff's goods.'

Thus the plaintiff was not held entitled to an injunction where the

---

21   *Payton & Co Ltd* v *Snelling, Lampard & Co Ltd* (1899) 17 RPC 48 (CA); (1900) 17 RPC 628 (HL); *JB Williams Co* v *H Bronnley & Co Ltd* (1909) 26 RPC 481 (Neville J)—in both cases the plaintiffs were the first to use the get-up, but failed to establish property in it; see also *Coleman & Co Ltd* v *Stephen Smith & Co* (1911) 29 RPC 81 (CA); see also cases referred to footnotes 15 and 16 above.
22   *M Saper Ltd* v *Specters Ltd* (1953) 70 RPC 173 at 174 (Harman J, striped boxes for confectionery).
23   Per Romer LJ in *Payton & Co Ltd* v *Snelling Lampard & Co Ltd* (1899) 17 RPC 48 at 55 (CA).

plaintiff had shown that the plaintiff was the only person who had used a picture of a particular fruit on wrappers as denoting the flavour of preparations, but had not been able to show that that particular device was identified with the plaintiff's goods (*White, Tomkins & Courage Ltd* v *United Confectionery Co Ltd* (1914) 31 RPC 430: Warrington J; see also footnote 21 above). And the get-up of cartons containing hooks and eyes, although a novelty, was held not to be associated in the minds of purchasers with the plaintiff's goods in particular (*De Long Hook & Eye Co Ltd* v *Newey Bros Ltd* (1911) 29 RPC 49: Warrington J).

Likewise in all the cases where the get-up was held to be common to the trade, it naturally followed that the plaintiff could not establish that it distinguished the plaintiff's particular goods in the eyes of the public. (See per Kekewich J in *Thomas Hubbuck & Son Ltd* v *William Brown Sons & Co* (1900) 17 RPC 148 at 154; and also p 94 above, in particular footnote 4.)

5 Any kind of get-up, if distinctive, may be protected

The following are examples of the types of get-up case held to constitute passing off.

5.1 Vehicles

One of the earliest cases was that of *Knott* v *Morgan* (1836) 2 Keen 213, where the defendant imitated the green decoration, general aspect and name of the plaintiff's omnibuses and the green livery and gold hat-bands of the coachmen and conductors. In granting an injunction Langdale MR, said, at 218, 'The law has been settled, from the year books downward, that a man has no right to trade under false colours, and to sell his goods as another's'.[24]

In *London General Omnibus Co Limited* v *Felton* (1896) 12 TLR 213 Chitty J said 'in these cases it is useless to compare the points of similarity one by one. What must be looked at as the most important consideration

---

[24] Followed in *London General Omnibus Co Ltd* v *Turner* (1894) 38 SJ 457; see also *London Road Car Co* v *Era Omnibus Association* (1898) *The Times*, 23 June and (1899) *The Times*, 28 April (where the defendant was restrained from running omnibuses with a flag affixed thereto, and in other ways got up like the plaintiff's without clearly distinguishing their omnibuses from the plaintiff's); see also *London General Omnibus Co Ltd* v *Haydon* (1900) *The Times*, 17 February cf with *London General Omnibus Co Ltd* v *Gillings* (1900) *The Times*, 1 June and 27 June, where an injunction was refused and *London General Omnibus Co Ltd* v *Lavell* (1901) 18 RPC 74 (where judge viewed the two buses and there was no independent evidence of a likelihood of deception).

was what caught the eye generally, and this was certainly not less important when it was born in mind that omnibuses were not merely stationary, but also moving objects.'

In *W & G Du Cros Ltd* v *Gold* (1912) 30 RPC 117 an injunction was granted by Swinfen Eady J restraining the defendant from so getting-up his taxicabs as to pass them off as and for the taxicabs of the plaintiff.

5.2 Shape of bottles or other receptacles

In *John Haig & Co Ltd* v *Forth Blending Co Ltd*[25] for many years the petitioner had sold a brand of whisky in distinctively shaped bottles technically known as 'three pinch decanters' but which had come to be known as 'Dimple' bottles and this brand was commonly asked for as 'Dimple' whisky. An interdict was granted restraining the respondent from selling whisky not blended by the petitioner in 'Dimple' bottles for consumption in the UK even though the respondent's labels were quite different to the petitioner's labels.

In the *Jif Lemon* case[24] the House of Lords upheld an injunction which Lord Bridge described as giving the plaintiffs a de facto monopoly of the use of a yellow plastic simulated lemon-shaped container for the packaging of lemon juice, albeit that the wording of such injunction merely prevented the defendants from marketing their product 'in any container so nearly resembling the plaintiff's Jif lemon-shaped container as to be likely to deceive without making it clear to the ultimate purchaser that it is not of the goods of the plaintiff', even though such a device could not at that time have been registered as a trade mark.

Apart from imitating the shape of the plaintiff's bottles there are also cases where the defendant has actually used the plaintiff's bottles for the defendant's own products. Thus in *Rose* v *Loftus*[26] it was held that an injunction would be granted to restrain a trader from filling and sending

---

[25] (1952) 69 RPC 323 (Court of Session); (1953) 70 RPC 259 (Court of Session); See also *Reckitt & Colman Products Ltd* v *Borden Inc* [1990] RPC 341 (the *Jif Lemon* case). Cf *John Haig & Co Ltd* v *Brooks & Bohm (Wine Shippers) Ltd* (1955) 72 RPC 247 (Roxburgh J) where interim injunction refused as defendant's bottles had no actual depressions and plaintiff had not shown there was any likelihood of the public buying by the shape of the defendant's bottles. See also *Coca-Cola Co* v *AG Barr & Co Ltd* [1961] RPC 387 (Court of Session) where interim interdict refused as respondent's drink of a different colour to petitioner's though bottles were of the same shape.

[26] (1878) 47 LJ Ch 576 (Malins V-C); see also *Andrew G Barr & Co* v *Mair & Dougall* (1904) 21 RPC 665 (Court of Session-OH, soda syphon); *Calor Gas (Distributing) Co Ltd* v *Cooper* [1962] RPC 16; and *Sodastream Ltd* v *Thorn Cascade Co Ltd* [1982] RPC 459 (CA, coloured gas cylinders).

out to the public articles of his own manufacture in bottles, casks or other receptacles having indelibly impressed thereon the name of another trader who manufactured an article of like description even though such trader placed on such bottles, casks or receptacles a label having his own name thereon.

5.3 Labels and get-up of packaging

The imitation by the defendant of the plaintiff's label or boxes is the most common way in which a defendant will try to benefit from the plaintiff's goodwill.[27]

5.4 Colour of article[28]

In *RJ Elliott & Co Ltd* v *Hodgson* (1902) 19 RPC 518 an interim injunction was granted by Buckley J restraining the defendant from selling cigars made in the plaintiff's distinctive flat-ended shape without distinguishing such cigars from the plaintiff's cigars. Compare *British American Glass Co Ltd* v *Winton Products (Blackpool) Ltd* [1962] RPC 230 (Pennycuick J)—see also pp 98–100 above.

In *F Hoffman-La Roche & Co AG* v *DDSA Pharmaceuticals Ltd* [1969] FSR 410 (CA) the defendant was restrained from selling the defendant's drug in green and black capsules which the defendant argued was the same drug as the plaintiff's. Harman LJ said 'now I myself never received from the defendants a satisfactory answer to the plain question why do they wish to market their goods in green and black? I can only answer that they wish to do so in order to attract to themselves some part of the plaintiffs' goodwill and trade on their reputation and in fact to represent to the public that their goods are the goods of the plaintiffs. That, in my judgment, is exactly the classic case of passing-off.'

However, in *John Wyeth & Brother Ltd* v *M & A Pharmachem Ltd* [1988] FSR 26 where plaintiffs' and defendants' tranquilliser pills in the shape of small torpedoes were coloured blue and yellow to denote different dosages. Whitford J held that there was no likelihood of deception on the

---

[27] Examples of recent cases where injunctions have been granted are: *Tavener Rutledge Ltd* v *Specters Ltd* [1959] RPC 355 (CA); *White Hudson & Co Ltd* v *Asian Organisation Ltd* [1965] RPC 45 (PC, known in Singapore as 'red cough sweets'); and *Lee Kar Choo* v *Lee Liam Choon* [1967] 1 AC 602 (PC). Cf where injunctions were refused:—*Saper Ltd* v *Specters Ltd* (1953) 70 RPC 173 (Harman J); and *Tetrosyl Ltd* v *Silver Paint & Lacquer Co Ltd* [1980] FSR 68 (CA, filler tubs).

[28] See p 105 above as to shape of article.

part of doctors or pharmacists, the pills only being available on prescription.[29]

5.5 Way in which name is written

The way in which a name is written may entitle it to protection even though the word itself is descriptive and has not acquired a secondary significance which will entitle it to rank as a trade name. Where the plaintiff put on the market corsets under the name of 'Erect Form', and this name was written in certain distinctive lettering with a flourish underneath, and the defendant copied the name and style of the lettering, it was held that although 'Erect Form', being descriptive, had not acquired a secondary meaning and could not be protected, yet taking into conjunction with it the imitation of the lettering the defendant could be restrained from selling or offering for sale corsets in boxes bearing the scroll or imitation of the scroll used by the plaintiff in connection with the plaintiff's corsets, or any corsets designated by show cards or labels bearing such scroll or imitation, or otherwise distinguished by such scroll or imitation (*Weingarten* v *Bayer* (1905) 22 RPC 341: HL).[30]

6 Whether get-up is deceptive[31]

In *Schweppes Ltd* v *Gibbens*[32] Lord Halsbury said 'the whole question in these cases is whether the thing—taken in its entirety, looking at the whole

---

[29] See also *Boots Co Ltd* v *Approved Prescription Services Ltd* [1988] FSR 45 (CA, magenta coloured pills, interlocutory injunction refused, pills available only on prescription, loss of sales adequate compensation. In *Imperial Group plc* v *Philip Morris Ltd* [1984] RPC 394, Whitford J refused injunction as black and gold get-up of John Player cigarettes held not to be distinctive. Likewise in *Rizla Ltd* v *Bryant & May Ltd* [1986] RPC 389, Walton J refused injuction to restrain use of blue, red and green boxes for cigarette papers sold by retailers and in *Scott Ltd* v *Nice Pak Products Ltd* [1989] FSR 100, CA, refused injunction to restrain use of rectangular blue tub to hold baby wipes, the colour blue being a preferred colour for baby goods.

[30] See also *T Wall & Sons Ltd* v *Wells Whip Ltd* [1964] RPC 197 (Buckley J, 'Walls' in characteristic script, defendant sold ice cream from vans similar in colour and style to the plaintiff's painted with the words 'WELLS WHIP' in a script resembling that of the plaintiff—held confusion was likely).

[31] See also pp 96–98 above.

[32] (1905) 22 RPC 601 (HL); see also per Cozens Hardy MR in *Coleman & Co Ltd* v *Stephen Smith & Co* (1911) 29 RPC 81 at 88 (CA, medicated wine in champagne bottles wrapped in pink paper with the name 'Wincarnis' on a label, get-up adopted by defendant held to be common to trade).

thing—is such that in the ordinary course of things a person with reasonable apprehension and with proper eyesight would be deceived.' This is a question of fact to be decided on the evidence before the court.

It is not necessary for the whole get-up of an article to be imitated so as to render deceit likely. Any imitation that is likely to deceive will be restrained.[33] Where the defendant takes some matter which forms a prominent part of the plaintiff's get-up, even if such matter is not distinctive per se, the likelihood of deception will be enhanced.

Where, however, the essence of a mark of origin is its particular colour, it does not follow that a similar mark of a wholly different colour would indicate a similar origin to the public. The fact that Dunhill pipes are known to the world generally by a white spot on the mouthpiece was held not to prevent another firm of pipemakers from marking their mouthpieces with a red spot (*Dunhill* v *Bartlett & Bickley* (1932) 29 RPC 426: Russell J).

The more necessarily similar articles are to one another the more the trader should be careful to distinguish, and a small similarity in get-up may, when added to the necessary similarities, amount to a passing off.

In *Cordes* v *R Addis & Son* (1923) 40 RPC 139 Eve J said 'the necessary similarity of the articles increases the risk of deception, one is not dealing with a class of article where the shape or the make or the colour is so distinctive as to render factors of similarity of little importance. We are dealing, as I say, with a common article, a common shape, with a word that is open to all the world; and it behoves manufacturers, in putting their products on the market, to be careful to avoid adopting any factors or elements which may be likely to confuse their article with the almost exactly similar article put on the market by another manufacturer.'

In that case it was held that the get-up of the defendant's tooth brushes, and the cartons enclosing them, were not calculated to mislead purchasers into thinking that they were buying the plaintiff's tooth brushes.

7 Similarity of get-up in addition to other features

Where the name given by the defendant to his wares is complained of as being similar to that of the plaintiff, the similarity of 'get-up' may make the difference. In *Woollam* v *Ratcliff* (1863) 1 Hem & M 259 at 261 (get up of bundles of silk) Wood V-C said 'I have before me the case of the Omnibus Companies,[34] where the words "Conveyance Company", the green

---

[33] See footnote 2 above, where mere imitation held not sufficient.

[34] *Knott* v *Morgan* (1836) 2 Keen 213 (Langdale MR).

omnibus, etc, were held sufficient together to entitle the plaintiffs to an injunction. The defendants might have had those words painted on a yellow omnibus without objection, and so of the other resemblances; the wrong lay in their accumulation, not in any one of them alone.'

Where the plaintiff had for many years sold paper with the water-mark 'British Bond' and a monogram underneath in a special lettering, and the defendant issued a paper with the water-mark 'British Dominion Bond' and a monogram underneath closely resembling the monogram and lettering of the plaintiff's monogram, it was held that the defendants must be restrained from using the name and lettering and monogram in conjunction.[35] And, similarly, an injunction was granted in a case where the defendant not only imitated the get-up of the plaintiffs' 'Liquid Veneer', polish, known as 'LV', but also called it 'Elvee' (*Liquid Veneer Co v Scott* (1912) 29 RPC 639, a case of fraudulent conduct: Swinfen Eady J).

---

[35] *Spicer Bros Ltd v Spalding & Hodge Ltd* (1914) 32 RPC 52 (Joyce J); see also *Lever v Goodwin* (1887) 4 RPC 492 (Chitty J, Sunlight 'Self-Washer Soap'; Goodwin's 'Self-Washing Soap', both wrapped in similar parchment paper wrappers).

Chapter 7

Imitation of Name of Business or Profession

The law of passing off will restrain one trader from trading under a name which is likely to deceive other members of the trade or members of the public into thinking they are dealing with some other trader or with some trader who is connected with that other trader. There must be some commercial activity on the part of the plaintiff whether it be trade or profession—see *Kean* v *McGivan* [1982] FSR 119 (CA), in which the Social Democratic Party failed to restrain the defendant from using the same name.

1 Rights of individuals

Where the plaintiff is an individual or group of individuals having some professional interest (for example journalist, actor, etc) well known to the public or having adopted and become known by some fanciful name, the courts will protect that person if injury is likely to occur to such name. In *Hines* v *Winnick*[1] the plaintiff, a conductor and composer, had been

---

[1] (1947) 64 RPC 113. See also *Marengo* v *Daily Sketch & Sunday Graphic Ltd* (1948) 65 RPC 242 (HL, plaintiff well known cartoonist able to restrain rival from using his signature 'Kem' or a confusingly similar signature); *Fleetwood Mac Promotions Ltd* v *Clifford Davis Management Ltd* [1975] FSR 150 (Goff J, plaintiff company owned and controlled by four individual musicians in group granted injunction to restrain use of 'Fleetwood Mac' by a different pop group formed by late manager of plaintiff group); *Henderson* v *Radio Corp Pty Ltd* [1969] RPC 218 (New South Wales, Full HC, injunction granted to professional dancing couple where without their consent defendants had used a photograph of them on the sleeve of a gramophone record even though no likelihood they would produce a record themselves, the damage being 'the wrongful appropriation of another's professional or business reputation'; considered in *Lego System AS* v *Lego M Lemelstrich Ltd* [1983] FSR 155 at 193: Falconer J); cf *Clark* v *Freeman* (1848) 11 Beav 112 (Sir James Clark, a well-known physician

employed by the defendant to appear in a musical act entitled 'Ignorance is Bliss' which was being broadcast by the BBC. When the defendant continued the act as 'Dr Crock and his Crackpots' with a conductor other than the plaintiff, it was held that the name 'Dr Crock' had become identified with the plaintiff and that an injunction should be granted restraining the defendant from passing off any musical act under the title 'Dr Crock and his Crackpots' as and for the plaintiff's musical performance. Vaisey J said at 117 'We are dealing with a personal matter connected with an art, and if a man, be he musician, portrait painter, or writer of articles in newspapers, gets to be known under a particular name, that name becomes inevitably part of his stock-in-trade . . . he is entitled to say that it is his name, and that anyone who adopts or causes the adoption of that name by some other person is inflicting upon him an injury.'

In *British Medical Association* v *Marsh* (1931) 48 RPC 565, where the defendant was restrained from carrying on business so as to represent to the public that it was in some way connected with the plaintiff by use of the letters BMA, Maugham J stated . . . '*Clark* v *Freeman* [see footnote 1] does not establish the proposition . . . that a doctor has no remedy if he establishes by proper evidence that the sale by the defendant of some quack medicine as the medicine of the plaintiff or recommended by the plaintiff will be injurious to the plaintiff by causing him to lose patients or not to gain other patients who would naturally come to him . . . What it is necessary in such a case to prove is, either positive injury, or, in a *quia timet* action, a reasonable probability of injury; and if that is done, I, for my part, see no reason why such an action should not succeed.'

1.1 Authors, artists

A well-known author or artist may prevent his name (real or assumed)

---

was unable to stop defendant chemist from selling 'Sir J Clark's Consumption Pills' as Sir James was not in trade or business, libel being his only cause of action: Langdale MR). See also *Tolley* v *Fry* [1931] AC 333 (HL, where there was a libel on a well known amateur golfer in the form of a caricature of him used to advertise the defendant's chocolate); *Alastair Sim* v *HJ Heinz Co Ltd* [1959] RPC 75 (CA, alleged libel and passing off by unauthorised imitation of actor's voice, interlocutory injunction refused following libel practice); *Derek McCulloch* v *Lewis May A May (Produce Distributors) Ltd* (1947) 65 RPC 58 (Uncle Mac, broadcaster, could not restrain Uncle Mac shreaded wheat: Wynn-Parry J); *Lyngstad* v *Anabas Products Ltd* [1977] FSR 62 (Oliver J, pop group Abba could not restrain use of name and likeness on T-shirts etc—no probability of deception); and *Harrison and Starkey* v *Polydor Ltd* [1977] FSR 1 (Walton J, injunction refused where plaintiffs (the Beatles) sought to restrain unauthorised use of photographs of them in connection with two records of interviews of plaintiffs: *Henderson* v *Radio Corp Pty Ltd* (above) distinguished).

from being used on works not executed by him (*Martin* v *Wright* (1833) 6 Sim 297: Shadwell V-C—case of distinguished artist; *Lord Byron* v *Johnson* (1816) 2 Mer 29: LC; *Wood* v *Butterworth* (1901-4) MCC 16). Thus a writer who had obtained great celebrity under the nom de plume of 'Mark Twain' was held entitled to restrain other persons from using such nom de plume;[2] so, too, an author may maintain an action for injury to his reputation against the publisher of an inaccurate edition of his work, falsely purporting to be executed by him, though the publisher be the owner of the copyright. In *Archbold* v *Sweet*[3] Lord Tenterden CJ said that the case bore a close analogy to 'those cases in which a person, having a reputation in the manufacture of a particular commodity, but not protected by a patent, brings an action against another for selling an inferior article in his name; there the sale of the commodity is affected, here the character of the author.' Furthermore, a known or an unknown author has a statutory right to prevent his name being falsely attributed to a work (literary, musical, dramatic or artistic) when it is not his, whether or not the same would also constitute a libel (Copyright Act, 1956 s 43). See *Moore* v *News of the World Ltd* [1972] 1 QB 441 (CA), in which the false attribution of words 'By Dorothy Squires talking to Weston Taylor', gave rise to a case of libel as well as breach of s 43.

1.2 Right of an individual to trade under his own name

With one exception the principle of law is the same as that applicable to goods. The exception is that 'a man must be allowed to trade in his own name and if some confusion results, that is a lesser evil than that a man should be deprived of what would appear to be a natural and inherent right'[4] provided that such use of his own name is done honestly. As was

---

[2] Sebastian's Digest 429. See also *Landa* v *Greenberg* (1908) 24 TLR 441 (Eve J, plaintiff entitled to protect nom de plume 'Aunt Naomi' as part of her stock-in-trade as an authoress and journalist); *Modern Fiction Ltd* v *Fawcett* (1949) 66 RPC 230 (Romer J, dispute over ownership of pen name 'Ben Sarto', held to belong to the author as against the plaintiff publisher); and *Forbes* v *Kemsley Newspapers Ltd* (1951) 68 RPC 183 (Wynn-Parry J, dispute between journalist and employer over pen name 'Mary Delane', held to belong to journalist in the absence of any special term in her contract of service); cf *Sykes* v *Fairfax* [1978] FSR 312 (Supreme Court of New South Wales).

[3] (1832) 1 Mach & Rob 162; but see *Lee* v *Gibbings* (1892) 67 LT (NS) 263 where Kekewich J said that the case was one of trade libel and refused an injunction.

[4] *Marengo* v *Daily Sketch & Sunday Graphic Ltd* (1948) 65 RPC 242 at 251 (HL, Lord Simonds); see also *Parker Knoll Ltd* v *Knoll International Ltd* [1962] RPC 265 (HL), Chapter 2, pp 38-39.

stated by Romer J in *Joseph Rodgers & Sons Ltd* v *WN Rodgers & Co*:[5]

> It is the law of this land that no man is entitled to carry on his business in such a way as to represent that it is the business of another, or is in any way connected with the business of another; that is the first proposition. The second proposition is, that no man is entitled so to describe or mark his goods as to represent that the goods are the goods of another. To the first proposition there is, I myself think, an exception: a man, in my opinion, is entitled to carry on his business in his own name so long as he does not do anything more than that to cause confusion with the business of another, and so long as he does it honestly. It is an exception to the rule which has of necessity been established . . . To the second rule, to which I have referred . . . it is not necessary that there should be an exception to that. It is perfectly legitimate for a man in the cutlery business to carry on business under his own name whatever that name may be, but I can see no necessity for his marking his cutlery with a name (although it be his own name) which may have the effect of passing off those goods as the goods of the plaintiffs.

This passage was considered by the Court of Appeal in *Baume & Co Ltd* v *AH Moore Ltd*[6] (a case involving marking of watches) where it was reiterated that there was no exception to the second rule. Of the first

---

[5] (1924) 41 RPC 277 at 291 (the defendant was restrained from carrying on a cutlery business under the name 'WN Rodgers & Co' without clearly distinguishing it from the plaintiff's business; it being found that the defendant had adopted such name to benefit from the plaintiff's goodwill and in any event the defendant was not carrying on under his own name, viz Wilfred Newbound Rodgers). See also *Turton* v *Turton* (1889) 42 Ch D 128 (CA, Thomas Turton & Sons, steel manufacturers, unable to restrain defendant and his sons trading in a similar business in the same town as John Turton & Sons. See also *Wishie Circus (Pty) Ltd* v *Brian Boswell Circus (Pty) Ltd* [1986] FSR 479 (S Africa) where held person using own name must use such means as are necessary to distinguish defendants' circus.

[6] [1958] RPC 226 (CA, Romer LJ gave the judgment of the court). See also *Wright, Layman & Umney Ltd* v *Wright* (1949) 66 RPC 149 (CA granted a qualified injunction not to use 'Wright' without clearly distinguishing the defendant's business where defendant was trading as 'Wright's Chemical Coy' and where defendant's own name was William Frederick Thomas Wright): In *Electromobile Co Ltd* v *British Electromobile Co Ltd* (1908) 25 RPC 149 at 154 (CA) Lord Halsbury said 'if in point of user a particular thing had become so identified with the proper name of a person who carried on business under his own name that he could establish, as a matter of fact, that the name had become associated with the particular manufacture, I do not deny that another person who set up in business under that name, although it might be that person's own proper name, might be restrained from carrying on business under that name').

113

proposition the Court of Appeal said 'whether or not the learned Judge may have expressed the exception of the first of the two rules too widely it is not necessary, for present purposes to consider'. However, in *Parker-Knoll Ltd* v *Knoll International Ltd* [1962] RPC 265 at 279, 284, 287, a majority of the House of Lords whilst observing (albeit obiter as the trading names of the respective parties were not in issue) that such exception exists, held that there was no such exception in respect of goods (Lord Denning dissenting).

This distinction between use in respect of goods and as a trading name seems to be one which is hard to enforce in practice. For when a man manufactures and sells articles they become automatically labelled with his name in the mind of a purchaser. If a man named Pears is allowed to carry on in his own name the business of manufacturing soap (as was suggested by Romer J in *Joseph Rodgers & Sons Ltd* v *WN Rodgers & Co*), all the soap that he sells is to the mind of the customer 'soap manufactured by Pears' or 'Pears' soap' and it is useless to forbid him to mark it as such (see *Wright, Layman & Umney Ltd* v *Wright* (1949) 66 RPC 149 (CA), where an injunction was granted in respect of name 'Wright's Chemical Company' as well as baby powder).[6] Perhaps the natural reluctance of the Court to interfere where the name complained of is the defendant's own name is best expressed by Lord Lindley MR in *Jamieson and Co* v *Jamieson* (1898) 15 RPC 169 at 181:

> Now, when we are asked to restrain a man who is carrying on business in his own name, we must take very great care what we are about. The principle applicable to the case, I take it, is this: The Court ought not to restrain a man from carrying on business in his own name simply because there are people who are doing the same and who will be injured by what he is doing. It would be intolerable if the Court were to interfere, and to prevent people from carrying on business in their own names in rivalry to others of the same name. There must be something far more than that, viz, that the person who is carrying on business in his own name is doing it in such a way as to pass off his goods as the goods of somebody else . . . In all cases in which a person has been restrained from carrying on business in his own name he has done something more than use his name; he has copied something from somebody else in the trade, or he has gone out of his way to make his things look like those of a rival in the trade . . .

In *Jamieson* the plaintiff failed to establish a secondary meaning of 'Jamieson' for a harness composition, and an injunction was refused. Where injunctions have been granted, generally the defendant has not been restrained absolutely from trading under his own name but in a manner without sufficiently or clearly distinguishing his business from that of the plaintiff.[7]

In all the above cases stress was laid on the right of the individual to trade honestly under his name.[8] In *Jay's Ltd* v *Jacobi* (1953) 50 RPC 132, the defendant Mrs Jacobi who was known locally in Hove as 'Miss Jay' started a shop there called 'Jays' which was objected to by the plaintiff, who was an old-established costumier of Regent St London. In refusing an injunction (on the grounds of no likelihood of confusion between the two businesses) Eve J observed that Mrs Jacobi had acquired the surname 'Jay' by reputation and was entitled to trade under such name so long as she was acting honestly. This case was distinguished by Whitford J in *Biba Group Ltd* v *Biba Boutique* [1980] RPC 413 (injunction granted, defendant's boutique named BIBA after nickname of the proprietor) where it was stated 'whatever the rights may be in respect of the use of a surname, it does not appear to me that those authorities go to the question of the use of the first name, let alone a nickname . . .'

2 Corporate rights

2.1 Position where use of personal name is by a company

Where there is no fraud, a limited company may adopt the name under which a business has already been carried on. See for example *Dunlop Pneumatic Tyre Co Ltd* v *Dunlop Motor Co Ltd* (1906) 23 RPC 761 (Court of Session–IH); (1907) 24 RPC 572 (HL), where it was held that there was no likelihood of confusion of the two businesses, one being a tyre company and the other a small motor repair business at Kilmarnock; see also *Waring & Gillow Ltd* v *Gillow & Gillow Ltd* (1916) 33 RPC 173 in which two promoters, one called Gillow, were held by Astbury J to have acted honestly in setting up defendant auctioneering business. As Farwell J said in *S Chivers & Sons* v *S Chivers & Co* (1900) 17 RPC 420 at 426 'to my mind, no element of suspicion of fraud attaches to the man who has established a business under his own name if he turns that business into a

---

7   See, eg, *J & J Cash Ltd* v *Cash* (1902) 19 RPC 181 (CA); *B Warsop & Sons Ltd* v *Warsop* (1904) 21 RPC 481 (Kekewich J); *Joseph Rodgers & Sons Ltd* v *W N Rodgers & Co* (1924) 41 RPC 277 (Romer J); *Wright, Layman & Umney Ltd* v *Wright* (1949) 66 RPC 149 (CA); cf *Montgomery* v *Thompson* (1891) 8 RPC 361 (HL); *Jamieson* v *Jamieson* (above); and *Teofani & Co Ltd* v *Teofani* (1913) 30 RPC 446 CA.

8   See *Croft* v *Day* (1843) 7 Beav 84 (Langdale M R); and *Clayton* v *Day* (1881) 26 SJ 43 (Chitty J), where persons of the name of Day and Martin went into partnership for making 'blacking' in order that they might get the benefit of a well known firm of that name.

limited company and applies to that limited company his own name with the word "limited", because the reasons for doing so is obvious, that he desires to retain the goodwill which he has gained for that name.'

Where, however, a new company is not formed to carry on an existing business it will not be able to adopt the name or names of its promoter or directors if confusion with some other established trader is caused thereby.

Thus in *MP Guimaraens & Son v Fonseca & Vasconcellos Ltd* (1921) 38 RPC 389, where the plaintiff's brand of port was known as 'Fonseca Co's Port', a defendant company was restrained from carrying on business as importers of or dealers in port under the name of 'Fonseca & Vasconcellos Ltd' or any other name in which the word 'Fonseca' formed a part although Fonseca was the name of one of the three directors of the defendant company. Younger LJ indicated that the plaintiff would not have been entitled to the injunction if the defendant had been a partnership instead of a limited company.

In *Kingston, Miller & Co Ltd v Thomas Kingston & Co Ltd*[9] one Thomas Kingston, who had been an assistant manager of the plaintiff company, left their service on the expiration of his agreement and formed the defendant company with the same objects as the plaintiff company, namely catering, and made himself a managing director. It was held that any goodwill generated by Thomas Kingston whilst employed by the plaintiff company was their goodwill and was not transferred to the defendant company. Warrington J stated 'the Defendants are not an individual born with the name of *Kingston*; the company does not incorporate the right which *Thomas Kingston* had to carry on business in his own name; the person of the name of *Thomas Kingston* is not transferring any business and goodwill, he is merely authorising the promoters to use his name as part of the title of their company.'

Where a company lawfully incorporated abroad seeks honestly to use its name in connection with a business in this country, it is an open question whether it may do so if deception is likely to result.[10]

---

[9] (1911) 29 RPC 289 (injunction granted); approved and applied by Astbury J in *WH Dorman & Co Ltd v Henry Meadows Ltd* [1922] 2 Ch 233; see also *(Madame) Tussaud & Sons Ltd v Tussaud* (1890) 44 Ch D 678 (where an injunction was granted by Stirling J to restrain the registration of a proposed new company 'Louis Tussaud Ltd' promoted by Louis Tussaud to carry on a wax-work exhibition with him as manager); and *Valentine Meat Juice Co v Valentine Extract Co Ltd* (1900) 17 RPC 673 (CA, where C R Valentine, managing director of defendant company, had attempted to get the benefit of plaintiff's reputation, defendant restrained from using name).

[10] See *Saunders v Sun Life Assurance Co of Canada* [1894] 1 Ch 537 (Stirling J) referred to in *Habib Bank Ltd v Habib Bank* [1982] RPC 1 at 32. Cf *Parker-Knoll Ltd v Knoll International Ltd* [1962] RPC 265 (HL) where honest use of own name was held not to be a good defence to use of a name used abroad in connection with goods.

2.2 Registration of names under the Companies Acts[11]

Since the coming into operation of the Companies Act 1981 on 26 February 1982, it is the duty of persons or a company seeking to register a name to avoid a name which is already on the index (kept by the Registrar of Companies) or differs only in immaterial respects (s 22(1)(*c*), (3)); now Companies Act 1985, s 26(1)(*c*), (3). Where a name is registered which is the same or too like a name which at the time of registration is, or should have been, on the index, the Secretary of State has power to direct the later registration to be changed if such power is exercised within 12 months of registration (s 24(2)).[12] In determining whether two names are too alike it is material to consider how similar are the respective businesses (*Aerators Ltd* v *Tollit* (1902) 19 RPC 418: Farwell J).

The provisions under the Companies Act have been invoked by a plaintiff where there would otherwise have been a breach, thereby preventing a defendant company not yet registered from so registering under an objectionable name. Thus in *Hendriks* v *Montague* (1881) 17 Ch D 638 the plaintiff, trading as the Universal Life Assurance Society, had established a substantial business in life assurance both here and abroad, and sought to restrain the defendant from inter alia 'applying to the Registrar of Joint Stock Companies in England for registration under the Companies Act of any company to be incorporated under the name of the *Universe Life Assurance Association*, or any other name likely to mislead or deceive the public into the belief that the company, being incorporated as aforesaid, is the same as the *Universal Life Assurance Society ...*' The Court of Appeal, overruling Jessel MR, gave the injunction asked for, holding that a company, although not itself registered, may prevent the registration of a projected new company which is intended to carry on the same business as itself, and to bear a name so similar to its own as to be calculated to deceive, and that there was no need for the plaintiffs to wait until the defendant company was actually registered—for equity provides a remedy without reference to the Companies Acts. Compare *Aerators Ltd*

---

[11] The Business Names Act 1916 whereby registration was required in respect of any business name used by a person, firm or company where that name was not the actual name of such person, firm or company was abolished by Companies Act 1981, Sch 4, s 119(5). The Register of Business Names has been replaced by a system of statutory requirements as to what words in names may not be used and the disclosure required where such business names are used—these requirements are embodied in the Business Names Act 1985.

[12] See the Business Names Act 1985 where a company carries on business under a name other than its corporate name, which provisions replace ss 28–35 of the Companies Act 1981, which repealed the Registration of Business Names Act 1916.

v *Tollit*, in which no injunction was granted, the names not being too alike due to different businesses.

When the defendant company has already been registered, an injunction may forbid the signatories of the Memorandum of Association to allow the company to remain registered under the name complained of. Thus in *Panhard et Levassor SA* v *Panhard-Levassor Motor Co Ltd* (1901) 18 RPC 405, the defendants, who were signatories of the Memorandum, were restrained from 'using the names of Panhard and Levassor, or either of them, or any title or description including those names or either of them, or otherwise colourably resembling the name of the plaintiffs, in connection with the manufacture, use, or sale of or other dealing in motor cars or parts thereof' and Farwell J ordered 'that they do not allow the defendant company to remain registered under its present name or any such title as aforesaid.' See also *Fletcher Challenge Ltd* v *Fletcher Challenge Pty Ltd* [1982] FSR 1 (Powell J, NSW) in which the plaintiff, a New Zealand company, was entitled to an order against an Australian shelf company of the same name to change its name, the Australian company have been incorporated to bar the plaintiffs from registering their name.

Where an injunction is granted it will generally be suspended for a short time, for example two to six weeks, to enable the company to make the necessary alteration to its name (see *Lloyd's* v *Lloyd's (Southampton) Ltd* (1912) 29 RPC 433 (CA); *Poiret* v *Jules Poiret Ltd* (1920) 37 RPC 177 (Younger J); cf *Harrods Ltd* v *R Harrod Ltd* (1923) 41 RPC 74 (CA)).

2.3 Adoption of name suggesting a connection or association with the plaintiff

A defendant will be restrained where the adopted name falsely suggests a connection or association with the business of the plaintiff. This may take a number of forms, the following cases being examples.

Amalgamation

In *North Cheshire & Manchester Brewery Co Ltd* v *Manchester Brewery Co Ltd*[13] an injunction was granted restraining the defendant from using the name or style of the North Cheshire and Manchester Brewery Company Ltd, Lord Halsbury stating 'when I see that in the name of the appellant company there is literally and positively the same name as that of the rival company, as I will call it, and that it is only prevented from being identical in name by having another name associated with it, I should think myself

---

[13] [1899] AC 83 (HL). See also *Mills* v *Chapman* (1930) 47 RPC 115 (Farwell J, Luxmoore J, London Olympia Circus able to restrain 'Chapman's London Olympia Zoo and Circus' from using London Olympia in their name).

that the inevitable result would be that which appears to have happened—that any one who saw the two names together would arrive at the conclusion without any doubt at all that the two companies, both with well-known names, both in the particular neighbourhood with which we are dealing, had been amalgamated.' But this does not mean that any company can be restrained from embodying the name of another company in its title. For if the words common to both companies are descriptive, the plaintiff company has no right to monopolise them, and the similarity is not likely to cause deception[14]. 'In considering whether a name is calculated to deceive,' said Farwell J in *Aerators Ltd* v *Tollit* (1902) 19 RPC 418, at 420, 'it is, as I have said, material to see what that name is, and if the name is simply a word in ordinary use representing a machine or an article of commerce, the probability of deception is out of all proportion less than it would be in the case of an invented or fancy word, or even of the name of a place. The latter may well point to a particular company; the former certainly points, *prima facie*, to the machine or article, and can only, under very exceptional circumstances and by a long course of usage point to the company rather than the thing itself. English-speaking people know 'aerators,' 'motors,' and the like as machines, not as companies, and the presence of such a word in the title of a company suggests that thing itself—a company that deals in those machines—not that it has anything to do with a company of that name.'

Branch, subsidiary or agency

In *Lloyd's* v *Lloyd's (Southampton) Ltd*[15] the defendant who carried on

---

[14] *Aerators Ltd* v *Tollit* (1902) 19 RPC 418 (Farwell J, Automatic Aerator Patents Limited); *British Vacuum Cleaner Co Ltd* v *New Vacuum Co Ltd* (1907) 24 RPC 641 (Parker J); *HE Randall Ltd* v *E Bradley & Son* (1907) 24 RPC 657 (Warrington J); 773 (CA, Anglo-American Shoe Co and American Shoe Co); *Electromobile Co Ltd* v *British Electromobile Co Ltd* (1907) 24 RPC 688 (Warrington J); (1908) 25 RPC 149 (CA); see also *My Kinda Town Ltd* v *Soll* [1983] RPC 407 (CA, 'Chicago Pizza' as part of plaintiff's and defendant's trading name held to merely denote that both businesses sold same commodity).

[15] (1912) 29 RPC 433 (CA, overruling Warrington J). See also *Wheeler & Wilson Manufacturing Co* v *Shakespear* (1869) 39 LJ Ch 36 (James V-C, false representation as to agent); *Ewing (trading as Buttercup Dairy Company)* v *Buttercup Margarine Co Ltd* (1917) 34 RPC 232 (CA); *Albion Motor Car Co Ltd* v *Albion Carriage and Motor Body Works Ltd* (1917) 34 RPC 257 (Astbury J); *Harrods Ltd* v *R Harrod Ltd* (1923) 41 RPC 74 (CA); *FW Woolworth & Co Ltd* v *Woolworths (Australasia) Ltd* (1930) 47 RPC 337 (Farwell J); *British Legion* v *British Legion Club (Street) Ltd* (1931) 48 RPC 555 (Farwell J); and *Computervision Corporation* v *Computer Vision Ltd* [1975] RPC 171. See also footnote 16 below.

business of buying and selling vessels and acting as shipping brokers was restrained from 'using the name *'Lloyd's (Southampton) Ltd'* or any other name calculated to induce the belief that the defendants' business is the business of, or an agency, branch, or department of the business of the plaintiffs, *Lloyd's.*' This was a case of fraud and Cozens-Hardy MR stated 'I think there is ample evidence on the part of the plaintiffs that this is not an honest case, but one in which serious damage might be done to *Lloyd's* and to *Lloyd's* agents at Southampton.'

Extension of business or some other connection with the plaintiff's business

Where the field of activity of the rival traders is allied but not the same, then just as in respect of goods, so also in respect of a business it is a question of fact whether the name in question falsely represents a connection with the plaintiff's business; such a question will depend largely on the distinctiveness of such name and the motive of the defendant in adopting the name.[16]

Where a business is extended beyond its original scope so that it encroaches on the rights of an already established business, the principles

---

[16] See *Dunlop Pneumatic Tyre Co Ltd* v *Dunlop Lubricant Co* (1898) 16 RPC 12 (Romer LJ); *Hulton Press Ltd* v *White Eagle Youth Holiday Camp Ltd* (1951) 68 RPC 126 (Wynn-Parry J, likely confusion of defendant's 'White Eagle Youth Holiday Camp' with plaintiff's 'The Eagle' magazine as a venture sponsored by or owned by the plaintiff); *Legal & General Assurance Society* v *Daniel* [1968] RPC 253 (see p 124 below); *Annabel's (Berkeley Square) Ltd* v *Schock* [1972] RPC 838 (CA, defendant's escort agency sufficiently allied to the plaintiff's well-known night club); *Ames Crosta Ltd* v *Pionex International Ltd* [1977] FSR 46 (Walton J, importation and sale of protective clothing and plaintiff's Pionex Division engaged in the control of industrial pollution sufficiently similar for people to think the plaintiff had expanded plaintiff's business); cf *Marathon Oil Co* v *Marathon Shipping Co Ltd* [1968] RPC 443 (Stamp J, interlocutory injunction refused on balance of convenience, risk of damage to plaintiff company negligible); *Granada Group Ltd* v *Ford Motor Company Ltd* [1973] RPC 49 (Graham J, Granada cars no association with plaintiff's TV, theatre, cinema and publicity activities); *Stringfellow* v *McCain Foods (GB) Ltd* (CA) [1984] RPC 501, 'Stringfellows' oven chips not likely to be associated with plaintiff's well known night club of same name); *Fortnum & Mason plc* v *Fortnam Ltd* [1994] FSR 438 (Harman J), defendant importer exporter of plastic goods from Far East nor likely to be confused with grocery business of plaintiff). *Harrods Ltd* v *The Harrodian School Ltd*, 13 May 1994, unreported (Harman J), defendant prep school located on one-time site of plaintiffs Harrodian Club, no likelihood of the public believing a connection between the two; see also footnotes 14 and 15 above.

applicable are those applicable to other cases.[17] Thus a defendant will be restrained who buys up a business of a certain name with the dishonest intention of extending its scope so as to manufacture something that may be passed off as the manufacture of a business of a like name (*Holloway* v *Clent* (1903) 20 RPC 525: Swinfen Eady J; *Mappin & Webb Ltd* v *Leapmann* (1905) 22 RPC 398: Farwell J). Thus in *Abel Morrall Ltd* v *Hessin & Co* (1903) 20 RPC 429 (CA) a defendant was restrained from buying the business of one Morrall, which did not manufacture needles to any extent, in order to extend it to the manufacture of needles, so as to get the advantage of the reputation of the plaintiff whose needles were known everywhere as 'Morrall's' needles. See also *Joseph Rodgers & Sons Ltd* v *FM Hearnshaw* (1906) 23 RPC 349, where Buckley J granted an injunction against the defendant who had bought the tool manufacturing business of Rodgers Bros and commenced to manufacture cutlery which the defendant sold under the Rodgers mark.

Late connection with business

Cases of deception sometimes arise when an employee or partner wishes to advertise his connection with a firm which he has left. A trader who has been a manager or partner in a firm of established reputation has a right on setting up an independent business to make known to the public that he has been with that firm; but he must take care not to do so in a way calculated to lead the public to believe that he is carrying on the business of the old firm or continues in any way to be connected with it.[18] In *Harrods Ltd* v *Schwartz-Sackin & Co Ltd* [1986] FSR 490 the defendant who operated the fine art department of Harrods under various concession arrangements could not be restrained from promoting his own showroom by reference to having been responsible for running the Harrods

---

[17] *Evans* v *Eradicure Ltd* [1972] RPC 808 (Goff J, expansion of rival businesses of wood preservation under similar names, no interlocutory injunction granted); cf *A Levey* v *Henderson-Kenton (Holdings) Ltd* [1974] RPC 617, (Foster J, defendant restrained from expanding business as retailers of furniture and furnishings under the name 'Kentons' to Newcastle as plaintiff was a well known departmental store of same name (at the time burnt down)).

[18] *Hookham* v *Pottage* (1872) 8 Ch App 91 (an injunction was granted where, after dissolution of the partnership whereby the business went to the plaintiff, the defendant painted over his door 'S. Pottage from Hookham and Pottage': the word 'Hookham' being in the most conspicuous position). See also *Glenny* v *Smith* (1865) 2 Drew & Sm 476 (an injunction granted by Kindersley V-C where a tradesman who had been employed by Thresher & Glenny put his own name over the shop but on the plates under the shop window and on the sun awning put 'from Thresher & Glenny', the 'from' being in much smaller letters, and when the awning was down it obscured the defendants' name).

department. Warner J applied the statement of Plowman J in *Pompadour Laboratories Ltd* v *Stanley Frazer* [1966] RPC 7 that it was 'clearly settled law that a defendant who formerly had a connection with a plaintiffs' business but had ceased to do so, although entitled to inform the world that he formerly had that connection, is not entitled to state that he still has such a connection if that in fact is not the case.

But it seems that the words 'late of' or 'from', even though small, may be sufficient, if fairly placed and not calculated to deceive (*Matthews* v *Hodgson* (1886) 2 TLR 899: North J and CA, injunction refused).

It is a question of fact in each case, whether the defendant is representing himself to have any continuing connection with the plaintiff's business, and the words 'late of' may represent such a connection. Thus where a son left his father's fish-sauce warehouse at 107 Strand and set up business on his own, describing himself and his business as 'late of 107 Strand', he was restrained from so describing himself (*Burgess* v *Burgess* (1853) DeGM & G 896: LJJ; see *Van Oppen & Co Ltd* v *Leonard Van Oppen* (1903) 20 RPC 617; Swinfen Eady J).

Successors in business

So, too, a representation that the plaintiff has gone out of business and that the defendant is continuing in his stead will be restrained (*Selby* v *Anchor Tube Co* [1877] WN 191; see also *Rickerby* v *Reay* (1903) 20 RPC 380 (Byrne J), where on the sale of his business to the plaintiff, the defendant—the son of one of the founders—was restrained from describing himself as 'late Reay and Carrick'). Two defendants were restrained from describing themselves on their doorplate as 'Scott and Nixon, late Robert and Walter Scott' (*Scott* v *Scott* (1866) 16 LT (NS) 143: Wood V-C). For although they carried on business at the same place as the firm of Robert and Walter Scott, they had no connection with the firm, and it was held that their inscription was a representation to the public that they had acquired the goodwill as well as the premises of Robert and Walter Scott, and that one or both of those partners had retired from business.

In a similar case the plaintiff and defendants were fireclay makers. When the plaintiff's lease of certain works where he carried on business, expired, the defendants managed to procure a lease of those works. The defendants thereupon inter alia circulated cards describing themselves as 'E.J. and J. Pearson (late Harper and Moore).' They were restrained by injunction on the ground that they were leading the public to suppose that they had succeeded to the business of the plaintiff (*Harper* v *Pearson* (1860) 3 LT 547: Wood V-C).

Similarly, where a person (or his trustee in bankruptcy) sells the goodwill of a business, he will be restrained from holding himself out as carrying on business in succession to or in continuation of the business he has sold (*Churton* v *Douglas* (1859) 28 LJ Ch 841 (Wood V-C); *Hudson* v *Osborne* (1869) 39 LJ Ch 79: James V-C).

2.4 Proximity of place of business to be considered

The fact that the defendant takes up his place of business near to or with an address likely to be confused with that of the plaintiff is very material, for it is often a strong indication of a deliberate intention to deceive and even if honestly chosen confusion is more likely to occur.[19] Where two persons called Day and Martin set up business in blacking at 901/2 Holborn Hill, so that they were likely to be confused with the famous makers of blacking, Day and Martin of 97 High Holborn, they were restrained by injunction (*Croft* v *Day* (1843) 7 Beav 84: Langdale MR). So a similarity in get-up may be enhanced by the fact that a defendant moves into the same neighbourhood as the plaintiff, or adds '& Co' to his name, although he has no partners, thereby making the name sound more like that of the plaintiff (*Fullwood* v *Fullwood* [1873] WN 93: Malins V-C; 185: CA). And an injunction was granted where the plaintiff had traded for many years in Pall Mall as the Guinea Coal Co, and the defendant, after trading as the Pall Mall Guinea Coal Co for some time in the Strand, moved into Pall Mall (*Lee* v *Haley* (1869) 5 Ch App 155: Malins V-C).

Also the location of the respective establishments may be material. Thus it was held that the Lyric Opera House was not likely to be mistaken for the Lyric Theatre as the former was in the suburbs and the latter in the heart of London (*Lyric Theatre Ltd* v *Cordingley* (1890) 90 LTJ 122).

3 Some more important cases

Set out below by way of subject matter are examples of cases where, although each case is a pure question of fact, a previous case may assist as to the courts' general approach to the particular topic.

---

[19] *Melachrino & Co* v *Melachrino Egyptian Cigarette Co* (1887) 4 RPC (Chitty J, a case of fraudulent trading); *Radio Rentals Ltd* v *Rentals Ltd* (1934) 51 RPC 407 (Clauson J, see p 124 below); *The Clock Ltd* v *The Clock House Hotel Ltd* (1936) 53 RPC 269 (CA, defendant's hotel some five miles from the plaintiff's 'The Clock' road house, injunction granted); *Bach & Jackson Ltd* v *Cowan* [1969] RPC 156 (Plowman J, defendant's hotel opposite restrained from being named 'The Pembridge Hotel'); cf *Laraine Day Ltd* v *Kennedy* (1953) 70 RPC 19 (Roxburgh J, even though the defendant's dress shop was only two doors away, no deception, no similarity of names).

3.1 Descriptive/geographical names

The locus classicus is the House of Lords decision in *Office Cleaning Services Ltd* v *Westminster Window and General Cleaners Ltd* (1946) 63 RPC 39 where Lord Simmonds set out certain considerations which will apply to this type of case, namely:

(i) the title being the use of words in common use—the courts will readily accept small differences to avoid such use, even though some members of the public will be confused

(ii) the motive of the choice of name of the defendants—if the intention is to deceive, it will readily be inferred that deception will result

(iii) whether the words in question have acquired a secondary meaning

(iv) the nature of the respective businesses and the way they are carried on.

Injunction granted

Association Booking Corporation a theatre booking agency in UK and USA able to restrain use of name 'Associated Booking Agency' (*Associated Booking Corp* v *Associated Booking Agency* [1964] RPC 372: Pennycuick J).

The Berkeley Hotel which was demolished in 1969 and was to be opened on a new site in autumn 1971 under the old name, was entitled to stop the hotel Berkeley International which was being built on the old Berkeley Street site (*Berkeley Hotel Co Ltd* v *Berkeley International (Mayfair) Ltd* [1972] RPC 237: Pennycuick J).

Computervision Corporation, an American company concerned with the manufacture and marketing of electronic equipment, able to restrain 'Computer Vision Ltd'; held members of the public would be led to think the defendant was an English subsidiary of the plaintiff (*Computervision Corp* v *Computer Vision Ltd* [1975] RPC 171: Plowman J).

Effluent Disposal Ltd, operating from Birmingham, able to restrain 'Midlands Effluent Disposal Ltd'—the word Midlands was no distinction at all (*Effluent Disposal Ltd* v *Midlands Effluent Disposal Ltd* [1970] RPC 238: Stamp J).

General Radio Company, an American company, able to restrain defendants from trading in electrical or electronic apparatus under any name containing the word 'General Radio Company' without distinguishing the defendant's business from the plaintiff, but this was not to prevent the use of General Radio Company (Westminster) Ltd if all parts of name of equal prominence (*General Radio Co* v *General Radio Co (Westminster) Ltd* [1957] RPC 471: Roxburgh J).

Legal & General, a well known insurance company, able to restrain the defendant (private investigators) from using the name 'Legal & General Enquiry Bureau' (*Legal & General Assurance Society Ltd* v *Daniel* [1968] RPC 253: CA).

Manchester Brewery Company able to restrain use of name North Cheshire and Manchester Brewery Company (*North Cheshire and Manchester Brewery Co* v *Manchester Brewery Co* [1899] AC 83: HL).

Midland Counties Dairy, also referred to as 'Midland Dairy' or 'Midland Dairies', able to prevent defendant, who also was wholesaler of ice cream, trading under 'Midland Dairies'—the name was held to have been dishonestly adopted (*Midland Counties Dairy Ltd* v *Midland Dairies Ltd* (1948) 65 RPC 429: Harman J; 437: CA).

Music Corporation of America, musical and entertainment agents whose name was naturally abbreviated to 'Music Corporation', were able to restrain defendant's use of name 'The Music Corporation (Great Britain) Ltd' (*Music Corp of America* v *Music Corp (GB) Ltd* (1947) 64 RPC 41: Wynn Parry J).

Pembridge Gardens Hotel, known also as 'The Pembridge Hotel', able to restrain 'the Pembridge Hotel' (*Bach & Jackson Ltd* v *Cowan* [1969] RPC 156: Plowman J).

Radio Rentals able to stop defendant company using the name 'Rentals' to carry on same business close by (*Radio Rentals Ltd* v *Rentals Ltd* (1934) 51 RPC 407: Clauson J).

Southern Music Publishing Co Ltd, music publishers whose name was customarily abbreviated to 'Southern' able to prevent defendant's use of name 'Southern Songs Ltd' as songwriters (*Southern Music Publishing Co Ltd* v *Southern Songs Ltd* [1966] RPC 137: Buckley J).

Injunction refused

Aerators Ltd failed to restrain defendant from registering a company under the name 'Automatic Aerator Patents Ltd', the plaintiff's action being held to be an attempt to monopolise a word in ordinary use in the English language (*Aerators Ltd* v *Tollit* (1902) 19 RPC 418: Farwell J, see p 119 above).

The American Shoe Company failed to prevent 'The Anglo-American Shoe Company' using the term 'Anglo-American', being descriptive of British made boots and shoes made after American models and methods (*H E Randall Ltd* v *E Bradley & Son* (1907) 24 RPC 773: CA).

'Chicago Pizza' as part of plaintiff's and defendant's trading name was held to merely denote that both businesses sold the same commodity (*My Kinda Town Ltd* v *Soll* [1983] RPC 407: CA).

Credit Management Company Ltd sufficiently different to Credit Management, being descriptive of the hire purchase firms with whom the parties were dealing (*Credit Management Co Ltd* v *Credit Management* [1961] RPC 157: Cross J).

Drive Yourself Hire Company (London) Ltd failed to stop defendant trading as 'Self Drive Cars' from inserting his name in the telephone directory as 'Drive Yourself (Self Drive Cars)', it not being established that 'Drive Yourself' meant the plaintiff's business (*Drive Yourself Hire Co (London) Ltd* v *AG Parish* [1957] RPC 307: Harman J).

The Electromobile Company Ltd failed to prevent the use of the name 'British Electromobile Company Ltd', it being held that 'Electromobile' was descriptive of a motor car driven by electricity (*Electromobile Coy Ltd* v *British Electromobile Co Ltd* (1907) 25 RPC 149: CA).

Furnitureland as trading style of 11 stores in South of England selling branded furniture, defendants in same business in same area trading under the style 'Furniture City': held plaintiffs could not succeed at the trial. *Furnitureland Ltd* v *Harris* [1989] FSR 536; Browne-Wilkinson V-C).

Hotel International at Lancaster Gate, London, failed to prevent much larger hotel in Cromwell Road, London, from using the name 'London International Hotel', it being held that 'International' was descriptive (*Park Court Hotel Ltd* v *Trans-World Hotels Ltd* [1972] RPC 27: Ungoed-Thomas J).

'Miss Great Britain' beauty contest, although a fancy expression, not likely to be confused with 'Miss Britain' (*Morecambe and Heysham Corp* v *Mecca Ltd* [1966] RPC 423: Buckley J; see also *Miss World (Jersey) Ltd* v *James Street Productions Ltd* [1981] FSR 309: CA).

Nationwide Building Society not entitled to restrain name 'Nationwide' being used for estate agents having no goodwill at date of writ in that name for estate agency although since the issue of the writ, it had purchased a number of estate agents. Browne-Wilkinson J in refusing interlocutory relief considered it would give the plaintiffs an unfair advantage if defendants not allowed to use name to expand and plaintiff were allowed to do so (*Nationwide Building Society* v *Nationwide Estate Agents Ltd* [1987] FSR 579).

'Office Cleaning Association' held to be sufficiently different from 'Office Cleaning Services' (*Office Cleaning Services Ltd* v *Westminster Windows and General Cleaners Ltd* (1946) 63 RPC 39: HL, Lord Simonds' speech is the leading authority on this topic).

The Tape Recorder Centre, a mainly mail order business in electronic equipment, failed to stop the defendant wholesalers from using the words 'Tape Recorder Centre', the differences in the respective businesses being held sufficient (*Sypha Sound Sales Ltd* v *Tape Recorders (Electronics) Ltd* [1961] RPC 27: Buckley J).

'Vacuum Cleaner' was held to be descriptive of the type of goods which the respective parties were trading in rather than distinguishing the plaintiff's business (*British Vacuum Cleaner Co Ltd* v *New Vacuum Cleaner Co Ltd* (1907) 24 RPC 641: Parker J, plaintiff known as 'Vacuum Cleaner Coy').

3.2 Clubs, restaurants, shops

Injunction granted

Ad-Lib Club, injunction granted against defendant calling itself by that name in relation to a club reopening on the same premises where the plaintiff had been forced to close some five years earlier (*Ad-Lib Club Ltd* v *Granville* [1972] RPC 673: Pennycuick J).

Annabels Club able to restrain Annabel's Escort Agency (*Annabel's (Berkeley Square) Ltd* v *Schock* [1972] RPC 838: CA).

Cavendish House, a well known departmental store in Cheltenham, was able to restrain defendant from opening a retail furniture shop under the name 'Cavendish' only some 200 yards down the road (*Cavendish House (Cheltenham) Ltd* v *Cavendish-Woodhouse Ltd* [1970] RPC 234: CA, strong prima facie case, interim injunction granted even though some five to six months unexplained delay).

Chelsea Man menswear entitled to prevent use of name by defendants with regard to the name of their retail shops to be located within or adjacent to their well known Chelsea Girl shops; *Chelsea Man Menswear Ltd* v *Chelsea Girl Ltd* [1987] RPC 189 (CA).

Injunction refused

'Bravingtons' the jewellers failed to stop the defendant from trading under his Christian name 'Barrington' in connection with a jewellers shop at 452, Strand, London, close to one of plaintiff's shops—general get-up of shop considered but not established that people likely to believe it was a branch shop of Bravingtons (*Bravingtons Ltd* v *Barrington Tennant* [1957] RPC 183: Upjohn J, interlocutory injunction refused due in part to undue delay in taking action, the defendant's shop having been open for some four months).

Chicago Pizza Pie Factory restaurant in London failed to stop defendant using name 'LS Grunts Chicago Pizza Company' or any other name including the phrase 'Chicago Pizza' (*My Kinda Town Ltd* v *Soll* [1983] RPC 407: CA).

Crazy Horse Saloon (Paris) failed to stop Crazy Horse Saloon (London) due to absence of goodwill in UK—mere dissemination of advertising material not being sufficient (*Alain Bernadin et Cie* v *Pavilion Properties*

Ltd [1967] RPC 581 (Pennycuick J); cf *Maxims Ltd* v *Dye* [1977] FSR 364: Graham J).

Dorothy Perkins, retailers of ladies' garments, failed to obtain an interlocutory injunction stopping defendant opening a self-service store for young ladies in Manchester under the name 'Polly Perkins of Piccadilly'; the plaintiff had no shop in Manchester and the defendant's price range was substantially higher than the plaintiff's so it was not a case where plaintiff's goodwill would be injured (*Dorothy Perkins Ltd* v *Polly Perkins of Piccadilly Ltd* [1962] RPC 153: Cross J).

Fortnum & Mason plc v *Fortnum Ltd* [1994] FSR 438 (Harman J), defendants' wholesale import/export business of plastic goods from Far East not likely to be connected with well-known grocery business of plaintiff.

Furnitureland stores selling branded furniture could not prevent defendants using the name 'Furniture City' for similar business (*Furnitureland Ltd* v *Harris* [1989] FSR 536).

Harrods Ltd v *The Harrodian School Ltd,* 13 May 1994, unreported (Harman J), defendant prep school situated on site at Barnes once used by the Harrodian Club of the plaintiff. Held there was no likelihood of public believing the school was connected with the plaintiff.

'The Over Six Club' sufficiently different to 'The Under Six Club' (*Deane* v *Schofield* [1962] RPC 179: Plowman J).

3.3 Hotels

Injunction granted

The Berkeley Hotel able to stop a new hotel on the old site at Berkeley Street, London, being called Berkeley International (see p 124 above).

'The Clock' road house on the Welwyn By-Pass able to stop defendants using the name 'The Clock House Hotel' on their hotel premises on the Barnet By-Pass some five miles south of the plaintiff (*The Clock Ltd* v *The Clock House Hotel Ltd* (1936) 53 RPC 269: CA).

Pembridge Gardens Hotel able to restrain hotel opposite calling itself 'The Pembridge Hotel', the plaintiff being also known as 'The Pembridge' and 'The Pembridge Hotel' (see p 125 above).

Sheraton Hotels, a chain of hotels in the USA and other countries, able to restrain the defendant company from trading as 'Sheraton Motels Ltd'—dishonest choice of name (*Sheraton Corp of America* v *Sheraton Motels Ltd* [1964] RPC 202: Buckley J).

Injunction refused

'Hotel International', Lancaster Gate, London, failed to stop defendant using the name 'London International Hotel' for a much larger new hotel opposite the West London Air Terminal (see p 126 above).

3.4 Charitable and professional associations

A body, whether incorporated or unincorporated, may stop a person from falsely representing himself to be a member of that body by attaching a certain description or certain initials to himself. In *Society of Accountants and Auditors* v *Goodway* (1907) 24 RPC 159, Warrington J said 'the ultimate question as to the use of the term in question ['incorporated accountant'] is one of fact, namely, did the term, in the contemplation of that section of the public who had dealings with accountants prior to the acts complained of, denote that the person to whom it was applied was a member of the plaintiff society, and does it distinguish him from other persons in the same profession?' As regards injury to the society the judge held it was a matter of pecuniary value that it should have as many members as possible.

Injunction granted

Dr Barnardo's Homes able to restrain defendant from publishing novelettes as 'a Barnardo' publication (*Dr Barnardos Homes* v *Barnardo Amalgamated Industries Ltd* (1949) 66 RPC 103: Vaisey J).

The British Legion, formed as a voluntary association in 1921, later incorporated by Royal Charter held entitled to restrain a non-political social club from the use of 'British Legion' in its name (*British Legion* v *British Legion Club (Street) Ltd* (1931) 48 RPC 555: Farwell J).

The British Diabetic Association having both charitable status and a business arm for its publications, granted an injunction against use of the name The Diabetic Society (*The British Diabetic Association* v *The Diabetic Foundation*, unreported, 15 April 1992; (Lindsay QC sitting as a Deputy High Court judge).

The British Medical Association, registered as a company not for gain, entitled to prevent misuse by the defendant of the initials BMA or other conduct likely to show some connection with the BMA (*The British Medical Association* v *Marsh* (1931) 48 RPC 565: Maugham J approving of *Society of Accountants* v *Goodway*, see above).

Use of the initials FSAA restrained (*Society of Incorporated Accountants* v *Vincent* (1954) 71 RPC 325: Vaisey J, judgment in default).

'Incorporated accountant' restrained (*Society of Architects* v *Kendrick* (1910) 26 TLR 433: Joyce J).

'Merchant Service Guild' and initials MSG restrained (*Toms and Moore* v *Merchant Service Guild Ltd* (1908) 25 RPC 474: Neville J).

'Registered Osteotherapist' and initials MRO restrained (*General Council and Register of Osteopaths* v *Register of Osteotherapists and Naturopaths* (1968) 112 SJ 443: Pennycuick J, osteotherapist held meaningless and deception likely).

Injunction refused

Use of initials BP of the British Pharmacopeia, no evidence as to what the public would understand by such letters (*AG* v *Barrett Proprietaries Ltd* (1933) 50 RPC 45: Bennett J).

British Association of Aesthetic Plastic Surgery failed to prevent use of name the Association of Aesthetic Plastic Surgery (*British Association Aesthetic Plastic Surgeons* v *Cambright Ltd* [1987] RPC 549 Scott J).

Unauthorised use of initials MSA not restrained (*Society of Architects* v *Kendrick* (1910) 26 TLR 433: Joyce J stating 'if the decision in *Society of Accountants and Auditors* v *Goodway* (see p 129 above) were right, it certainly ought not to be extended').

National Canine Defence League failed to stop an ex-secretary of the League operating a rival organisation under the style 'World Dog Defence Campaign', the two names not being confusingly similar (*Workman and Persson* v *Johns* [1960] RPC 265: Russell J, leaving open whether the council of an unincorporated charitable association can sue for passing off).

Society of Motor Manufacturers of Traders, a trade protection society, failed to prevent an insurance company calling itself 'Motor Manufacturers' and Traders' Mutual Insurance Ltd', the words in common being descriptive and there being no charge of fraud (*Society of Motor Manufacturers and Traders Ltd* v *Motor Manufacturers' and Traders' Mutual Insurance Co Ltd* (1925) 42 RPC 307: CA).

Chapter 8

Other Misrepresentations as to Business or Products

1 Imitation of name of premises

It is well established that there can be no exclusive right to the name of a private house and thus no right to prevent an adjoining house from taking the same name although confusion may arise therefrom (*Day* v *Brownrigg* (1878) 10 Ch D 294: CA). Nor can one business restrain another from using a telegraphic address likely to be confused with its own if the two businesses are so different that there could be not misrepresentation caused thereby (*Street* v *Union Bank of Spain & England* (1885) 30 Ch D 156: Pearson J).

A trader may, however, protect the name of his premises in the same way he can protect his trade name.[1] Thus in *The Clock Ltd* v *The Clock House Hotel Ltd* (1936) 53 RPC 269 (CA) the plaintiff, whose road house with a clock was known as 'the Clock', was able to restrain a hotel about five miles away from calling itself 'Hotel Clock House', a prominent feature of which was a tower carrying a clock.

However, where the name of the premises have acquired a reputation, it is sometimes a difficult question as to whether the name remains with the premises (even on demolition with new premises on the old site) and thus whether a purchaser of the goodwill of the business can prevent the successors in title to the premises from using such name. In *J and W*

---

[1] *R & J Pullman Ltd* v *Pullman* (1919) 36 RPC 240 (Lawrence J, plaintiff deer leather producers, whose factory was known as 'Westbrook Mills' at Godalming, were entitled to a declaration that the defendant was not entitled to use the name 'Westbrook' in connection with his business of a deer leather merchant).

Nicholson & Co Ltd v *Buchanan*[2] the plaintiff had acquired the goodwill in the business of a gin distillery at Nos 25 and 26, Holborn, which displayed an effigy of a black swan outside the distillery and had become known as the 'Black Swan distillery'. The freehold of the distillery was sold to the defendant, a whisky distiller, who pulled down the old buildings and erected new buildings which were used as stores and a London office. The defendant placed the effigy of a black swan on the front and used as his address the 'Black Swan Distillery, 26, Holborn'. It was held that no dishonest motive on the part of the defendant had been established and that the risk of deception was too small to justify an injunction. However, in *Berkeley Hotel Co Ltd* v *Berkeley International (Mayfair) Ltd* [1972] RPC 237 (Pennycuick J) the plaintiff succeeded in preventing the defendant from using the name 'Berkeley International' on a new hotel being erected on the old site of the plaintiff's well known hotel 'The Berkeley' which was in the course of being rebuilt elsewhere.

Where the name is part of the structure of a building which is let or sold, (whether it is carved on the lintel or fixed on it in iron letters) whatever may be the predecessor's rights to prevent him from trading under the name, he cannot compel him to remove such name without a covenant to that effect. As Farwell J said in *Townsend* v *Jarman*[3] 'if a man chooses to sell a shop with his name carved thereon, and takes no covenant from the purchaser to alter the building in that respect I can see no equity whatever which will afterwards enable him to compel the purchaser to do so.'

Prima facie, it seems that in the case such as an hotel, a large part of the goodwill must remain with the building itself so that anyone acquiring the building may continue to use the name. Thus in *Mason* v *Queen* (1886) 23 SLR 641 (Court of Session) it was held that the purchaser of the goodwill of the 'Waverley' hotel who had moved the hotel to another part of the same town had not obtained an exclusive right to 'the use of a name which is not the name of a firm or of an individual but of a place where a business was carried on' and thus failed to prevent the old premises being re-let as a hotel and using the name 'Waverley'. In *Boussod, Valadon & Co* v *Marchant* (1908) 25 RPC 42 (CA) Fletcher Moulton LJ said:

---

[2] (1900) 19 RPC 321 (Stirling J). See also *Royal Insurance Co* v *Firehurst Ltd* (1984) unreported (Whitford J, The Cavern, Liverpool home of the Beatles, was demolished in 1973; the plaintiff who purchased the site and rebuilt it in 1983/84 failed to restrain the defendant from simultaneously using the name for a punk rock club opposite, the club having taken over the original Cavern members, and being variously called The New Cavern Club, The Revolution, Erics and at the time Brady's).

[3] (1900) 17 RPC 649; approved in *Boussod, Valadon & Co* v *Marchant* (1908) 25 RPC 42; CA, Goupil Galley).

in selling these premises, all such advantage for carrying on business as is due to the notoriety of the premises, under the name by which they are known, automatically passes, and is intended to pass to the purchasers. I can quite imagine that in many cases that is the most valuable part of a goodwill, and I do not think the Court should hold that a purchaser is in any way going beyond his rights if he exploits to the full, without misrepresentation, that which I might call the goodwill of the locality. Supposing, for instance, that the persons who owned the freehold of some noted restaurant, like the Café Royal in Regent Street, were to sell the building. Supposing they sold without a covenant that they would not set up business in a way which might interfere with the business of a restaurant carried on by the purchaser on those premises, the Court would hesitate to say that the purchaser might not still call it Café Royal, the name by which it was known, the name fixed up on the premises.

2   Franchisor's rights: character merchandising[4]

Without goodwill to protect, a person who franchises a well-known fictional character, whether as creator of the character or as producer of a TV series or other material by which the character has become known, will not be able to prevent someone else adopting that character for his own purposes. Thus in *Conan Doyle* v *London Mystery Magazine Ltd* (1949) 66 RPC 312 the executor of the late Sir Conan Doyle was unable to stop the defendants from stating 'The London Mystery Magazine, 221B, Baker Street NW1. Dear Reader, you will have noticed that we are writing to you from the address of the late Sherlock Holmes, Esq. . .', it being held by Wynn-Parry J that there was 'no right of property except the goodwill which is vested in the plaintiff . . . in the actual stories relating to "Sherlock Holmes" which Sir Arthur wrote in his lifetime'.

Equally instructive are two cases decided by Walton J within a week of each other. In *Wombles Ltd* v *Wombles Skips Ltd* [1977] RPC 99 the plaintiff who was a franchisor of the copyright material (for example pictorial representations) of the 'Wombles', being fictitious animals the subject of a TV series, failed to stop the defendant from using the name 'Wombles Skips' in connection with the leasing of rubbish skips, there being held to be no 'common field of activity'. In *Tavener Rutledge Ltd* v

---

4   See also Chapter 2, p 34.

Trexapalm Ltd[5] the plaintiff who had been selling lollipops for some months under the mark 'Kojakpops' was able to restrain the defendant, who was the exclusive licensee of the proprietors of the TV series, from selling lollipops under the mark 'Kojak lollies', it being held (against the defendant) that there was no property in a word or name per se and that it was not enough to show that the public would think that the plaintiff was licensed by the owners of the TV series. It would be necessary to go further and prove that the fact of quality control was so well known that the public would rely on the licence as a guarantee of the product's quality.

These cases should be contrasted with *Lego System AS* v *Lego M Lemelstrich Ltd* [1983] FSR 155 where Falconer J said, at 194, in respect of damage to the plaintiff's goodwill in the mark 'Lego', 'obviously, the possibility of licensing or franchising another trader to use 'Lego' in the gardening equipment area would be lost if the defendants are allowed to continue using 'Lego' in this country in relation to their products. The effect, therefore, of the defendants continuing to use 'Lego' in this country in relation to their products would be to destroy that part of the plaintiffs' reputation in their mark 'Lego' and goodwill attached to it which extends to such goods.' Also in *IPC Magazines Ltd* v *Black and White Music Corp* [1983] FSR 348, although refusing an interlocutory injunction (damages by way of a licence fee being adequate), Goulding J held that the unauthorised use of the plaintiff's cartoon character 'Judge Dredd' on a gramophone record was likely to cause people to wrongly believe that the plaintiff had endorsed the record, there being evidence that 'Judge Dredd' had a wide cult following and had been the subject of character merchandising agreements between the plaintiff and others.

In *Mirage Studios* v *Counter Feat Clothing Co Ltd* [1991] FSR 145 Browne-Wilkinson V-C granted interlocutory relief restraining the defendant from licensing manufacturers of T-shirts and other clothes to reproduce illustrations of cartoon characters called Teenage Mutant Ninja Turtles, which had been created in the USA by the first plaintiff and licensed in the UK by the second and third plaintiffs. Following the Australian case *Children's Television Workshop Inc* v *Woolworths (NSW) Ltd* [1981] RPC 187 as sound law, Browne-Wilkinson V-C held that there had been a misrepresentation by the reproduction of a famous cartoon or television character on unlicensed goods; namely that a substantial number of the public would expect such reproduction to be the result of a licence granted by the owner of the rights in that character. To market

---

[5]   [1977] RPC 275. See also *Lyngstad* v *Anabas* [1977] FSR 62 (Oliver J, where 'Abba' failed to obtain interlocutory relief against the defendant who was using the plaintiff's name and likenesses in connection with T-shirts and key rings).

goods which the public mistake for the genuine article necessarily involved a misrepresentation to the public that they were geniune.

However, there was no requirement that the public, in purchasing T-shirts carrying Turtle pictures would rely on such misrepresentation. The damage to the plaintiff resulted from the depreciation of the Turtle image being fixed to inferior foods, which might well reduce the value of the licensing rights. Brown-Wilkinson V-C went on to observe that 'I do not find anything in [*Lyngstad* v *Anabas Products Ltd* [1977] FSR 62] inconsistent with the Australian cases. Again, it was concerned with licensing rights in a name as opposed to licensing rights in what is undoubtedly copyright material. It may be that different factors apply in such a case, though those cases may, given the change in trading habits, require reconsideration on a future occasion if the evidence before the court is different.'

3 Appropriation to own business or products, testimonials, patents and prizes of a rival

A trader may not pass off his business or goods by applying to them testimonials or honours which have been awarded to a rival or falsely claim to work under a patent of a rival. Thus in *National Starch Manufacturing Co* v *Munn's Patent Maizena and Starch Co* (1894) 11 RPC 281 (PC) Maizena was a kind of cornflour manufactured by the plaintiff and a prize medal had been awarded to Maizena manufactured by the plaintiff at the International Exhibition in London in 1862. The defendant made and sold cornflour which the defendant called Maizena, claiming that it was a word descriptive of a certain preparation of cornflour, and on the defendant's wrappers pointed out that Maizena alone of all cornflours received a prize at that exhibition. Lord Asbourne at 294, giving the judgment of the Privy Council, said 'If "Maizena" in the Colony had come to denote a certain article simply, there would be nothing wrong in any one in the trade advertising that such and such prizes had been awarded to "Maizena", though the successful article was not of his own manufacture. But then the advertiser ought to make it perfectly clear that he claims no connection with the successful article beyond similarity in the process of manufacture and practical identity in the substance produced'. An undertaking in that case was given by the defendants to discontinue the objectionable statement. And in *Franks* v *Weaver* (1847) 10 Beav 297 (Langdale MR) the plaintiff invented and sold a medicine under his own name as 'Frank's Specific Solution of Copaiba.' The defendant also made and sold a similar medicine, and on his labels he used the plaintiff's name and certain certificates given by distinguished doctors as to the efficiency of the plaintiff's medicine in such an ingenious manner as, prima facie, though not in fact, to appropriate and apply them to his own medicine. It was held that although there were other differences in the method of selling, the proceeding was wrongful, and the defendant was restrained by injunction from 'using the name or testimonials of the plaintiff for the purpose of securing to himself an unjust advantage to which he has no title'. See also *Copydex Ltd* v *Noso Products Ltd* (1952) 69 RPC 38, where the defendant was restrained by Vaisey J from falsely advertising the defendant's goods 'as shown on television').

However, where there is no passing off, no injunction will be granted[6] even though untrue statements are made (unless made 'maliciously' and therefore subject to an action for injurious falsehood). See Chapter 1, p 11.

Similarly in *Lawrie* v *Baker* (1885) 2 RPC 213 the defendant was restrained by Day J from selling as 'patent' articles which were not patent, where the only patent article answering to the description was a patent article of the plaintiff's with the result that customers believed the defendant's article to be the plaintiff's. This case should be contrasted with *Ormond Engineering Co Ltd* v *Knopf* (1932) 49 RPC 634 where the defendant sold condenser dials, not manufactured or licensed by the plaintiff bearing the words 'Manufactured under Ormond Patent No 273,392'. It was held by Clauson J that assuming the words complained of were untrue, there was no evidence that the plaintiff was making or selling goods of the kind in question so no passing off and the action was dismissed.

4 Claim to be the original inventor when rival really is

The original inventor of a new manufacture and persons claiming under him are alone entitled to call their manufacture 'original'. If they have been in the habit of so calling it, an injunction will be granted to restrain another manufacturer from applying the word to his goods (*Cocks* v *Chandler*

---

[6] See, eg, *Tallerman* v *Dowsing* [1900] 1 Ch 1 (Stirling J, appraisal of plaintiff's hot air treatment for diseases contained in an article, used to promote defendant's rival system but admitted that no attempt had been made by the defendant to pass off his system as the plaintiff's, action failed); see also *Serville* v *Constance* (1954) 71 RPC 146 (Harman J, plaintiff although the true 'Welter-weight champion of Trinidad' could not prevent defendant masquerading as such in UK, plaintiff had no reputation here; query whether injurious falsehood would have succeeded); and *Morecambe and Heysham Corp* v *Mecca Ltd* [1966] RPC 423 (Buckley J, similarity of respective titles of beauty contests Miss Britain and Miss Great Britain could have been a ground for relief if confusion had been established).

(1871) LR 11 Eq 446: Romilly MR). So defendants have been restrained from calling their goods 'The Original Reading Sauce' and 'The Original Lazenby's Sauce' in two cases where the plaintiffs were successors to the business of the original makers (*Lazenby* v *White* (1871) 41 LJ Ch 354 n: LJJ).

5 Claim to be the authorised distributor

In *Sony* v *Saray Electronics (London) Ltd* [1983] FSR 302 at 307 Lawton LJ ordered the defendants to make clear to customers that they were not the authorised agents of the plaintiff and that if and when they sell equipment which has been modified other than by the plaintiff (Sony), that it is made clear that that is the fact. To enable such an order to be complied with it was ordered that the defendants should apply sticky labels to such effect. This case was followed in *Nistuka Coporation* v *Goodchild* [1990] FSR 371 (Knox J).

Similarly where, after the death of the inventor of a blister ointment, known as 'Lieut James's blister', the recipe for which was a valuable trade secret but not patented, his nephew discovered the secret and made and sold the ointment under the name of the original inventor in competition with the inventor's successors in business, describing his own as the only genuine ointment, it was held that he was entitled to make and sell it as Lieu. James's blister, but not to do anything calculated to make the public think that he was the original inventor or the successor of the inventor or to represent that his was the only genuine preparation (*James* v *James* (1872) LR 13 Eq 421: Romilly MR).

But if there is no evidence that by holding out his article as the 'original' a trader is likely to deceive the public into taking his goods for those which really are the original, the plaintiff cannot obtain an injunction on the grounds of passing off,[7] though he may do so on the ground of trade libel.[8]

---

[7] *Browne* v *Freeman* (1863) 12 WR 305; Wood V-C.
[8] *Browne* v *Freeman* [1873] WN 178: LJJ).

Chapter 9

Interlocutory Relief

1 Interlocutory injunctions

It is common for interlocutory injunctive relief to be sought when a passing off action is commenced, 'The very life of a trade-mark depends upon the promptitude with which it is vindicated'.[1]

1.1 Principles upon which relief is granted

The principles which the Court now follows in deciding whether or not to grant such relief are those set out by the House of Lords in *American Cyanamid Co v Ethicon Ltd*.[2] Earlier cases must be regarded with caution as different tests were formerly applied. The plaintiff must show an arguable case that passing off has occurred or is likely to occur, but it need not (subject to what is said below) be an overwhelming or strong one. There must be prospects of success which in substance and reality exist (*Mothercare v Robson Books* [1979] FSR 466: Megarry V-C). But where the Court finds for example that only 'a moron in a hurry' would be misled (so that the plaintiff has no real chance of success at trial), then it will not grant interlocutory relief.[3] It is for the plaintiff to adduce sufficient evidence at

---

[1] The headnote in *Johnston v Orr Ewing* (1882) 7 App Cas 219 (HL); a quotation from the decision of the Court of Appeal, but the sentence itself does not appear to have been used by any members of the House of Lords.

[2] [1975] RPC 513. See *Alfred Dunhill Ltd v Sunoptic SA* [1979] FSR 337 (CA) and *County Sound plc v Ocean Sound Ltd* [1991] FSR 367 (CA) where is has been held that the principles of *American Cyanamid* apply to passing off actions; cf *Newsweek v BBC* [1979] RPC 441 (CA); and *Athletes Foot Marketing Associates Inc v Cobra Sports* [1980] RPC 343 (Walton J), where *American Cyanamid* has been distinguished.

[3] *Morning Star Co-op Society v Express Newspapers Ltd* [1979] FSR 113 (Foster J). See also *Fisons v E J Godwin (Peat Industries)* [1976] RPC 653 (Brightman J); *Tetrosyl Ltd v Silver Paint & Lacquer Co Ltd* [1980] FSR 68 (CA); and *McCain International Ltd v Country Fair* [1981] RPC 69 (CA).

the interlocutory stage to demonstrate that he has at least an arguable case: where he cannot show a case on the materials put before the Court then relief will be refused (*Thrustcode Ltd* v *W W Computing Ltd* [1983] FSR 502: Megarry V-C, a copyright case).

1.2 Strength of case required where motion will determine proceedings

If an injunction is granted, this will usually have the effect of causing the defendant to change his trading style of which complaint is made. Once this is done, he will begin to acquire goodwill in any new trading style which he adopts, and once this stage is reached, a defendant seldom finds it worthwhile to continue to contest the action. Similarly, a plaintiff who has succeeded in forcing such a change seldom considers it worthwhile to pursue the action for the sake of damages alone (for if the application for interlocutory relief was heard and brought promptly, the actual damages involved are unlikely to be great). Thus it is that settlement is usually achieved once an interlocutory hearing has taken place.

In *NWL Ltd* v *Woods* [1979] 1 WLR 1294 (HL), a trade dispute case, Lord Diplock said, at 1307:

> Where, however, the grant or refusal of the interlocutory injunction will have the practical effect of putting an end to the action because the harm that will have been already caused to the losing party by its grant or refusal is complete and of a kind for which money cannot constitute any worthwhile recompense, the degree of likelihood that the plaintiff would have succeeded in establishing his right to an injunction if the action had gone to trial, is a factor to be brought into the balance by the judge in weighing the risks that injustice may result from his deciding the application one way rather than the other.

although he was at pains there to point out (at 1306 F–G) that such cases were exceptional.

In *Elan Digital System Ltd* v *Elan Computers Ltd* [1984] FSR 373 at 386 (CA), Lord Donaldson said that the effect of an interlocutory injunction on a defendant adopting a different name is a factor to be taken into account.

Thus, the Court generally is more circumspect in granting an interlocutory injunction in a passing off action where it appears that this would in effect determine the outcome of the proceedings. In such circumstances the plaintiff must do somewhat better than establish merely an arguable case (*Parnass/Pelly Ltd* v *Hodges* [1982] FSR 329 (Whitford J); *Athletes Foot Marketing Associates Inc* v *Cobra Sports* [1980] RPC 343: Walton J; *Boots* v *APS Ltd* [1988] FSR 45: CA). Thus, the Court has of late been prepared to consider the merits of the plaintiff's case more robustly in concluding that no arguable case was disclosed.[4] The relevance at the interlocutory stage of the strength of the party's cases is further discussed below.

1.3 Damages an adequate remedy

Once the hurdle of showing that there is an arguable case has been overcome, the Court must then establish (1) whether damages are adequate compensation to the plaintiff assuming he were successful at the trial or whether pending the trial he is likely to suffer irreparable loss or injury; and (2) whether the defendant, if he were successful at the trial and therefore wrongly injuncted, would be adequately compensated by damages in the form of the cross-undertaking given by the plaintiff. If the answer to both these questions is in the negative the Court will then consider whether the 'balance of convenience' is in favour of the grant of interlocutory relief or not. Generally in passing off cases damages will *not* provide adequate compensation to the plaintiff, damage to goodwill being notoriously difficult to quantify.[5] However, where the only real damage is likely to be a loss of sales, such damage will be quantifiable and relief will be refused (see, eg, *John Wyett* v *M & A Pharmacen* [1988] FSR 26: Whitford J; *Boots* v *APS* [1988] FSR 45: CA). Simliarly, where the plaintiff is a franchisor and is in the habit of granting licences, damage will generally be quantifiable even where a licence has been refused to the particular defendant.[6] The terms of settlement with earlier infringers may also be material in establishing whether or not a plaintiff may suffer irreparable damage pending trial.[7]

Furthermore there must be a real prospect that damage to the plaintiff's goodwill is likely to result, mere possibility of confusion not being sufficient (*John Hayter Motor Underwriting Agencies Ltd* v *RBHS Agencies Ltd* [1977] FSR 285: CA; *British Association of Aesthetic Plastic Surgeons* v *Cambright Ltd* [1987] RPC 549: Scott J). Where the goods involved are pharmaceutical products supplied only on prescription, there may be

---

[4] See, eg, *Rizla* v *Bryant & May* [1986] RPC 389: Walton J; *Mothercare* v *Penguin* [1988] RPC 113: CA; *Solaglas* v *Bridgewater* (unreported) CA, 27 July 1988; *Management Publications Ltd* v *Blenheim Exhibitions Group* [1991] FSR 348 (Hoffman J) at 550 (CA).

[5] See, eg, *Sodastream* v *Thorn Cascade* [1982] RPC 459 at 471, lines 3–4: CA.

[6] *IPC Magazines* v *Black and White Music Corp* [1983] FSR 348 (Goulding J); cf *Mirage Studios* v *Counter Feat Clothing Co Ltd* [1991] FSR 145, where applied to inferior goods.

[7] *Smith Kline & French* v *Higson* [1988] FSR 115, a trade mark case. Cf *Reckitt & Coleman* v *Borden* [1987] FSR 278.

particular difficulties in showing damage for which monetary compensation would be inadequate.[8]

To establish that the plaintiff is good for the cross-undertaking, evidence of the plaintiff's financial standing should be adduced in chief so that the defendant has an opportunity to challenge it (*Brigid Foley Ltd* v *Ellott* [1982] RPC 433; Megarry V-C). In the case of a foreign plaintiff with no assets in the UK, or an impecunious plaintiff, some form of security such as a bank guarantee may be an acceptable method of providing the cross-undertaking as to damages. The cross-undertaking is given to the Court and is not a matter of contract between the parties.[9]

In the case of an impecunious defendant the Court will consider an offer to keep accounts of sales and/or to provide some form of security, for example by payment of a notional royalty into a joint account of the parties' solicitors or some kind of bank guarantee.[10]

Some heads of damage to the defendant will be quantifiable, in particular, the cost of reprinting, eg, labels or stationery if the injunction causes him to change his trading name or style. However, if the effect of the injunction would be to cause a major disruption to his business or shut him out of a potential market altogether, then it may not be possible after trial to predict what his level of business would have been and thus what profits he has lost.

1.4 Balance of convenience

Often in passing off cases the balance of convenience will lie in favour of the plaintiff, for if the action is properly brought he will ex hypothesi have an established goodwill, while if the interlocutory proceedings are brought swiftly then the defendant will not. Thus harm to the defendant if an injunction is granted may simply be confined to the reprinting of, say, labels or stationery, and therefore be quantifiable.

However, each case must depend on its own facts—in particular upon the nature and scale of the respective businesses of the parties and the likelihood of unquantifiable damage by reason of the likelihood of deception. Thus where there was only a possible risk of damage to the plaintiff if relief was refused, but a certainty of damage to the defendant if it was granted, an interlocutory injunction was refused (*John*

---

[8] *Boots* v *APS* [1988] FSR 45; see also *SKF* v *Higson* (above), a trade mark case.
[9] *Fletcher Sutcliff Wild* v *Burch* [1982] FSR 64: Powell J, NSW).
[10] See, eg, *Coco* v *A N Clarke (Engineers) Ltd* [1969] RPC 41; and *Vernon & Co (Pulp Products Ltd)* v *Universal Pulp Containers Ltd* [1980] FSR 179 (Megarry V-C), a copyright case.

Walker & Sons Ltd v *Rothmans International Ltd* [1978] FSR 357: Brightman J).[11]

A question arises as to how far the court should determine the likelihood of confusion that will occur pending the hearing of the trial in assessing the unquantifiable loss to the plaintiff. In *Blazer plc* v *Yardley & Company Ltd* [1992] FSR 501 Aldous J distinguished his earlier judgment in *The Financial Times Ltd* v *Evening Standard Co Ltd* [1991] FSR 8. In the earlier case he stated that 'if the risk of persons being misled . . . is small, then the risk of any substantial damage pending the hearing of the motion must also be small'. In the later case Aldous J stated '. . . it is not the right approach when it entails a "not-so-mini" trial on affidavit evidence of an issue of fact which is in dispute. In this case I believe the correct approach is to accept that there is a serious issue to be tried and to go on and apply *American Cyanamid* principles without resolving what is the likelihood of deception'.

Where the defendant's goods are of poorer quality than the plaintiff's and confusion between the two may lead the public to believe that the plaintiff has lowered his standards, this may be very material. But the fact that the defendant's goods are of equal or even superior quality may not assist him, and it affords no defence in the action. Where, as a result of the grant or refusal of relief, one party is likely to lose business not just in the goods the subject of the action but in other goods, because customers place multiple orders with a single source, this will affect the balance.

Where the defendant has acted with his eyes open and ought to have realised that the plaintiff would object, this fact may be relevant to the balance of convenience (*Hymac* v *Priestman Bros* [1978] RPC 495: Walton J).

Where the act of passing off complained of is an alleged misrepresentation in the nature of an injurious falsehood or libel and if the defendant states an intention to justify the same at trial in deciding whether to refuse interlocutory relief, the test to be applied is whether a jury could reasonably conclude that the statement in issue was true. In other words, is there a serious issue to be tried as to whether the alleged falsehood is true (see *Compaq Computer* v *Dell Computer* [1992] FSR at 93 98 and 100 (Aldous J)). In such a case the court considers that the value of freedom of speech is such that it will not generally interfere and stifle any statement

---

[11] See also *Management Publications Ltd* v *Blenheim Exhibitions Group plc* [1991] FSR 348 (Hoffmann J) affirmed at 550 (CA).

that it has no means of knowing whether it can be justified or not (see *Microdata* v *Rivendale* (CA), 11 September 1984, unreported).[12]

It is sometimes argued by the plaintiff that if an injunction is refused, other infringers may be encouraged to enter the market causing further damage (the 'snowball effect'). However, this argument has not generally found favour, at least in the absence of convincing evidence of such effect.[13]

It should be remembered that in a passing off action, it is the injury to the goodwill that matters, and not the precise mode in which the injury is inflicted (*BBC* v *Talbot Motor Co Ltd* [1981] FSR 228: Megarry V-C). Thus if a likelihood of injury pending trial can be shown, it should be taken into account when considering the balance of convenience irrespective of the manner in which this injury may be caused.

1.5 Status quo

Where other factors appear to be evenly balanced, then the Court will take such measures as will preserve the status quo (*American Cyanamid Co* v *Ethicon Ltd* [1975] RPC 513 at 542 (HL) line 3 et seq). The question arises whether this is to be tested at the time when the cause of action arose, when the writ was issued, when the motion is heard, or what other time.

In *Garden Cottage Ltd* v *Milk Marketing Board* (1984) AC 130 at 140 Lord Diplock stated, albeit obiter, that the status quo is the state of affairs existing during the period immediately preceding the issue of the writ or if there be unreasonable delay between the issue of the writ and the motion for an interlocutory injunction, the period immediately preceding the motion.

In *Alfred Dunhill Ltd* v *Sunoptic SA* [1979] FSR 337 at 376 (CA) Megaw LJ suggested that 'the relevant point of time for purposes of the status quo may very well vary in different cases'. In *Metric Resources Corp* v *Leasemetrix Ltd* [1979] FSR 571 Megarry V-C explained, at 582, that the term 'status quo' is an abbreviation for 'status quo ante bellum'. He said (obiter):

> If the metaphor is pursued, then it may well be that the true status quo ante bellum is the state of affairs which existed immediately

---

12 See also *Alastair Sim* v *H J Heinz Co Ltd* [1959] RPC 75 (CA), *Lord Brabourne* v *Hough* [1981] FSR 79 (Slade J), *Consorzio del Proscuitto di Parma* v *Marks & Spencer* [1990] FSR 530 at 536–538 (Morritt J), and *Ciba-Geigy* v *Parke Davis* [1994] FSR 8 at 21 (Aldous J).

13 See, eg, *Reckitt & Coleman* v *Borden* [1987] FSR 228; *John Wyett* v *MCA Pharmaceuticals* [1988] RPC 26; *Boots* v *APS* [1988] FSR 45; Cf *EAR Corp* v *Protector Safety Products* [1980] FSR 574 (Graham J, a patent case) at 578–9.

before the act which constitutes the casus belli, unless hostilities are delayed so long that the act becomes part of the status quo. I would, I think, regard the act of the defendants in commencing business under a name closely resembling that used by the plaintiff company as constituting the casus belli, and the status quo to be preserved (since the plaintiff company moved so promptly) as being the state that existed immediately before the defendants began business in this way.[14]

Judging the state of affairs at such a date may be compared with the test that the date for determining whether a plaintiff has established the necessary goodwill or reputation to be able to sue is the date of the conduct complained of (*Elida Gibbs Ltd* v *Colgate-Palmolive Ltd* [1983] FSR 95 (Goulding J); following *Cadbury-Schweppes Pty Ltd* v *The Pub Squash Co Ltd* [1981] RPC 429: PC).

1.6 Relevance of respective strength of parties' cases

Where all other factors appear to be evenly balanced then the Court may be justified in also taking into consideration any views which it may have formed as to the relative merits of the parties' cases. In *American Cyanamid* [1975] RPC 513 at 542 lines 19 et seq, Lord Diplock said:

> if the extent of the uncompensatable disadvantage to each party would not differ widely, it may not be improper to take into account in tipping the balance the relative strength of each party's case as revealed by the affidavit evidence adduced on the hearing of the application. This, however, should be done only where it is apparent on the facts disclosed by evidence as to which there is no credible dispute that the strength of one party's case is disproportionate to that of the other party. The court is not justified in embarking upon anything resembling a trial of the action upon conflicting affidavits in order to evaluate the strength of either party's case.

The phrase 'balance of the risk of doing an injustice' has been used in place of 'balance of convenience' (*Cayne* v *Bank*, unreported, 25 August 1982 (CA); cited by Megarry V-C in *Thrustcode Ltd* v *W W Computing Ltd* [1983] FSR 502 at 508).

The *American Cyanamid* decision is to be read as setting out guidelines, and is not to be applied rigidly in the manner of a statute; justice, as best it can be administered between the parties prior to a formal trial, is the

---

[14] See also *J C Penney Co Inc* v *Penney's Ltd* [1975] FSR 367 (CA); *John Walker & Sons Ltd* v *Rothmans International Ltd* [1978] FSR 357.

ultimate aim. But it should be borne in mind that, as Lord Diplock said in *American Cyanamid* itself at [1975] RPC 541:

> It is no part of the court's function at this stage of the litigation to try to resolve conflicts of evidence on affidavit as to facts on which the claims of either party may ultimately depend nor to decide difficult questions of law which call for detailed argument and mature considerations. These are matters to be dealt with at the trial. One of the reasons for the introduction of the practice of requiring an undertaking as to damages upon the grant of an interlocutory injunction was that 'it aided the court in doing that which was its great object, viz abstaining from expressing any opinion upon the merits of the case until the hearing.

Thus where the facts were clear and undisputed, and unlikely to alter at trial, the Court will give weight to what it considered the prospects of ultimate success (*Office Overload Ltd* v *Gunn* [1977] FSR 39: CA; *Newsweek* v *BBC* [1979] RPC 441: CA; *Athletes Foot Marketing Associates Inc* v *Cobra Sports* [1980] RPC 343: Walton J; *BBC* v *Talbot Motor Co* [1981] FSR 228: Megarry V-C); *Mothercare* v *Penguin* [1988] RPC 113 (CA); *Solaglas v Bridgewater*, unreported, 25 July 1988 (CA).

1.7 Delay

Delay in bringing an application for interlocutory relief will usually be fatal, on two grounds. First, if it is culpable in the sense that the plaintiff delayed after knowing of the defendant's conduct complained of, equity will not grant relief. But even if he was unaware of that conduct, the delay may have permitted the defendant to establish a trade and a goodwill of his own, and if this was innocently done then it may be enough to tip the balance of convenience in his favour and establish the status quo as being a position in which the defendant is on the market. In *Cavendish House (Cheltenham) Ltd* v *Cavendish-Woodhouse Ltd* [1968] RPC 448 (Stamp J) there was a delay of nine months in bringing the proceedings, at least four months of which was not satisfactorily explained, but a very strong prima facie case of passing off was found. The Court balanced the delay against the prospects of success and granted relief. See also *Great American Success Co* v *Kattaineh* [1976] FSR 554 (Slade J), in which there was five months' delay while ascertaining the defendant's identity.

1.8 Form of relief

Where an injunction is granted, it should specify as nearly as possible the precise conduct of the defendant which is forbidden[15] so that the injunction can be enforced if necessary, and so that any inquiry on the plaintiff's cross-undertaking in damages can readily be taken. It is generally undesirable to restrain the defendant at the interlocutory stage from 'passing off by' doing some particular act, for at any hearing to enforce the injunction it will be necessary to determine whether the conduct complained of did in fact constitute passing off, and this before the trial of the action. However, the Court can and will determine such matters when necessary (see, eg *Chanel Ltd* v *FGM Cosmetics* [1981] FSR 471, at 476 (Whitford J)). It is usual, where the action concerns a name or mark, to restrain the defendant from using the name or mark complained of or any other name or mark 'the same as or substantially similar to' the plaintiff's mark; the Court will not assist by indicating to the defendant how he may circumvent the order. See *Parker-Knoll Ltd* v *Knoll International Ltd* [1962] RPC 243 at 261 (HL); see also Chapter 10, footnote 45.

However, the broader the injunction which is sought, the more reluctant the Court may be to grant it. Where an injunction was sought to restrain the use of the colour blue in relation to tubs of baby products (but was refused), Walton J observed that blues can range from almost milky white to indigo and had an injunction been granted, some method of defining the forbidden range of blues would have had to be devised (*Scott* v *Nice Pak Products* [1988] FSR 125 at 137).

Where the defendant was restrained from using a converted or modified version of the plaintiff's car, the injunction was modified to permit him to use the car for purely domestic purposes (*Rolls-Royce Motors Ltd* v *Zanelli* [1979] RPC 148 (CA); cf *Rolls-Royce Motors Ltd* v *Dodd* [1981] FSR 517: (Whitford J)).

2 Disclosure of names of suppliers and customers

The Court has power to order a defendant who is a 'middleman' or otherwise tortiously mixed up in the torts of others to disclose to the plaintiff the names of his suppliers, and in appropriate circumstances this can be ordered at an interlocutory stage.[16] Discovery of the names of *customers*, however, is less often granted at an interlocutory stage because such early discovery will not normally assist a plaintiff to advance his case

---

[15] *Biro Swan Ltd* v *Tallon Ltd* [1961] RPC 326 (Russell J).

[16] *RCA Corp of America* v *Reddington's Rare Records* [1975] RPC 95 (Goff J); see also *EMI Ltd* v *Sarwar* [1977] FSR 146 (CA) where it was part of an Anton Piller order.

or safeguard his interests, and is likely to prejudice the defendant[17] but it may later become relevant if any inquiry as to damages is ordered.

Even where no independent cause of action exists against a person, that person can be ordered to disclose the names of tortfeasors known to him if he has in some way become mixed up in their torts, albeit innocently, and through no fault of his own. In *Norwich Pharmacal Co* v *Commissioners of Customs and Excise* [1974] RPC 101 (HL), the plaintiff sought the identity of persons who had imported a chemical alleged to infringe the plaintiff's patent; the Commissioners had published statistics which revealed infringing importation but declined to disclose the names of the importers, which they knew. Lord Reid said:

> if through no fault of his own a person gets mixed up in the tortious acts of others so as to facilitate their wrongdoing he may incur no personal liability but he comes under a duty to assist the person who has been wronged by giving him full information and disclosing the identity of the wrongdoers. I do not think that it matters whether he became so mixed up by voluntary action on his part or because it was his duty to do what he did. It may be that if this causes him expense the person seeking the information ought to reimburse him. But justice requires that he should co-operate in righting the wrong if he unwittingly facilitated its perpetration.

In a subsequent action against one of the infringing importers whose name was disclosed as a result of that judgment, the costs of bringing the 'discovery' action were held to be forseeable and reasonably incurred, and thus recoverable from that defendant (*Morton-Norwich Products Inc* v *Intercen* [1981] FSR 337).

3   Ex parte relief

It is normal when seeking interlocutory relief to give notice to a defendant by serving proceedings together with a notice of motion in the usual way (RSC Ord 8, r 2). However, the Court will entertain an application for ex parte relief, that is relief without notice to the other side, in appropriate circumstances. These may be, first, in a case of real urgency, such as for example where the defendant is about to launch his product at an important exhibition or by major advertising, and real and immediate

---

[17] *Harry Freedman* v *Hillingdon Shirts Co Ltd* [1975] FSR 449 (Walton J suggested that a defendant resisting such disclosure would be wise to put in evidence that he could satisfy an award of damages at trial); *Sega Enterprises Ltd* v *Alca Electronics* [1982] FSR 516 (CA).

harm to the plaintiff's goodwill is apprehended; secondly, where it is feared that the defendant may conceal or destroy evidence of his torts or of their extent should any notice of the plaintiff's complaint be given; and thirdly, where the defendant may remove his assets from the jurisdiction in order to avoid satisfying any judgment given against him. In the first case an ordinary injunction may be given over a short period; in the second the form of order which has come to be known as the Anton Piller order is appropriate; and in the third case a 'Mareva' injunction would be suitable.

The Court will not grant an ex parte injunction save where there is a real prospect of substantial damage being caused to the applicant over the period in which notice of motion would usually be given. Any party affected may apply to set it aside (RSC Ord 8, r 2(1)). Such an injunction will often form part of an Anton Piller order so as to prevent the defendant from disposing of any stock pending a proper inter partes hearing. It is of particular importance that full disclosure of all material facts be made to the Court on such an application and failure to do so may result in the order being set aside without further consideration of its merits (*Thermax v Schott Industrial Glass* [1981] FSR 289: Browne-Wilkinson J; cf *Gallery Cosmetics* v *Number 1* [1981] FSR 556: Nourse J; and *Yardley & Co Ltd* v *Higson* [1984] FSR 304 CA)) and *Hoechst UK Ltd* v *Chemiculture Ltd* [1993] FSR 270, Morritt J.

In *Naf Naf SA* v *Dickens (London) Ltd* [1993] FSR 424 Hoffmann J held, in discharging the ex parte order, that whilst evidence obtained as a result of an improperly obtained Anton Piller order was admissible evidence, there was jurisdiction to order the plaintiffs not to make use of such evidence and he so ordered in that case.

3.1 Anton Piller orders[18]

This form of order, named after the action *Anton Piller KG* v *Manufacturing Processes Ltd* [1976] RPC 719 (CA) in which its form was first fully considered, consists in its normal form of a mandatory injunction requiring the defendant to permit the plaintiff's representatives to enter premises[19] for the purpose of searching for and removing infringing material and evidence of dealings in such material. Such an order will only be made if there are real grounds for believing that the defendant is likely to conceal or destroy such matter if given notice of proceedings against him, and thus the order will invariably be made in

---

[18] See White Book 1993, Ord 29, r 2, footnotes 29/2–3/6 et seq.
[19] Which should be specified: *Protector Alarms Ltd* v *Maxim Alarms Ltd* [1978] FSR 422 (Goulding J).

camera. As well as showing such grounds, the plaintiff must make out a very strong prima facie case that an infringement of his rights has taken place, and that the potential damage to him is very serious.[20] Because the order is obtained ex parte, full and frank disclosure of all relevant facts to the plaintiff must be given in the affidavits in support. Relevance is a matter for the judge not the plaintiff's solicitors, and in cases of doubt the affidavits should err on the side of excessive disclosure.[21]

The order is a draconian one, and thus requirements will be imposed for the defendant's protection. It is the duty of counsel for the plaintiffs to ensure (usually by putting a draft minute of order before the judge) that the order sought contains all proper safeguards.[22] Under the Practice Direction (Ex parte Mareva injunctions and Anton Piller orders) dated 28 July 1994,[23] guidelines have now been laid down which provide standard forms for such orders. The order must be drawn so as to extend no further than the minimum extent necessary to serve its purpose.[24] The order should be served on the defendant by an experienced solicitor, together with the evidence relied upon in support.[25] In *Universal Thermosensors Ltd v Hibben* [1992] FSR 361 at 387 Nicholls V-C has indicated that judges in the future should give serious consideration to the desirability of ensuring that the order should be served and its execution supervised by a solicitor other than a member of the firm of solicitors acting for the plaintiff and that such solicitor should be an experienced solicitor having some familiarity with Anton Piller orders. Under the Practice Direction if the judge does not think it appropriate for the order to be served, by a supervising solicitor his reasons should be expressed in the order itself. Nicholls V-C also stated that the solicitor should prepare a written report on what occurred when the order was executed and that a copy of the report should be served on the defendant. Also, such report should be presented to the Court at the inter partes hearing following execution. An opportunity should be afforded to the defendant to consider the order and to take legal advice before complying and the order must permit the defendant to apply to the Court to discharge.[26] In order for such opportunity to be of use the order should normally be served only on

---

[20] See per Ormrod LJ at [1976] RPC 726.
[21] *CBS* v *Robinson* [1986] FSR 367. See also *Guess? Inc* v *Lee Seck Mon* [1987] FSR 125.
[22] *Booker McConnell* v *Plascow* [1985] RPC 425 at 442 (CA).
[23] See *The Times*, 2 August 1994.
[24] *CBS* v *Robinson* (supra).
[25] See *International Electronics Ltd* v *Weigh Data Ltd* [1980] FSR 423 at 427 (Graham J).
[26] Per Lord Denning at [1976] RPC 725.

working days in office hours and if it is to be executed at a private house only when a solicitor can be expected to be available. In the case of service on a woman, the solicitor serving the order must be accompanied by a woman.[27] The solicitor will be required to undertake to explain the meaning of the order in simple language, and to specifically advise the defendant of his right to take legal advice before complying. A detailed list of the material taken should always be made by the solicitor before it is removed, and the defendant should be given an opportunity to check the list at the time of removal. No material should be taken unless it is clearly covered by the terms of the order. The plaintiff's solicitors will be required to keep safe any articles or documents removed when the order is executed. Once copies have been taken, the material should be returned to its owner; where ownership is in dispute, it should be handed over to the defendants' solicitors on their undertaking for its safe custody and production.[28] A cross-undertaking in damages from the plaintiff will be necessary. If the defendant refuses to permit access, then force cannot be used but he will be in contempt[29] unless the order is set aside.[30] As Lord Denning said in the *Anton Piller* case itself at [1976] RPC 724:

> But the order sought in this case is not a search warrant. It does not authorise the plaintiffs' solicitors or anyone else to enter the defendant's premises against his will. It does not authorise the breaking down of any doors, nor the slipping in by a back door, nor getting in by an open door or window. It only authorises entry and inspection by the permission of the defendants. The plaintiffs must get the defendant's permission. But it does do this: It brings pressure on the defendants to give permission. It does more. It actually orders him to give permission—with, I suppose, the result that if he does not give permission, he is guilty of contempt of court.

An Anton Piller order will usually require that the defendant confirm on oath within a short period after service that he has complied with its terms. It can be coupled with an order for discovery of the names of suppliers,[31] with a Mareva injunction,[32] an order that the defendant does not disclose the existence of the proceedings against him to anybody other than his

---

[27] *Universal Thermosensors Ltd* v *Hibben* [1992] FSR 361, 386 (Nicholls V-C).
[28] *CBS* v *Robinson* [1986] FSR 367.
[29] *Chanel Ltd* v *3 Pears Wholesale Cash and Carry Co* [1979] FSR 393 (Walton J).
[30] *Hallmark Cards Inc* v *Image Arts Ltd* [1977] FSR 150 (CA).
[31] *EMI Ltd* v *Sarwar* [1977] FSR 146 (CA).
[32] *Johnson* v *L & A Philatelics* [1981] FSR 286 (Robert Goff J), where the order is set out.

legal advisers,[33] and even with an order that the defendant discloses all his assets and delivers up certain of them to the plaintiff's solicitors.[34] When suppliers' names are disclosed it is legitimate to rely upon such disclosure for the purpose of bringing new actions, or criminal proceedings, against the suppliers or other wrongdoers involved in the handling of the offending goods (*Sony Corp v RS Anand* [1981] FSR 398: Browne-Wilkinson J).[35] Templeman LJ said in *Sega Enterprises Ltd v Alca Electronics* [1982] FSR 516 at 525:

> discovery is frequently included in *Anton Piller* orders which are made against record pirates. The order for discovery in those cases is made because there is a well-founded fear that unless the record pirate against whom proceedings are brought is obliged to disclose the names of his suppliers and customers as soon as he is served with an *ex parte* injunction and is injuncted to keep silent, he will be able to warn his suppliers and customers who are reasonably suspected to be record pirates themselves, and they will immediately disperse and get rid of the infringing copies in their possession, so that the plaintiff will not be able to obtain an effective remedy against them. It is necessary to make an order which enables the plaintiff at once to discover and to proceed against the companions in tort of the defendant against whom an *Anton Piller* order is made.

But he (and the other members of the Court of Appeal) went on to warn that such orders should be regarded with great caution, and should not be granted unless the Court is reasonably satisfied that the plaintiff will, or probably will, suffer irreparable damage if there is any delay in ordering discovery. They should only be made in special circumstances and not as a matter of course.

The remedy is an effective one in dealing with piracy. As Graham J said in *International Electronics Ltd v Weigh Data Ltd* [1980] FSR 423 at 426:

> I would in this connection like to confirm as a Patent Judge that justice in many industrial property cases, such as those involving patents, trade marks, copyright and confidential information, can often only satisfactorily be dispensed if, as the Master of the Rolls

---

[33] See, eg, *Chanel Ltd v 3 Pears Wholesale Cash and Carry Co* [1979] FSR 393 (Walton J); *Universal Thermosensors v Hibben* [1992] FSR at 387 (Nicholls V-C), one week for too long.

[34] *CBS UK Ltd v Lambert* [1983] FSR 127 (CA), where the defendant was deliberately conducting his lifestyle in a manner calculated to prevent judgments against him from being effectively enforced.

[35] See also *Power v S & J Perfume* [1987] FSR 159 and *Naf Naf SA v Dickens (London) Ltd* [1993] FSR 424 (Hoffmann J)

urged in the *Rank* case, *Anton Piller* orders are made. There are many unscrupulous pirates in these fields and *Anton Piller* orders or something equivalent are necessary to prevent offending parties disposing of vital evidence before normal discovery is obtained. Such orders must of course be granted with great care, and hedged with all proper restrictions so as to avoid oppression. They have however in my experience worked well in practice and I have no knowledge of any oppressions having been caused.

The privilege against self-incrimination, which the House of Lords held in *Rank Film Distributors Ltd* v *Video Information Centre* [1981] FSR 363 would protect a defendant served with an Anton Piller order from having to produce documents or answer interrogatories which might tend to expose him to criminal proceedings, has now been curtailed by statute. Section 72 of the Supreme Court Act 1981 removes the privilege from answering any question put in, or complying with any order in, inter alia, proceedings in the High Court for infringement of rights pertaining to any intellectual property or for passing off.

A defendant served with such an order who believes that it has been improperly made may apply to have it discharged, as will usually be expressly provided on the face of the order. The fact that the order has already been executed is no reason for not discharging it.[36] An application to discharge, rather than an appeal to the Court of Appeal, should be made in the first instance.[37] However, where the order has already been fully executed, the application may be adjourned to be heard at the trial of the action.[38] Where a defendant succeeded in having an Anton Piller order set aside on the grounds that the evidence disclosed no cause of action against them, the plaintiff was ordered to pay the defendant's costs on a higher scale (*AB* v *CDE* [1982] RPC 509 (Lord Hooson QC)). Where the order was oppressively executed in flagrant disregard of the defendant's rights, £10,000 was awarded under the cross-undertaking by any of the compensatory and aggravated damages (*Columbia Pictures* v *Robinson* [1986] FSR 367 (Scott J)). The order may in particular be set aside where the plaintiff failed to disclose material facts to the court on the plaintiff's application—see p 148 above. Where the order was set aside on the grounds of serious non-disclosure, the Court exercised its discretion to exclude further evidence obtained as a result of execution of the order.[39]

---

[36] *Booker McConnell* v *Plascow* [1985] RPC 425 at 442.
[37] *WEA Records* v *Visions Channel 4* [1983] 1 WLR 721.
[38] *Booker McConnell* v *Plascow* (supra) at 443.
[39] *Guess* v *Lee Seck Mon* [1987] FSR 125 (CA, Hong Kong); but cf *WEA Records* (above).

Further, even where no application to set aside the order is made, if it subsequently emerges that sufficient grounds for seeking the order were not available then the plaintiff may be refused the costs of the order. Thus in *Systematica Ltd* v *London Computer Centre Ltd* [1983] FSR 313 (Whitford J), although at the inter partes hearing the Court was satisfied that grounds for seeking a simple ex parte injunction had been available, but not grounds for the more far-reaching Anton Piller relief which was actually obtained, that part of the costs of the interlocutory proceedings was refused.

3.2 Mareva injunctions[40]

Where the defendant has assets within the jurisdiction but there are grounds for fearing that these might either be removed from the jurisdiction or disposed of within the jurisdiction before a judgment can be entered and enforced, the Court has power to grant an interlocutory injunction restraining the dealing with those assets (*Mareva Compania Naviera SA* v *International Bulk Carriers SA* [1980] 1 All ER 213 (CA); see also *Ninemia Maritime Corp* v *Trave Schiffahrts GmbH* [1984] 1 All ER 398 (CA) for a review of the cases and principles to be applied). The jurisdiction is recognised by s 37(3) of the Supreme Court Act 1981. The injunction and ancillary order for discovery should be limited to assets within the jurisdiction (*Ashtiani* v *Kashi* [1986] 3 WLR 647). Again, as the relief is granted ex parte, supporting affidavits must give full disclosure of all material facts, and they should specify the assets (often monies in a bank account) sought to be preserved and give reasons for a belief that the defendant may abscond or those assets may be removed (*Third Chandris* v *Unimarine* [1979] QB 645 (CA); *Barclay-Johnson* v *Yuill* [1980] 1 WLR 1259 (Megarry V-C); *Rahman (Prince Abdul) bin Turki al Sudairy* v *Abu-Taha* [1980] 1 WLR 1268 (CA)). The mere fact that the defendant is abroad will not be enough.

Where the defendant, a 'record pirate' resident in the UK, was deliberately conducting his lifestyle in a manner calculated to prevent judgments against him from being effectively enforced (by concealing and dissipating his assets rather than removing them), an order was made requiring disclosure of and delivery up of assets (*CBS UK Ltd* v *Lambert* [1983] FSR 127 (CA)). The Court of Appeal said (at 131):

On the facts put before us this was not a case of a plaintiff seeking to

---

[40] See White Book 1993, Ord 29 r 1, footnotes 29/1//20–29/1/23, and Practice Direction (Ex parte Mareva injunctions and Anton Piller orders) 28 July 1994 for the standard forms to be used in any application therefor.

freeze a defendant's assets pending trial in anticipation of getting judgment. It was one which seemed to us to show that the defendant Steven Lambert was conducting his affairs with intent to deprive anyone who got judgment against him of the fruits of his victory.

The *Mareva* injunction was brought into use to make this kind of behaviour in commercial cases unprofitable.

The report sets out the form of order made, together with guidelines to which regard is to be had when such an exceptional order is to be made.

The injunction does not give any priority over other creditors, and may be qualified or limited where the defendant can show that he requires the funds for the bona fide payment of other creditors or otherwise to carry on his normal business (*Iraqi MOD* v *Arcepey Shipping Co SA* [1980] 2 WLR 488 (Donaldson J); *Third Chandris Shipping Corp* v *Unimarine SA* [1979] QB 645 (CA)). Thus, third parties are entitled to intervene to exercise any rights of set-off which they may have, and to seek variations in the form of the order accordingly (*Project Development* v *KMK Securities* [1982] 1 WLR 1470; *The Theotokos* [1983] 1 WLR 1302).

A Mareva injunction may in a proper case be granted after judgment to facilitate execution, or continued after judgment if originally made before (*Orwell Steel* v *Asphalt and Tarmac* [1984] 1 WLR 1097; *Stewart Chartering* v *C & O Managements* [1980] 1 WLR 460).

4 Interlocutory procedure[41]

4.1 Letter before action

There is no requirement that warning be given before the action is brought,[42] but it is usual that a letter before action is written unless there be good reason; for example real urgency, or an intention to seek ex parte relief in any of the forms discussed above.

Such a letter before action will set out the plaintiff's alleged reputation, in what way his trading style is alleged to have become distinctive, and the defendant's specific conduct of which complaint is made; and will seek an undertaking that such conduct will be discontinued. Depending upon the circumstances, it may also be appropriate in such a letter to seek disclosure of the names of the defendant's suppliers, or his customers; disclosure of

---

[41] See also Chapter 10, as to parties, forum and evidence.
[42] *Upmann* v *Forester* (1883) 24 Ch D 231 (Chitty J); cf *Deane* v *Schofield* [1962] RPC 179 (Plowman J); *Ucan* v *Hilti* [1968] FSR 248 (Cross J, where the defendant showed that he would have given a suitable undertaking had the facts relied upon and matters complained of been brought to his notice, the plaintiff was refused the plaintiff's costs).

the extent of the acts complained of; delivery up, destruction or obliteration of offending material and payment of damages.

4.2 Submission to judgment

Where a defendant does not contest the action but submits to judgment, a plaintiff is entitled to an order made in open court, it being desirable that publicity be given to such orders[43] but the plaintiff through counsel may not make a public statement.[44]

4.3 General procedure for interlocutory relief

Usually, the plaintiff will issue his writ and serve this together with a notice of motion setting out the interlocutory relief which he seeks. There should be at least two clear days between the date of service and the date fixed for the hearing of the motion (RSC Ord 8, r 2(2)). But in cases of urgency the Court can give leave for shorter notice to be given, and where ex parte relief is required, the matter will be heard without any notice being given, in which case any relief will be granted over only a short period during which notice in the usual way can be given.

When the matter comes before the Court on notice, it is usual for the defendant to seek an adjournment of the hearing of the motion to give him time to put in evidence in answer to that of the plaintiff. Directions may then be given as to a timetable for evidence and the date of the resumed hearing. If the defendant declines to offer any undertakings over the adjourned period, and the plaintiff can make out a case that he will suffer harm in the interim, then the plaintiff may move ex parte for relief. The defendant will usually be given an opportunity to be heard on such application (but this is a matter for the discretion of the Court).

On the full hearing of the motion, the plaintiff will open his case, and the evidence is read. The plaintiff then closes his case and the defendant presents his case. Although the plaintiff has no absolute right of reply, he is usually permitted to reply. If relief is granted the plaintiff will be required to give a cross-undertaking in damages to the Court; that is, an undertaking that he will pay any damages sustained by the defendant as a result of the order which the Court is subsequently of the opinion that the plaintiff should pay. If the plaintiff fails at trial, or the action is

---

[43] *Fox* v *Luke* (1925) 43 RPC 37 (Tomkin J); *Smith* v *Service, Reeve* (1914) 31 RPC 319; cf the copyright cases *Savory* v *The World of Golf* [1914] 2 Ch 566; *PRS* v *Ciryl* [1924] 1 KB 1.

[44] *Showerings* v *Mecca* [1957] RPC 217 (Roxburgh J).

discontinued, then the defendant may seek an inquiry as to damages under this undertaking.

If the parties come to terms in respect of the motion before it is heard, the defendant may give undertakings to the Court, in which case the cross-undertaking in damages is implied into the order (Practice Note [1904] WN 203, 208; *Supreme Court Practice 1988*, note 29/1/13). Or if terms disposing of the entire action are reached, then the parties may agree to treat the motion as the trial of the action and thereupon seek an order for judgment in agreed form, thus saving further costs.

If, having received the defendant's evidence on the motion, the plaintiff chooses not to move the motion, it may be stood over to the trial of the action, the costs being reserved. There is conflicting authority as to whether the plaintiff has an absolute right to have the motion stood over[45] or whether it is a matter for the Court's discretion.[46] But the discretion, if there is one, will usually be exercised in favour of the party wishing to stand over the matter to trial, because the question of who should be liable to pay the costs cannot sensibly be determined without going into the merits of the motion (but see *Kodak* v *Reed* [1986] FSR 477, where Harman J took a more robust view, and *Kitchens International SA* v *Paul Kettle Agencies Ltd* [1990] FSR 436, where Hoffman J ordered costs of an abandonment motion to be taxed and paid forthwith).

4.4 Prosecution of action on grant of interlocutory relief

The courts have consistently emphasised the need to prosecute actions with due diligence, particularly where the plaintiff has obtained interlocutory injunctive relief. If a plaintiff fails to do so the court may discharge the interlocutory order, even though the action itself is not strikable for undue delay—see *Newsgroup Newspapers Ltd* v *The Mirror Group Newspapers (1986) Ltd* [1991] FSR 487.[47]

---

[45] *Simon Jeffrey Ltd* v *Shelana Fashions Ltd* [1977] RPC 103 (Walton J).

[46] *Simons Records Ltd* v *WEA Records Ltd* [1980] FSR 35 (CA); *Société Francaise D'Applications Commerciales et Industrielles SARL* v *Electronic Concepts Ltd* [1977] RPC 106 (Oliver J).

[47] See also *County Sound plc* v *Ocean Sound Ltd* [1991] FSR 367 at 371 (CA).

Chapter 10

Practice

(See also Checklist at pages 179 and 180)

1 Parties

1.1 Who should be plaintiff

A passing off action protects goodwill, and the plaintiff should be the person who owns the goodwill in this country which is sought to be protected. Where more than one person shares the goodwill then, provided the person(s) in question can establish damage as a result of the deceptive use, such person(s) may bring proceedings as a representative action in accordance with RSC Ord 15, r 12, without joining in all those entitled to share such goodwill.[1] As Lord Diplock stated in *Erven Warnink BV* v *J Townend & Sons (Hull) Ltd* [1980] RPC 31 at 95 (HL):

> The larger the class the more difficult it must also be for an individual member of it to show that the goodwill of his own business has sustained more than minimal damage ... As respects subsequent additions to the class, mere entry into the market would not give any right of action for passing off; the new entrant must have himself used the descriptive term long enough on the market in connection with his own goods and have traded successfully enough to have built up a goodwill for his business.

---

[1] *Erven Warnink BV* v *J Townend & Sons (Hull) Ltd* [1980] RPC 31 at 93, 95, and 106 (HL); *J Bollinger* v *The Costa Brava Wine Co Ltd* [1960] RPC 16 (Danckwerts J); *Dent* v *Turpin* (1861) 2 John & H 139 (Wood V-C); cf *J Bollinger SA* v *Goldwell Ltd* [1971] RPC 412 (Megarry J, where plaintiff held not entitled to sue in a representative capacity because part of the claim (estoppel) was not appropriate); see also *Consorzio del Prosciutto di Parma* v *Marks & Spencer plc* [1991] RPC 351 (CA), where the plaintiff consortium and the producers of Parma ham did not have identity of interest so that it could not represent the producers.

157

Difficulties may sometimes arise in determining which of two or more persons is the true owner of the relevant goodwill, as for example where the goods imitated are made by a foreign manufacturer or licensor but marketed in this country by an exclusive distributor or licensee. In such cases it is advisable that both parties should be before the Court, and that such a course should not be penalised in costs unless the joinder of both was clearly unreasonable. Such a joinder may be advantageous in other respects, for example by increasing the quantum of damages recovered or in respect of any interlocutory application tilting the 'balance of convenience' in the plaintiff's favour; thus apart from injury to goodwill in the name, the loss to a foreign manufacturer or licensor may be quantifiable by reference to loss of revenue from sales, but the loss to the local distributor may be less quantifiable, for example by loss of position in market place, effect on sales of other goods, etc.

1.2 Who should be defendant

In the normal course of events, the defendant will be the person who makes the misrepresentation which results in the commission of the tort. However, liability will also fall upon those who, while not deceiving their own customers (who may be middlemen who are well aware of with whom they are dealing), put into the hands of others the 'instruments of deception' which may be used to deceive an ultimate consumer. As Lord Watson said in *Johnson* v *Orr Ewing*,[2] 'no man, however honest his personal intentions, has a right to adopt and use so much of his rival's established trade-mark as will enable any dishonest trader, into whose hands his own goods may come, to sell them as the goods of his rival.' Sums recovered from such persons may well be greater than those recovered from persons further down the chain of supply, for it will be assumed that every sale made by them was wrongful, whereas for example the retailer may be able to show that a portion of his customers were not confused. See *My Kinda Town Ltd* v *Soll* [1983] RPC 15 at 49 to 53 (Slade J) for a review of the more important cases of where an account of profits has been ordered against a defendant who sells to middlemen.

Where the act of passing off is committed by a limited company, the directors of the company may themselves also be personally liable for the tort if it can be shown either: (1) that the company was formed for the express purpose of doing the wrongful acts; or (2) that the directors

---

[2] (1882) 7 App Cas 219 at 232 (HL); see also Chapter 1, p 12, para 8.

expressly directed the wrongful act.[3] But such direction may not be inferred merely from the fact that they are sole directors,[4] at least some further evidence will be required.

In *Mentmore Manufacturing Co Ltd* v *National Merchandising Co Inc* (1978) 89 DLR 195, a patent case, the Canadian Federal Court of Appeal concluded that before a director could be made personally liable for corporate acts it had to be shown that he deliberately or recklessly pursued a course of conduct likely to constitute infringement. That case has been followed and approved in this country in *Hoover Plc* v *George Hulme (Stockport) Ltd* [1982] FSR 565, a copyright case, and *White Horse Distillers Ltd* v *Gregson Associates Ltd* [1984] RPC 61, Nourse J, a passing off case. However in *C Evans & Sons Ltd* v *Spritebrand Ltd* [1985] FSR 267 (CA), a copyright case, after reviewing these and other cases it was held that except in those cases where a particular state of mind or knowledge is required to be proved, a director is liable for the tortious acts of the company if he directs or procures the act whether or not he acted deliberately or recklessly in the knowledge that the act was tortious.

As a matter of practice, it would be unusual to join directors unless they had guilty knowledge, and there were grounds for believing either that the acts might be repeated under the guise of a new company or that the company might be unable to satisfy any judgment debt in the action. Adequate particulars of the facts relied upon in support of the allegation that they personally directed the acts complained of should be given.

2 Forum

By reason of s 61 of the Supreme Court Act 1981 and Sch 1, para 1 thereof all cases and matters relating to trade marks are assigned to the Chancery Division of the High Court—see also RSC Ord 100, r 1.

While there is no express rule to that effect with regard to an action for passing off, nevertheless such action should be brought in the Chancery Division, because of the experience of the judges of that division in deciding actions of that type. In *McCain International Ltd* v *Country Fair Foods Ltd* [1981] RPC 69 at 82 (CA) Templeman LJ said:

---

[3] *Rainham Chemical Works Ltd* v *Belvedere Fish Guano Co* [1921] 2 AC 465 (HL); *Performing Right Society Ltd* v *Ciryl Theatrical Syndicate* [1924] 1 KB 1 (CA); *Pritchard and Constance (Wholesale) Ltd* v *Amata Ltd* (1924) 42 RPC 63 (Romer J); *T Oertli AG* v *E J Bowman (London) Ltd* [1956] RPC 282 (Roxburgh J); [1957] RPC 388 (CA).
[4] *British Thomson-Houston Ltd* v *Sterling Accessories Ltd* (1924) 41 RPC 311 (Tomlin J).

Speaking for myself it seems to me that this is the sort of action which ought usefully to be brought in the Chancery Division in conformity with current practice. In that Division judges deal with passing off actions every week. They have built up a fund of expertise, knowledge and practice which is of assistance to the judges themselves, of great assistance to this Court and of great assistance to litigants. In the Queen's Bench Division, though there may be other advantages, generally speaking there is not the time or opportunity for full references to the authorities, and this is a disadvantage which does not attach to the hearing of interlocutory injunctions in the Chancery Division, where in relation to the authorities, the judges themselves will have previous knowledge. It was suggested that one reason for litigating in the Queen's Bench Division might be the factor of speed. It does not accord with my experience that the Chancery Division is any slower than the Queen's Bench Division at issuing *ex parte* and some interlocutory orders. So far as I am aware, that situation has not altered—it would be lamentable if it did alter—and although as I understand it there is no jurisdictional bar on a plaintiff beginning a passing off action in the Queen's Bench Division, in all the circumstances and in view of the present practice which may have changed since the turn of the century, it seems to me it would be more convenient for a case of this nature to be begun in, or to be transferred to the Chancery Division;

and Stephenson LJ agreed.

By reason of s 15(1) of the County Court Act 1984, the county courts have jurisdiction to hear any action founded on tort. Under the High Court and County Court Jurisdiction Order 1991 there are no financial limits to such jurisdiction. Thus, although the county court has no jurisdiction to hear trade mark matters, it can at least in principle hear passing off actions. It seems likely that the special jurisdiction of the Patents County Court which has jurisdiction to hear patent and design matters may be extended in the future to include trade mark matters.[5]

3 Evidence

3.1 Reputation

The plaintiff must show he has a reputation in the UK in the name or style

---

[5] cf *PSM Int plc* v *Specialised Fastener Products (Southern) Ltd* [1993] FSR 113. Ford J held he had jurisdiciton to hear copyright matters.

relied upon. This is best established where the business has been carried on for some time by reference to the turnover of the business in question and to any promotional literature and expenditure relating thereto. Independent trade evidence and/or evidence from members of the public is often adduced. Also, survey evidence is admissible (see p 163).

3.2 Deception

As Lord Parker stated in *A G Spalding & Bros* v *A W Gamage Ltd*[6] 'It was ... contended that the question whether the advertisements were calculated to deceive was not one which your Lordships could yourselves determine by considering the purport of the advertisements themselves, having regard to the surrounding circumstances, but was one which your Lordships were bound to determine upon evidence directed to the question itself. I do not take this view of the law. There may, of course, be cases of so doubtful a nature that a judge cannot properly come to a conclusion without evidence directed to the point; but there can be no doubt that in a passing-off action the question whether the matter complained of is calculated to deceive, in other words, whether it amounts to a misrepresentation, is a matter for the judge, who, looking at the documents and evidence before him, comes to his own conclusion.'

In *General Electric Co (of USA)* v *General Electric Co* [1973] RPC 297 at 321–322 Lord Diplock in a trade mark case observed that where goods are of a kind not normally sold to the general public but in a specialised market, evidence of persons accustomed to dealing in that market as to the likelihood of deception or confusion is essential, but where goods are sold to the general public for consumption or domestic use, the question whether buyers would be likely to be deceived is a 'jury question' and the judge's approach should be the same as a jury, as a potential buyer of the goods he should give effect to his own opinion as to the likelihood of deception which need not be confined to the evidence of the witnesses—but being alert to the danger of allowing his own idiosyncratic knowledge to influence his decision.

Thus witnesses may not be asked whether the imitation complained of is calculated to deceive, this being a matter for the Court to decide (*Payton & Co Ltd* v *Snelling, Lampard & Co Ltd* (1900) 17 RPC 628 at 635: (HL)). As Lord Halsbury said in *North Cheshire & Manchester Brewery Co* v

---

[6] (1915) 32 RPC 286; followed in *Electrolux Ltd* v *Electrix Ltd* (1953) 71 RPC 23 (CA, a trade mark case).

Manchester Brewery Co[7] 'Is this name so nearly resembling the name of another firm as to be likely to deceive? That is a question upon which evidence, of course, might be given, as to whether or not there was another brewery either in the one place or in the other, or whether there were several breweries nearly resembling it in name; what the state of the trade was, and whether there was any trade name: all those are matters which are proper to be dealt with upon evidence; but upon the one question which your Lordships have to decide, whether the one name is so nearly resembling another as to be calculated to deceive, I am of opinion that no witness would be entitled to say that, and for this reason: that that is the very question which your Lordships have to decide.'

But although a witness may not be asked whether the public are likely to be deceived, since this is merely his opinion about a conclusion to which the court is to arrive, he may be asked the question whether he himself, being in the trade and familiar with the subject matter concerned, would be misled.[8] But it is obviously hard to get a witness to say this. 'Nobody quite likes to admit that he is so extremely foolish, as in many cases he would have to do'.[9] More obliquely he may be asked whether he would stock the plaintiff's and rival's goods in the same shop and if not, why not. In *Sodastream Ltd* v *Thorn Cascade Ltd* [1982] RPC 459 at 468 Kerr LJ observed that 'it is perfectly proper and admissible for someone in the trade to express opinions about the likely reaction of others in relation to matters which are within his or her sphere of work; indeed it is part of their responsibility to form a view on such matters.'[10]

The strongest evidence is that which shows that several persons have in fact been deceived. For if intelligent persons have been deceived this is very strong evidence that the action complained of is likely to deceive. But even if evidence is brought that someone has in fact been deceived, the court

---

[7] [1899] AC 83 (HL). See also *Perry & Co Ltd* v *Hessin & Co* (1912) 29 RPC 509 at 533 (CA), especially Buckley LJ's observations on relevant evidence in a get-up case.

[8] Per Lord Loreham LC in *Claudius Ash, Sons & Co Ltd* v *Invicta Manufacturing Co Ltd* (1912) 29 RPC 465 at 476 (HL).

[9] Per Farwell J in *Bourne* v *Swan & Edgar Ltd* (1903) 20 RPC 105 at 118.

[10] See also *Guccio Gucci SpA* v *Paolo Gucci* [1991] FSR 89 at 91 Browne-Wilkinson V-C held that where a judge is ignorant of the specific market it is legitimate to produce evidence of the likelihood of confusion of customers from those skilled in such market.

may ascribe it to the folly of the witness and hold that there is no probability of deceit.[11]

The absence of such evidence is by no means fatal,[12] especially where there are obvious difficulties in the way of obtaining such evidence, for example from abroad, of if the action is *quia timet* and thus the defendants' goods have never been placed on the market.[13] But the absence of it may afford grounds for comment. 'If there is a doubt on the subject as to whether a mark is likely to deceive or is calculated to deceive or not, the production of two or three cases of deception would be of the utmost importance, and I cannot fail to attach some weight to the fact that there being great doubt in other respects, no case of deception of any kind is found.'[14] Where the two articles have been for some time on the market together, and there is no evidence of actual deception, there is a stronger inference that no deception is likely to be caused.[15]

In addition to the foregoing, evidence may be called and interrogatories may be asked[16] as to whether certain features are common to the trade, what names are common to the trade, how intending purchasers describe certain articles,[17] who the intending purchasers are likely to be, for example, natives,[18] or illiterate people.[19]

3.3 Public opinion or survey evidence

To ascertain the extent of the reputation of a particular name or style

---

[11] See, eg, *Civil Service Supply Association* v *Dean* (1879) 13 Ch D 512 (Malins V-C); see also *Rolls Razor Ltd* v *Rolls Lighters Ltd* (1949) 66 RPC 29 (CA, where purchasers of the defendant's lighters who had brought them to the plaintiff for repair was admissible as evidence of confusion even though the motives of such persons could not be investigated).

[12] *Compania General de Tobacos* v *Rehder* (1887) 5 RPC 61 (Kay J): See also *Reddaway* v *Bentham Hemp Spinning Co* (1892) 9 RPC 506 (CA); and *Liebig's Extract of Meat Co Ltd* v *Chemists' Co-operative Society Ltd* (1896) 13 RPC 736 (CA).

[13] *Cowie* v *Herbert* (1897) 14 RPC 436 at 477 (Court of Session—IH).

[14] Per North J in *Baker* v *Rawson* (1890) 8 RPC 89 at 107; see also *Smith's Potato Crisps Ltd* v *Paige's Potato Crisps Ltd* (1928) 45 RPC 36 at 46 (Eve J).

[15] See *Edge & Sons Ltd* v *Gallon & Son* (1900) 17 RPC 557 at 564 (HL); *Re Holbrooks Ltd's Application* (1909) 26 RPC 791 (Joyce J, Eve J); *City Link Travel Holdings Ltd* v *Lakin* [1979] FSR 653 (Whitford J, where a few cheques/invoices were misdirected, but over a number of years of trading side by side).

[16] *Perry & Co Ltd* v *Hessin & Co* (1910) 28 RPC 108 (Eve J).

[17] *Imperial Tobacco Co* v *Purnell & Co* (1904) 21 RPC 598 (CA).

[18] *Wilkinson* v *Griffith Bros & Co* (1891) 8 RPC 370 (Romer J).

[19] See Chapter 3, footnotes 4 and 5.

amongst members of the public, or the effect of the defendants' proposed trading style, market research surveys have been held to be admissible in evidence. The market researcher who conducted the survey gives his expert testimony of the opinion held by members of the public, which is not subject to notice as hearsay evidence under the Civil Evidence Acts 1968 and 1977 and the provision of RSC Ord 28, rr 21–4.[20] Such evidence may in a suitable case be adduced by either side, and is admissible in principle in both interlocutory applications and at trial.[21]

However, survey evidence of this kind has not often been found helpful by the Court. The related questions of whether there is a misrepresentation, and whether there is a likelihood of deception, are ultimately to be answered by the Court and not by the witnesses.[22] Thus, in *Mothercare* v *Penguin Books*, Dillon LJ said:

> It has become rather a fashion latterly for large companies involved in passing off actions to have surveys carried out, with the results put in evidence, to show public reaction to the defendant's product, when, as here, the question of misrepresentation or likelihood of deception is a question for the Court. I do not for my part find such surveys helpful . . .

But in *Reckitt & Coleman* v *Borden (No 3)* [1987] FSR 505 at 511–512, Walton J accepted that although on the issue of the likelihood of confusion he was bound to decide the case for himself and not merely accept the evidence of witnesses, the question was not whether the judge himself would be confused but whether the judge was persuaded that the ordinary shopper would be deceived under typical trading conditions. He accordingly gave weight to the survey evidence (which was supported by oral evidence). Survey evidence may thus be of more assistance to the Court where the circumstances of the trade are in some way unusual, and of less relevance where the action concerns an ordinary consumer item.

Where there was a dispute between pollsters as to the validity of the methodology involved, the Court gave no weight to survey evidence adduced on an interlocutory application.[23] Survey evidence has been rejected where it results in an unnatural question being asked in an

---

[20] *Lego* v *Lego M Lemelstrich* [1983] FSR 155 at 173–179.

[21] The defendants relied upon survey evidence at the interlocutory stage in *Reckitt & Coleman* v *Borden* [1987] FSR 228, but its reliability was challenged and the Court of Appeal gave no weight to it (at 237).

[22] *Reckitt & Coleman* v *Borden (No 3)* [1987] FSR 505 at 511; *Mothercare* v *Penguin Books* [1988] RPC 113 at 116 (CA); see also *Parker Knoll* v *Knoll International* [1962] RPC 243 at 285, lines 13–27.

[23] *Nationwide Building Society* v *Nationwide Estate Agents* [1987] FSR 579 at 588.

unnatural surrounding,[24] or leads a witness to speculate as to something about which he might not have bothered with unless questioned.[25] The use of a tachistoscope (a device used in perception studies) was rejected as having no evidential value, for 'trade marks have to be considered in a business context and not in the context of laboratory experiments'.[26]

Even where survey evidence has been accepted, it has usually taken a secondary role to live oral evidence from members of the public.[27]

Whitford J gave guidance in *Imperial Group* v *Philip Morris* [1984] RPC 293 at 302–3 as to the requirements to be fulfilled for survey evidence to have validity. He held that:

(i)   the survey must be done fairly and by a method such that a relevant cross-section of the public is interviewed;

(ii) it must be of a sufficient size to produce a statistically significant result;

(iii) where several surveys are carried out, full disclosure must be given to the other side of their number, the methodology and the numbers of persons involved;

(iv) the totality of all answers given to all surveys must be disclosed and made available to the other side;

(v)   the questions should neither be leading, nor should they direct the interviewee into a field of speculation upon which he would never otherwise have embarked;

(vi) the exact answers must be recorded, not an abbreviation or digest;

(vii) the instructions given to those carrying out the interviews, and to those who subsequently code the answers if computer coding is used, must be disclosed.

It is unusual to call as witnesses the organisers of the survey, those persons who carried out the survey, and a sample of the respondents.[28] Such respondents may be selected from those whose answers indicated that they were confused, and although by reason of such selection they are not a representative sample of the public at large, nevertheless they may be regarded as representing a substantial part of the public.[29]

---

[24] *Mothercare* v *Penguin Books* (above) at 117.

[25] *Imperial Group* v *Philip Morris* [1984] RPC 293, followed in *Scott Ltd* v *Nice Pak Products Ltd* [1989] FSR 100 (CA). 'Have you ever seen or bought this make of baby wipe?' based on false premise as it was not on the market.

[26] *Laura Ashley* v *Coloroll* [1987] RPC 1 at 11.

[27] *Lego* v *Lego M Lemelstrich* [1983] FSR 155 at 165; *Reckitt & Coleman* v *Borden (No 3)* [1987] FSR 505 at 511.

[28] As was done in both *Lego* and *Reckitt & Coleman*, above, where the survey evidence was accepted but given less weight than the oral evidence.

[29] *Lego* v *Lego M Lemelstrich* (above) at 171–2.

In addition to survey evidence, questionnaires are frequently sent out to a sample of the relevant section of the public or relevant trade, and a smaller sample of those who have given favourable answers are called as witnesses. In *Bailey & Co Ltd* v *Clark, Son & Morland Ltd* [1938] 55 RPC 253 (HL) (the 'Glastonbury' case, a trademark case) it was observed that where it is desired to prove that those selected were fairly chosen, the proper course would be to adduce evidence of the number of those questioned, the number of replies received and to give the opposing party an opportunity of inspecting the replies not verified under oath.

Evidence of the results of market research surveys not prepared for the purposes of legal proceedings has been held not to be expert opinion evidence and thus not subject to the requirements of RSC Ord 38, r 36.[30] However, this may fall to be decided on the facts of each case, depending on the nature of the survey concerned and the conclusion sought to be drawn from the results.

Of course, evidence of actual confusion is always admissible and will usually be highly material. Evidence that complaints or enquiries intended for the other party have been received in error may be given by the person who received them and such evidence is not hearsay; the person who actually made the complaint need not be called.[31] However, greater weight may naturally attach to such evidence if the actual complainant is called, for such a witness may go on to state the reasons for such confusion having arisen.

3.4 'Trap orders'[32]

In the case of passing off by retailers, evidence may be given where in response to orders placed by the plaintiff (or his agents) for the genuine goods the defendant has substituted other goods. In such circumstances as the plaintiff or his agent is pretending to be somebody he is not, care must be exercised to see that such orders are fair. Thus in *Procea Products Ltd* v *Evans & Sons Ltd*[33] Roxburgh J stated 'trap orders . . . must be scanned with a special degree of severity . . . it seems to me that the burden upon a

---

[30] *Reckitt & Coleman* v *Borden (No 2)* [1987] FSR 407.

[31] *Nationwide Building Society* v *Nationwide Estate Agents* [1987] FSR 579 at 589–590.

[32] See *Marie Claire Album SA* v *Hartstene Hosiery Ltd* [1993] FSR 692, Chadwick J accepted the legitimacy of trap orders in principle.

[33] (1951) 68 RPC 210 at 211 (Procea bread made by bakers supplied with plaintiff's ingredients and to plaintiff's formulation). See also *Showerings Ltd* v *Blackpool Tower Co Ltd* [1975] FSR 40 (Goff J); cf *California Fig Syrup Co* v *Taylors Drug Co Ltd* (1897) 14 RPC 341 (Kekewich J); 564 (CA, trap orders unsatisfactory, injunction refused).

person executing a trap order does not extend beyond this; that he must be absolutely fair (a thing that I agree is not always easy when executing a trap order, and that is why they have to be so carefully scrutinised), he must give the order in circumstances such that he has the undivided attention of the persons to whom he is giving the order (that is to say, he must not interpose a question when in the middle of a queue or something of that kind and take some random answer as a passing off; he must see that he has the undivided attention of the assistant), he must, of course, do absolutely nothing which might be calculated to induce the person whom he is seeking to trap to fall into the trap (that, of course, would be a fatal objection to a trap order) and he must endeavour, so far as possible, to reproduce the conditions which would prevail if, instead of being a trap order, it was a genuine order; that is to say, if, as I think, in this sort of trade is usual, bread is ordered verbally, I can see no reason why the order should not be verbal.'

However, where appropriate it is wiser to send a written order. But whether it is done by word of mouth or in writing it must be shown that the order was clear and unambiguous (*Carr* v *Crisp* (1902) 19 RPC 497 at 500 (Byrne J)). It should also be given to a person of responsibility (*Wakefield & Co Ltd* v *Board* (1928) 45 RPC 261 (Tomlin J)).

When the trap order has been executed and the victim caught, he should be put on notice of the fact straight away so that he may recall his recollection of the circumstances.[34]

3.5 Isolated cases of deception

The Court will refuse to grant an injunction where only isolated instances of deception have occurred and are not likely to be repeated,[35] although in

---

[34] *Ripley* v *Griffiths* (1902) 19 RPC 590 at 597 (Farwell J, 'Oval Blue') approved by Byrne J in *H P Truefit Ltd* v *C J Edney* (1903) 20 RPC 321. See also *Cellular Clothing Co Ltd* v *G White & Co Ltd* (1952) 70 RPC 9 at 14 (Harman J, no notice given to the defendant, held traps orders unsatisfactory); cf *Showerings Ltd* v *Cheltenham & Hereford Breweries Ltd* [1958] RPC 446 (Elwes J).

[35] *Leahy, Kelly and Leahy* v *Glover* (1893) 10 RPC 141 (HL, '2D' cigars, a single instance of sale by one of the defendant's employees who had since left the defendant's employ); see also *Burberrys* v *Watkinson* (1906) 23 RPC 141 (Warrington J, isolated mistake no injunction, no order as to costs); and *Hilti AG* v *Ucan Development Ltd* [1963] RPC 160 (Wilberforce J, interlocutory injunction refused, isolated incident, defendant former selling agent of plaintiff progressively selling off stocks of plaintiff's goods); see also *Hilti AG* v *Ucan Development Ltd* [1964] RPC 206; cf *Bostitch Inc* v *McGarry & Cole Ltd* [1964] RPC 173 (Cross J, where the defendant was a former distributor of the plaintiff and the name 'Bostitch' had thus become associated with the defendant, on the basis of certain trap orders, an interlocutory injunction was granted).

such a case the defendant may not obtain his costs (*Kodak Ltd v Grenville* (1908) 25 RPC 416 (Eve J)). In such circumstances the Court may be prepared to grant a declaration in lieu of an injunction (*Treasure Cot Co Ltd v Hamleys Bros Ltd* (1950) 67 RPC 89 (Harman J)).

3.6 Intention to deceive

Whilst intention to deceive is not a necessary element of passing off, nevertheless if established, likelihood of deception will more readily be inferred.[36] See Chapter 3, p 48.

Valuable evidence may sometimes be obtained from the letters written to or by the defendant. In *Reddaway v Banham* (1896) 13 RPC 218 (HL) the case was largely influenced by a letter written to the defendant. 'The writer' said Lord Halsbury in that case, 'who doubtless knew what he was doing, specially desires that the thing which he is ordering should bear no other stamp than "Camel Hair Belting," and if he gets that, he adds, "I think I can take this order from Reddaway's." My Lords, I think with this letter before them the jury were perfectly right, and that my *prima facie* impression from the words being only descriptive of the article sold would have been wrong. The result is, in my mind, that the proof is satisfactory, and that one man's goods are being sold as if they were the goods of the other.' There was a similar letter in *McAndrew v Bassett* (1864) 33 LJ Ch 561 (Wood V-C), from a retailer to the defendant, enclosing a bar of the plaintiff's liquorice as a model of the way in which the defendant was to stamp his bars.

3.7 Injury to goodwill

As to the type of injury likely to be suffered by the plaintiff, see Chapter 4, above.

Where the defendant's goods or services are of inferior quality the plaintiff may need to conduct tests or survey evidence to establish such fact.

4 Defence of acquiescence or estoppel

A defendant may set up a defence of acquiescence or estoppel where 'it

---

[36] See *RHM Foods Ltd v Bovril Ltd* [1983] RPC 275 (CA), in which discovery relating to the defendant's intentions to deceive was refused before service of a statement of claim.

would be unconscionable for a party to be permitted to deny that which, knowingly or unknowingly, he has allowed or encouraged another to assume to his detriment . . .' (see *Habib Bank Ltd* v *Habib Bank AG Zurich* [1982] RPC 1 at 36 (Oliver LJ)). A narrower formulation propounded in the same case was that for the defendant to succeed the defence must establish at least three things, namely:

(i) the defendant was unaware that what he was doing constituted an invasion of the plaintiff's rights;
(ii) the plaintiff encouraged that course of action either by statements or conduct; and
(iii) the defendant acted upon the plaintiff's encouragement to his detriment.

There can be no acquiescence where there is no knowledge, thus it must be shown that the plaintiff was aware of the defendant's conduct (*Weldon* v *Dicks* (1878) 10 Ch D 247 at 262 (Malins V-C)). When a trader does know that a rival is passing off as his goods the goods of that other and has taken no action it will be a question of fact how far this inaction constitutes acquiescence. Merely threatening the defendant without taking proceedings is not sufficient to avoid the defence of acquiescence; for if the plaintiff stands by and allows a man to carry on business in the manner complained of and to acquire a reputation at great expense, he cannot then turn round and demand that the business be stopped (*Rowland* v *Mitchell* (1896) 13 RPC 457 at 464 (Romer J)). However, other circumstances may show that he was justified in taking no proceedings and that he did not acquiesce thereby (*Rowland* v *Mitchell*, above).

Mere delay does not bar plaintiff's action

Mere delay in bringing an action for passing off does not disentitle the plaintiff to relief if there has been no acquiescence. As Fry J said in *Fullwood* v *Fullwood* (1878) 9 Ch D 176 at 178–9:

'Delay . . . is not sufficient to deprive the plaintiff of his rights. The right asserted by the plaintiff in this action is a legal right. He is, in effect, asserting that the defendants are liable to an action for deceit. It is clear that such an action is subject to the *Statute of Limitations*, and it is also clear that the injunction is sought merely in aid of the plaintiff's legal right. In such a case the injunction is, in my opinion, a matter of course if the legal right be proved to exist. In saying that I do not shut my eyes to the possible existence in other cases of a purely equitable defence, such as acquiescence or acknowledgment, and the various other equitable defences which may be imagined. But mere lapse of time, unaccompanied by anything else (and to that I confine my observations) has, in my judgment, just as much effect, and no more, in barring a suit for an injunction as it has in barring an action for deceit.'[37]

But delay in policing one's rights may mean that the mark in question no longer distinguishes the plaintiff's goods or business and therefore the same has become publici juris (see Chapter 2, pp 30, 31). Furthermore delay will generally debar a plaintiff's right to interlocutory relief (see Chapter 9, p 145).

5 Forms of relief in passing off action

The relief which will be granted to the plaintiff in a passing off action may comprise an injunction, an account of profits or an inquiry as to damages, and delivery up of the articles complained of, or erasure of the mark complained of from the articles. A declaration has seldom been asked for in that until a defendant has been on the market for some time, evidence as to likelihood of deception will be hypothetical. See *Bulmer Ltd* v *Bollinger* [1978] RPC 79 where a declaration was sought that the plaintiffs were entitled to use the expressions 'Champagne Cider' and 'Champagne Perry'.

5.1 Injunction

The injunction may vary with the circumstances of each case, but in general there are two kinds, absolute prohibitions against using a name or mark[38] and qualified prohibitions against doing so, for example using without clearly distinguishing the goods from those of the plaintiff[39] or using it so as to represent that the goods are those of the plaintiff.[40]

---

[37] See also *Electrolux Ltd* v *Electrix Ltd* (1953) 71 RPC 23 (CA); cf *Vine Products* v *Mackenzie & Co Ltd* [1969] RPC 1 (Cross J, use of expressions such as 'British Sherry', 'South African Sherry' which had been in use for 100 years or so could not be stopped by producers of 'sherry'); and *Cluett, Peabody & Co Inc* v *McIntyre Hogg Marsh & Co Ltd* [1958] RPC 335 (Upjohn J, 'Arrow Shorts', 30 years' delay).

[38] See *Montgomery* v *Thompson* (1891) 8 RPC 361 (HL).

[39] *Powell* v *The Birmingham Vinegar Brewery Co Ltd* (1897) 14 RPC 720 (HL, Yorkshire Relish Case); *Reddaway* v *Banham* (1896) 13 RPC 218 (HL).

[40] *Johnston* v *Orr Ewing* (1882) 7 App Cas 219 (HL); *Siegert* v *Findlater* (1878) 7 Ch D 801 at 810, 814 (Fry J).

Injunctions to retailers will be in a form that prohibits them from supplying goods not of the plaintiff's manufacture in response to an order for goods under the name of ... (the trade name).[41]

Absolute injunctions

Such injunctions are granted where there is no real possibility of using the mark in question in a manner which will differentiate the defendant's goods or business from the plaintiff's. As Lord Macnaghten said in the 'Stone Ale' case in justification of an absolute injunction, 'thirsty people want beer not explanations'. (See footnote 38 above.) This will generally apply where the mark is a wholly distinctive mark of the plaintiff's goods or business.

Where the plaintiff has established a reputation in a particular area only, the court may still grant an injunction which covers the entire jurisdiction, extending beyond the boundaries within which the reputation has been proved (*Chelsea Man* v *Chelsea Girl* [1987] RPC 189 (CA).

Qualified injunctions

Such injunctions are granted where it is possible to foresee that some other use by the defendant of the mark may be perfectly proper and honest (for example where the mark relates to a surname, or a geographical name or is descriptive and thus the plaintiff may not be able to claim it exclusively).[42]

The words 'without sufficiently or clearly distinguishing' have been held

---

[41] *Kerfoot* v *Cooper* (1908) 25 RPC 508 (Eve J) where form of injunction was discussed. See also *Havana Cigar & Tobacco Factories Ltd* v *Oddenino* (1924) 41 RPC 47 (CA, where 'Corona' meant plaintiff's brand of cigar but was also used to denote size or shape of a cigar, the defendant was restrained from using the name 'Corona' 'unless it was first clearly ascertained that the customer ... did not require cigars of the Corona brand or unless it was made clear to him ... that the cigars supplied were of a brand other than the plaintiffs' brand'); applied in *Treasure Cot Co Ltd* v *Hamleys Bros Ltd* (1950) 67 RPC 89 (Harman J). See also *Sony KK* v *Saray Electronics (London) Ltd* [1983] FSR 302 (CA, where the defendant dealt in Sony goods, but was not an authorised dealer; and was ordered to make clear to Sony customers that (1) defendant was not an authorised dealer and (2) altered goods were not covered by the Sony guarantee, followed in *Nishika Corpn* v *Goodchild* [1990] FSR 371 (Knox J)).

[42] *Parker-Knoll Ltd* v *Knoll International Ltd* [1961] RPC 346 at 362 (CA) and [1985] FSR 349 (Whitford J), alleged breach of such order; see also footnote 39 above.

to mean that 'as a matter of commercial possibility'[43] there is a sufficient distinction. Thus once a particular mark has been adjudged to be deceptive (or it is conceded that the same is deceptive) then on committal the court will not be concerned with such issue (which is res judicata) but only whether the new use sufficiently and/or clearly avoids the deception (see footnote 58 below).

A disclaimer such as 'not connected or associated with the plaintiff' will generally not suffice, either because it will not be read or it will not reach those likely to be deceived or even if it does they will not know which are the genuine goods or business.[44]

The court will not assist a defendant in providing guidelines as to how to circumvent the order.[45] It is a question of fact and degree in each case and where the name of the plaintiff's goods has become well known it may be that no amount of differentiation of get-up or adding other matter will suffice. See, eg, *Powell* v *Birmingham Brewery Co Ltd* (1897) 14 RPC 720 (HL).

Directors

The directors of a company formed with a name too similar to that of the plaintiff can be ordered to secure a change of name of the company (*Panhard et Levassor SA* v *Panhard-Levassor Motor Co Ltd* (1901) 18 RPC 405 (Farwell J); see also *Exxon* v *Exxon Insurance Consultants International Ltd* [1982] RPC 69 at 80 (Graham J) where the company itself was restrained from allowing its name to remain on the register in its present form, although none of the directors were defendants). Equally directors will be liable for committal where they fail to carry out an order of the court. In *Ronson Products Ltd* v *Ronson Furniture Ltd* [1966] RPC 497

---

[43] *Parker-Knoll Ltd* v *Knoll International Ltd* [1962] RPC 243 (CA) where the mere addition of the defendant's address was held not a sufficient distinction. See also *F Reddaway & Co Ltd* v *Hartley* (1931) 48 RPC 283 (CA) where 'Lechat's Camel Hair Belting' was held not to be a sufficient distinction.

[44] *Mothercare Ltd* v *Robson Books Ltd* [1979] FSR 466 at 469 (Megarry J); *Associated Newspapers Group* v *Insert Media Ltd* [1991] FSR 380 (CA); cf *Brittain Publishing Co (London) Ltd* v *Trade & Commercial Press Ltd* [1957] RPC 271 (Harman J); *Parker-Knoll Ltd* v *Knoll International Ltd*, [1985] FSR 349: Whitford J, 16 July 1984, where such words have been used to avoid a qualified injunction in the rather special facts of this case; *Sony UK* v *Saray Electronics (London) Ltd* [1983] FSR 302 (see footnote 41, above).

[45] *Wright, Layman & Umney* v *Wright* (1949) 66 RPC 149 at 152 (Greene MR, 'honest men do not sail close to the wind'); see also, eg, *Parker-Knoll Ltd* v *Knoll International Ltd* [1961] RPC 346 at 366–370 where a declaration that certain steps would avoid the injunctions imposed was refused; see also ibid [1962] RPC 243 at 261.

directors were found guilty of contempt having had notice of an undertaking given by the company to the court although not served personally with an order embodying the same.

Injunction overseas

An injunction can be granted by the court to restrain passing off in a foreign jurisdiction, provided that evidence is adduced that the acts sought to be restrained would be unlawful (*John Walker & Sons Ltd* v *Henry Ost Ltd* [1970] RPC 489: (Foster J); *Alfred Dunhill Ltd* v *Sunoptic SA* [1979] FSR 337 at 368–369 (CA)). Such an injunction could of course only be enforced in the English Court. It may be granted at an interlocutory stage (*Alfred Dunhill Ltd* v *Sunoptic SA*, above).

5.2 Damages

A plaintiff may elect whether to proceed with an inquiry as to damages or an account of profits from the defendant.[46] The first remedy is to compensate him for his loss. The second is based on the equitable principle that a wrongdoer may not profit from his wrong. The two remedies may be claimed in the alternative in the writ, and the plaintiff makes his election at the time when judgment is given. The usual practice in the Chancery Division is to determine liability and quantum separately, and thus a successful plaintiff will be awarded not damages but an inquiry as to damages (unless he elects for an account, which will again be taken by the master after liability has been established at trial), with the costs of the inquiry reserved to the master who conducts it.

Even where the passing off has been found and an injunction has been granted, a plaintiff has no automatic right to an enquiry, for the court has a discretion to refuse to order one if satisfied that it would be fruitless (see *McDonald's Hamburgers* v *Burgerking (UK)* [1987] FSR 112). But if there is an arguable case that damages may be recovered, the court should order an enquiry.

As Lord Parker stated in *Spalding* v *Gamage* [1915] 32 RPC 273 at 287 'It is sufficient to say that the misrepresentation being established and being in its nature calculated to produce damage, the plaintiffs are prima

---

[46] *Weingarten* v *Bayer* (1905) 22 RPC 341 (HL); cf *Van Zeller* v *Mason, Cattley & Co* (1907) 25 RPC 37 at 41 (where Joyce J held it was a matter of court's discretion); see also *Electrolux Ltd* v *Electrolix Ltd* (1953) 70 RPC 158 (where Lloyd-Jacob J refused an account of profits but allowed an inquiry as to damages).

facie entitled both to an injunction and to an enquiry. As to damage, the enquiry, of course, being at their own risk in respect of costs.'[47]

At the inquiry the task of the master is not to make precise calculations on detailed evidence, but rather to decide upon a figure which is, in all the circumstances of the case, of the right order of magnitude (per Warner J in *Unik Time Co Ltd* v *Unik Time Ltd* [1983] FSR 121 at 123). The damages compensate for injury to the plaintiff's goodwill (ibid, at 124).

The enquiry as to damages in certain cases may be limited to where sales of the articles result from the passing off (*Singer Manufacturing Co* v *British Empire Manufacturing Co Ltd* (1903) 20 RPC 313 at 320 (Kekewich J). But in general the damages are such as are the natural and direct consequence of the unlawful acts of the defendant[48] including 'any loss of trade actually suffered by the plaintiffs, either directly from the acts complained of, or properly attributable to injury to the plaintiffs' reputation, business, goodwill, and trade and business connection caused by the acts complained of; in other words, such damages as flow directly, and in the usual course of things, from the wrongful acts, excluding any speculative and unproven damage.'[49]

It would seem that such damages will be awarded against an innocent passer-off (*AG Spalding & Bros* v *A W Gamage Ltd* (1918) 35 RPC 101 (CA); cf *Slazenger* v *Spalding* (1910) 27 RPC 20).

Where the misrepresentation gives rise to a false connection or association between the defendant and plaintiff, the injury to the plaintiff will be in the shape of the blurring or dilution of its goodwill (see, eg, *Taitinger SA* v *Allbev Ltd* [1993] FSR 641 at 669 (CA). The quantum of damages will depend on the degree the plaintiff's goodwill has been depreciated or debased, which is not easy to determine (see Interlocutory Relief, Chapter 9, para 1.3).

In *Dormeuil Frères SA* v *Feraglow Ltd* [1990] RPC 449 (Knox J), the court was not satisfied that damages should be assessed on a royalty basis on the ground that such a basis or principle of assessment used to determine damages suffered by a patentee only arises where every sale a defendant makes in violation of a patent is a damage to the patentee. Such was not true on the facts before Knox J because it could not be presumed (indeed it was conceded by the plaintiff) that the spurious goods sold by the

---

[47] Considered in *Gillette UK Ltd* v *Edenwest Ltd* [1994] RPC 279 at 288–289 (Blackburne J).

[48] *AG Spalding & Bros* v *A W Gamage Ltd* (1918) 35 RPC 101 (CA).

[49] Ibid, per Swinfen Eady LJ at 117. See also *Halsbury's Laws of England* (4th ed) Vol 48, para 268 where it is stated that the form of order should be limited to damage suffered by the plaintiff through the defendant's wrongful acts as distinct from damage caused by mere trade competition.

defendant would but for the defendant's unlawful use of the plaintiff's mark have been sold by the plaintiff. Not every sale by the defendant necessarily constitutes a misrepresentation to the purchaser or consumer, so that computation on a royalty basis would not seem to be directly applicable to a passing off case. This may be contrasted with the infringement of a registered trade mark, where every sale or use of the mark would constitute an infringing act (similar to infringement of a patent).

In the case where the plaintiff merely licenses his mark, logo or character, then it would seem that a royalty based on such licence rate would be an appropriate basis, subject to questions of quality of the unlawful goods and the extent such goods may have damaged the plaintiff's goodwill.[50]

5.3 Account of profits

In the case of passing off of goods, the account of profits extends to all the goods sold, whether in England or elsewhere[51] and when sold to middlemen, whether sold in mistake for the plaintiffs' goods or not.[52] However, apart from the sales to middlemen cases, a plaintiff is not entitled to all of the defendants' profits, but only those which can be regarded as having been improperly made by reason of the act of passing off. The master taking the account should seek by reasonable approximation rather than mathematical exactness to ensure that neither party will have that which justly belongs to the other.[53]

In *My Kinda Town v Soll*[49] the plaintiff, at first instance, succeeded in restraining the defendant from using a trade name in connection with the defendant's restaurant business, and elected to take an account of profits. The plaintiff sought to recover all the profits made by the defendant during the period that the name was used; relying on a number of earlier authorities, the plaintiff argued that the acts which had been restrained by the injunction were ex hypothesi unlawful, that the whole operation of the defendant's business was therefore unlawful, and that the defendant was

50 See *IPC Magazines Ltd v Black & White Music Corp* [1983] FSR 348 (Goulding J); *Mirage Studios v Counter-Feat Clothing Co Ltd* [1991] FSR 145 (Browne-Wilkinson V-C).
51 *Weingarten v Bayer* (1903) 20 RPC 289 at 303 (Joyce J); (1905) 22 RPC 341 (HL).
52 *Lever v Goodwin* (1887) 4 RPC 504 (CA).
53 *My Kinda Town v Soll* [1983] RPC 15 (Slade J, although reversed on appeal on the question of passing off, Court of Appeal did not consider the question of the account of profits).

therefore liable to the plaintiff for all of the defendant's profits, regardless of what proportion of customers had actually been confused. The defendant contended that there was liability only for those net profits improperly made, in other words those constituting unjust enrichment only. Slade J, in finding in the defendant's favour, and differentiating those authorities where all the profits had been awarded, held:

> The purpose of ordering an account of profits in favour of a successful plaintiff in a passing off case is not to inflict punishment on the defendant. It is to prevent an unjust enrichment of the defendant by compelling him to surrender those profits, or those parts of those profits, actually made by him which were improperly made and nothing beyond this . . . The facts of many particular cases may justify the conclusion that the whole of the relevant profits should be so treated. The facts of the present case, however, do not in my judgment justify such a conclusion . . .
>
> To ascertain the profits which have been improperly made by the defendants, it is therefore necessary to ascertain how much of the profits made by the defendants over the relevant period are properly attributable to the use of the name Chicago Pizza Co. Clearly, profits made by the defendants by the sale of meals to customers who were *not* confused by this name are not attributable to this use.

5.4 Delivery up

Where an injunction has been granted, to assist the enforcement of the same, an order is frequently made for the delivery up[54] or destruction on oath of any offending material or articles in the defendant's possession, custody or control, which if used would involve a breach of the injunction. Such an order will be made where it is not possible to use the material or articles in question in an unobjectionable manner, for example a pirate supplier of instruments of fraud. However, if the offending name or mark can be satisfactorily removed or obliterated then generally this will be ordered instead—at the very least the defendant will be given the choice. See, for example, *Slazenger & Sons* v *Feltham & Co* (1889) 6 RPC 531,

---

[54] Cf *Lissen Ltd* v *Mutton* (1929) 46 RPC 10 (Romer J held plaintiff not entitled to an order for delivery up in a passing off case); see also *County Chemical Co Ltd* v *Frankenburg* (1904) 21 RPC 722 (where an order for delivery up was refused by Alverstone LJJ on account of delay in bringing the action the boxes in question having other uses, and *Baume & Co Ltd* v *A H Moore Ltd* [1988] RPC 226 at 236 (CA), no order for delivery up or destruction on oath pressed for after discussion as to whether such order could be made in a passing off action (as opposed to a trade mark action).

where the Court of Appeal ordered delivery up of the offending tennis racquets *or* in the presence of the plaintiff satisfactory erasure of the name 'Demotic'. The defendant will be required (in the case of a limited company by a proper officer) to swear an affidavit verifying that any such order for delivery, destruction or obliteration has been fully complied with.

A limited company will not be ordered to deliver up or destroy or obliterate its company seal, its statutory books, or any other articles or documents which by law it is required to keep undefaced in its possession.

5.5 Costs

Costs will normally be awarded to the successful party, to be taxed on the standard basis if not agreed. The court has discretion to order payment of costs on an indemnity basis, but this is seldom exercised save in contempt cases. Where a charge of fraud or amounting to fraud (for example that a name was deliberately chosen with an intention to deceive) is not made out, then in principle, in the court's discretion costs may be awarded against an unsuccessful plaintiff on a higher scale, but the court will require a very special case such as some deliberate dishonesty in the prosecution of the action.[55] Where a successful party succeeds on some issues but fails on others, then only a proportion of costs may be awarded (see, eg, *McDonald's Hamburgers* v *Burgerking (UK)* [1987] FSR 112).

6 Breach of injunction

Committal proceedings will lie in the ordinary way. Being of a quasi-criminal nature[56] the acts alleged to constitute the breach must be strictly proved (*Chelsea Man* v *Chelsea Girl (No 2)* [1988] FSR 217). Thus if the order itself is ambiguous, no breach of it will arise if only on one of two possible constructions (*Redwing* v *Redwing Forest Products* (1947) 64 RPC

---

[55] Cf *Harrods Ltd* v *The Harrodian School Ltd*, 13 May 1994, unreported (Harman J), where only costs on the standard basis were awarded. See *Berkeley Administration Inc* v *McClelland* [1990] FSR 565 (Wright J), a breach of confidence case where it was held that vigourous presentation and conduct was different in nature from overt or deliberate dishonesty in the prosecution of an action and does not attract taxation on a higher basis; such basis of assessment was confirmed by the Court of Appeal (1990) QB 407).

[56] *Comet Products UK Ltd* v *Hawke & Plastics Ltd* [1972] RPC 691 (CA, where it was held a defendant is not a compellable witness and even where he has given affidavit evidence there is a discretion as to whether to allow cross-examination).

67 (Jenkins J)).[57] Also the notice of motion must specify the precise breaches of the order so that the alleged contemnors are afforded full knowledge of the allegations they have to face (*Chanel Ltd* v *FGM Cosmetics* [1981] FSR 471 (Whitford J). Where the breach is of an order obtained in default of appearance or defence or by consent the defendant is deemed to have admitted those essential characteristics which would justify the order made.[58] This may be compared with the case where there has been an adjudication, where the Court will not reopen the issues already decided, being, of course, res judicata (*Parker-Knoll Ltd* v *Knoll International Ltd* [1962] RPC 243 (Wilberforce J) at 255 (CA)).

Where the injunction is so worded as to restrain the defendant from 'passing off' by the doing of a particular act, then the Court will have to decide the substantive question of whether the further act complained of did amount to passing off even when the order being breached is an interlocutory one. See p 145, 146 above; *Chelsea Man* v *Chelsea Girl (No 2)* [1988] FSR 217; cf *Spectravest* v *Aperkrut* [1988] FSR 161 (a copyright case).

A man does an act 'by his servants, or agents' if (1) the persons who did the act were his servants or agents; (2) the acts were done in the course of the service or agency; and (3) he either authorised the acts or could reasonably have foreseen them and failed to take all reasonable steps to prevent them (*Hone* v *Page* [1980] FSR 500 (Slade J) see also *Showerings Ltd* v *Fern Vale Brewery Co Ltd* (1958) RPC 484 (Danckwerts J, servant failed to follow instructions)). As to the position of directors, see p 172 above.

---

[57] See also *Wilson & Whitworth Ltd* v *Express & Independent Newspapers Ltd* [1969] RPC 165 (Plowman J), where terms of compromise (not to encroach further than at the time of the commencement of the action) were too vague to be enforced by the court.

[58] *Ripley* v *John Arthur & Co* (1902) 19 RPC 443 (CA); see also *Brittain Publishing Co (London) Ltd* v *Trade & Commercial Press Ltd* [1957] RPC 271 (Harman J); *Moore* v *Thomson* (1890) 7 RPC 325 (HL, defendant estopped from questioning the validity and previous infringement of a patent when once he has submitted to injunction).

Checklist

A *For Commencing Proceedings*

(1) Parties: ensure proper plaintiff and defendant. See Chapter 10, paras 1.1 and 1.2.

(2) Forum: High Court or County Court. See Chapter 10, para 2.

(3) Relief Sought: interim or final:

    (a)   If interim relief, whether ex parte or inter partes. See Chapter 9, paras 1 and 3.

    (b)   If final relief whether absolute or qualified relief sought. See Chapter 10, para 5.1.

(4) Prepare Evidence:

    (a)   As to plaintiff's reputation, see Chapter 10, para 3.1.

    (b)   As to deception, see Chapter 10, paras 3.2–3.6.

    (c)   As to damage to goodwill, see Chapter 4 and Chapter 10, para 5.2.

(5) Consider what Discovery must be given in respect of each of the issues viz reputation, deception and damage to goodwill.

B *For Defending Proceedings*

(1) Decide whether to challenge or admit proper parties, forum and/or reputation.

(2) Has defendant made concurrent use of its mark, name or get-up? See Chapter 5, para 3.

(3) Has plaintiff acquiesced in defendant's use? See Chapter 10, para 4.

(4) Are goods of plaintiff's origin and has plaintiff thereby consented to the use? See Chapter 5, paras 4 and 5.

(5) What concurrent use has been made of similar marks (names or get up) by competitors?

(6) How and why was mark name or get up chosen. See Chapter 3, para 2.

(7) With regard to interlocutory proceedings:

    (a) Has plaintiff delayed in bringing proceedings to the detriment of the defendant? See Chapter 9, para 1.7.

    (b) What damage will defendants suffer if injuncted by having to give up or change the offending mark, name or get up? See Chapter 9, para 1.3.

    (c) Is there a satisfactory alternative mark, name or get up or modification to the one complained about?

(8) Prepare evidence as to the unlikelihood of a misrepresentation occurring both from those knowledgeable in the market place and consider survey evidence as to the reaction of the public. See Chapter 10, paras 3.2 and 3.3.

(9) Consider what discovery must be given.

Appendix

Precedents

---

1. Writ

2. Notice of Motion

3. Statement of Claim

4. Defence

5. Minute of Order

Whilst the precedents are drafted in terms of passing off of goods the same will apply mutatis mutandis to business names or services.

IN THE HIGH COURT OF JUSTICE   CH 19[   ] X No

CHANCERY DIVISION

BETWEEN:

XX LIMITED

Plaintiff

and

EX EX LIMITED

Defendant

WRIT

The Plaintiff's claim is for:

1. An injunction to restrain the Defendant whether acting by its directors, officers, servants or agents or any of them or otherwise howsoever from passing off (or attempting to pass off) widgets not being widgets of the Plaintiff as or for such widgets or widgets associated or connected with the Plaintiff by the use in relation thereto of the name "Ex Ex" or any other name or mark colourably or confusingly similar to "XX".

2. An Order for the delivery up or destruction upon oath of all articles and material in the power, possession, custody or control of the Defendant the use of which would offend against the foregoing injunction or alternatively the erasure or obliteration upon oath of the name "Ex Ex" from all such articles and material.

3. An enquiry as to the damages suffered by the Plaintiff or at the Plaintiff's option an account of profits accrued to the Defendant by reason of its acts of passing off.

4. An order for the payment of all sums found due upon such enquiry or account together with interest thereon pursuant to Section 35A of the Supreme Court Act 1981 or due under the Court's inherent jurisdiction.

5. Further or other relief.

6. Costs.

IN THE HIGH COURT OF JUSTICE   CH 19[   ] X No

CHANCERY DIVISION

BETWEEN:

XX LIMITED

Plaintiff

and

EX EX LIMITED

Defendant

NOTICE OF MOTION

TAKE NOTICE THAT this Honourable Court will be moved before the Chancery Motions Judge sitting in the Motions Court, Royal Courts of Justice, Strand, London WC2A 2LL on   day the   day of   at 10.30am or so soon thereafter as Counsel may be heard by Counsel for the Plaintiff for the following orders:

1. That the Defendant be restrained until judgment in this action or further order in the meantime, whether acting by its directors, officers, servants, agents or any of them or otherwise howsoever from doing the following acts or any of them, that is to say:

   (i) selling, offering for sale, or distributing widgets under or by reference to the name or mark "Ex Ex"; and/or

   (ii) otherwise passing off widgets not being widgets of the Plaintiff as or for such widgets or widgets associated or connected with the Plaintiff in the course of trade by the use in relation thereto of the name "Ex Ex" or any other name or mark colourably or confusingly similar to "XX"

2. An order that the Defendant by a proper officer makes, swears, and serves on the Plaintiff forthwith an affidavit (exhibiting all relevant documents) setting out the names and addresses of all the persons (a) to whom the Defendant has supplied and (b) from whom the Defendant has received widgets bearing the name "Ex Ex", together with the quantities so supplied and received.

3. Further or other relief.

4.   Costs.

Dated this   day of   1994

<u>Solicitors for the Plaintiff</u>

TO the Defendant
at [*address*]

AND TO [*name*] their solicitors
at [*address*]

IN THE HIGH COURT OF JUSTICE   CH 19[   ] X No

CHANCERY DIVISION

BETWEEN:

XX LIMITED

Plaintiff

and

EX EX LIMITED

Defendant

STATEMENT OF CLAIM

---

1. The Plaintiff has for many years offered for sale and sold widgets under and by reference to the name "XX". In the course of so doing the Plaintiff has carried out substantial advertising and marketing under the said name. By reason thereof the Plaintiff has become the owner of a substantial goodwill and reputation in the name or mark "XX" when it is used in connection with widgets.

PARTICULARS

> [Set out, if necessary by way of a schedule, a resumé of annual sales and promotional expenditure]

2. In the premises the use of the name or mark "XX" in connection with widgets denotes to members of the public (and has so denoted at all material times) the Plaintiff's widget or a widget associated or connected with the Plaintiff.

3. The Defendant carries on business, inter alia, selling widgets.

4. Prior to the issue of the writ herein and since [*date*] the Defendant has in the course of trade passed off (or attempted to pass off) widgets not being widgets of the Plaintifff or widgets associated or connected with the Plaintiff as and for such widgets by using in relation thereto the name "Ex Ex".

PARTICULARS

Pending discovery and/or interrogatories herein the Plaintiff will rely on:

[Set out particulars of all instances of deception/confusion and all instances of use complained of]

5. By reason of the matters aforesaid the Plaintiff has suffered loss and damage.

6. The Defendant threatens and intends to continue to do the acts complained of by reason of which the Plaintiff will suffer further loss and damage.

7. The Plaintiff is entitled to interest on all sums found to be due at such rate and for such period as the court thinks fit pursuant to section 35A of the Supreme Court Act 1981 or due in equity.

AND the Plaintiff claims:

1. An injunction to restrain the Defendant whether acting by its directors, officers, servants or agents or any of them or otherwise howsoever from passing off (or attempting to pass off) widgets not being widgets of the Plaintiff as or for such widgets or widgets associated or connected with the Plaintiff by the use in relation thereto of the name "Ex Ex" or any other name or mark colourably or confusingly similar to "XX".

2. An Order for the delivery up or destruction upon oath of all articles and material in the power, possession, custody or control of the Defendant the use of which would offend against the foregoing injunction or alternatively the erasure or obliteration upon oath of the name "Ex Ex" from all such articles and material.

3. An enquiry as to the damages suffered by the Plaintiff or at the Plaintiff's option an account of profits accrued to the Defendant by reason of its acts of passing off.

4. An order for the payment of all sums found due upon such enquiry or account together with interest thereon pursuant to Section 35A of the Supreme Court Act 1981 or due under the Court's inherent jurisdiction.

5. Further or other relief.

6. Costs.

Served etc.

IN THE HIGH COURT OF JUSTICE   CH 19[   ] X No

CHANCERY DIVISION

BETWEEN:

XX LIMITED

Plaintiff

and

EX EX LIMITED

Defendant

DEFENCE

---

1. It is admitted and averred that the Plaintiff has carried on a business selling blue widgets for many years under the mark "XX". Save as aforesaid paragraph 1 of the Statement of Claim is not admitted. The Plaintiff is put to strict proof of the existence of its alleged goodwill and reputation in the mark "XX" in relation to any widgets other than blue widgets.

2. Save that it is admitted that the mark "XX" denotes the Plaintiff's blue widgets paragraph 2 of the Statement of Claim is denied.

3. It is admitted that the Defendant carries on business, inter alia, selling red widgets. The Defendant does not and never has sold blue widgets.

4. It is admitted that the Defendant has sold red widgets under the name "Ex Ex" during the period specified in paragraph 4 of the Statement of Claim. However it is denied that the said acts amount to passing off or attempting to pass off as alleged or at all.

5. The Defendant denies that the particulars referred to in paragraph 4 of the Statement of Claim constitute acts of passing off or any

misrepresentation as alleged or at all. The Defendant will refer to the circumstances surrounding such particulars to explain their true import at the trial hereof. By the date hereof there has been no or no relevant confusion between the Plaintiff's blue widgets and the Defendant's red widgets.

6. It is denied that the Defendant has caused the Plaintiff the alleged or any loss or damage. The extent of the same is not admitted.

7. It is admitted that the Defendant intends lawfully to continue to use the mark "Ex Ex" in relation to red widgets. Save as aforesaid paragraph 6 is denied.

Served etc.

IN THE HIGH COURT OF JUSTICE   CH 19[   ] X No

CHANCERY DIVISION

BETWEEN:

XX LIMITED

Plaintiff

and

EX EX LIMITED

Defendant

MINUTE OF ORDER

UPON HEARING the Application by the Plaintiff by Motion dated [   ]

AND UPON READING the letter from the Defendant's solicitors dated [   ] consenting to this Order

AND UPON HEARING Counsel for the Plaintiff

AND UPON READING the documents listed in the Court file as having been read

BY CONSENT

IT IS ORDERED

1. That the Defendant be restrained until judgment in this action or further order in the meantime, whether acting by its directors, officers, servants, agents of any of them or otherwise howsoever from doing the following acts or any of them that is to say:

   (i) selling, offering for sale, or distributing widgets under or by reference to the name or mark "Ex Ex"; and/or

   (ii) otherwise passing off widgets not being widgets of the Plaintiff as or for such widgets associated or connected with the Plaintiff in the course of trade by the use in relation thereto of the name "Ex Ex" or any other name or mark colourably or confusingly similar to "XX".

2. That the Defendant by a proper officer makes, swears, and serves on the Plaintiff within seven days an affidavit (exhibiting all relevant documents) setting out the names and addresses of all the persons (a) to whom the Defendant has supplied and (b) from whom the Defendant has received widgets bearing the name "Ex Ex", together with the quantities so supplied and received.

3. Costs reserved.

Index